MR W. H.

Mr W. H.

LESLIE HOTSON

London
RUPERT HART-DAVIS
1964

Printed in Great Britain by Richard Clay and Company, Ltd.,
Bungay, Suffolk

TO
THE PROVOST AND FELLOWS
OF KING'S COLLEGE
CAMBRIDGE

ACKNOWLEDGEMENTS

This work has been in progress for many years, but I am in no danger of forgetting how much I have owed throughout to the skill and devotion of my friend Miss Nellie O'Farrell in the labour of expert excavation, both in the archives and the manuscript-collections. Of late I have also gratefully drawn on the expert knowledge of archivists in the North: at Lincoln, Mrs Joan Varley, Dr Mary Finch, Mr Michael Lloyd; and at Grimsby, Mr Edward Gillett and Mr Peter Shaw. And without the Staffs of the Public Record Office, the British Museum, Bodleian, and Yale University Libraries, nothing could have been done.

At critical moments generous friends have been quick to help— Mrs Stephen Wilson in London, John Horden at Oxford, and Dr A. N. L. Munby at Cambridge. The book has greatly bene-fited in its final stages by the fruitful suggestions of my friends Rupert Hart-Davis, Richard Garnett, and Nicolas Barker. Over the years, the warm encouragement of such friends as Miss Margaret Brooke, Dr C. Veronica Wedgwood, Mrs Ellery Sedgwick, Mrs Sidney Withington, Sir John Neale, and Thornton Wilder has kept me up to the mark. Above all, without the ever present aid and comfort of my wife, with her incredibly patient copying as my right hand, and the inspiring support of my friend Mrs Winifred Bryher, this study would never have been begun, far less carried through.

L. H.

CONTENTS

ILLUSTRATIONS

I

THE CASE OF THE EMBARRASSING PHANTOM

'SOME day, you know, someone's going to find out about Shakespeare's friend—this unknown Master W. H.'

Twenty-five years ago, in Great Russell Street, I tossed this remark idly to a very knowing bookseller.

'Oh, sir! I 'ope *not!*'

'Why?'

'Why, that would spoil all the *fun!*'

One must admit that he had a point, beyond all apprehended damage to the book trade. For from the literary quarter Mr Lawrence Durrell later voiced the same feeling: 'It will be a great day for the Elizabethan detectives,' he wrote, 'when the central mystery of the Sonnets is cleared up, but it will also be an unlucky one, since it will deprive us of one of the most enjoyable of literary pastimes.'

It is hard not to sympathize with the view. With Criticism heavily shutting the door against pleasure, and literary fun in painfully short supply, who would be a spoil-sport? Still, every great acquisition must involve some drawback or other. Even Splitting the Atom has spoilt the fun of vainly trying to split it. Furthermore—to set against the loss of an enjoyable literary pastime—will anyone deny that the gains yielded by what the press calls *the biggest prize yet to be unearthed in Shakespearean investigation* would excite the literate world? They might even be very great. And at the least, as Ivor Brown remarks, 'If anybody can discover a new and effective key to the locked rooms of these poems of strange provenance, abstruse meaning, and ever-debated significance, what a number of unnecessary books he will avert.' What if the identity of W. H. should prove to be that key?

Since I am one of those who believe that identifying Shakespeare's Friend could not fail to throw a flood of light upon important matters both of meaning and of poetic quality, as well as upon the poet's life and work, I hold its significance paramount. But that one thing which could prove our belief sound—or on the other hand expose it as an over-sanguine hope—still hangs in clouds, a great Obscurity.

No Wanted Man has ever cut so prominent a figure in any police gazette as Shakespeare's Friend (long hid in death's dateless night), whose offence is recalled with sorrow in Sonnet 120—

how once I suffer'd in your crime.

For all the world asks, *Who* can he be?

The fugitive enjoys a longish start of his present pursuers: some three hundred and fifty years. And conspicuously lacking in this doubtful chase through the bewildering woods of history is the policeman's frequent resource in a modern man-hunt, the confidential informant or 'contact'. What would we not give for a chance to suborn for our own purposes that odious *Informer* of Sonnet 125? No; it is only too plain that here we cannot take impressive short cuts, as they do at Scotland Yard, by 'acting on information received'.

But what sort of man are we looking for? That is obviously our first question. In the absence of photographs, aliases, and fingerprints, what start can we make towards forming a verbal description, a *portrait parlé*?

Let us see. The Sonnets themselves make it clear that this Friend, younger than the poet, is a most graceful and glorious young gentleman, excellent in beauty. Other poets besides Shakespeare write in his praise. Further, his hair—resembling *buds of marjoram*—is curls of a warm brown. And his name, like Shakespeare's own, is Will. There you have the sum of solid information gleaned from the poet's text.

What can be added? Well, when in 1609 *Shake-speares Sonnets* at length come to be printed—with no definite sign of the author's co-operation—their publisher inscribes the volume *To the onlie begetter of these insuing sonnets Mr. W. H.* And he wishes him *that eternitie* of fame which in these ensuing sonnets was repeatedly *promised by our ever-living poet* to his young Friend, Will. In 1609, then, Shakespeare's Will is still alive, a gentleman or squire, without knighthood or title of nobility, and his surname begins with the letter H.

If we are going to give up in despair, now is the time to do it. For where shall we find an Elizabethan Whitaker, listing the winners of young gentlemen's beauty-contests? Or where a complete roster of gentry junior to the poet, classified by hair-colour? And of course, as E. B. Reed pointed out, 'Shakespeare must have had many friends whose very names, to say nothing of initials, Time has effaced.'

Yet this glimmer of additional light shed by a gentleman's second initial in 1609 is all the modern world has got from the publisher, Thomas Thorpe. Beyond this, not a clue. Not a hint from Thorpe of the date when the Sonnets were written. No detail or circumstance which might help us in the search for Master William H———. Since we have nothing to chew upon, small wonder that Scepticism pours in its gas of doubt—'W. H. is a Mrs. Harris'—, and (since the unknown is ever magnified) that Snobbery puffs the problem up with airy titles of nobility, with Southamptons, with Pembrokes, the Earl of This, or the Earl of That—and every Will followed proves a Will o' the Wisp.

If we had *less* than we have, perhaps we could bear it better. But to be tantalized on what *feels* like the very threshold of knowledge is intolerable. Where Shakespeare is concerned, we refuse to live lives of quiet desperation. Hot for certainties about our supreme poet, and imploring *Let me not burst in ignorance, but tell!* —we get only an endless train of answers, all different, all dusty. Like Ovid's Erysichthon cursed with hunger, the Shakespearean

> *dreams of feasts, extends his idle jaws,*
> *With labouring teeth fantastically chaws,*
> *Deludes his throat by swallowing empty fare,*
> *And for affected food devours the air.*

As Scotland Yard would put it, every line of inquiry has blown out. 'Solutions' unnumbered have been advanced, ranging from the serious far into the nonsensical, and what Richard Grant White told our grandfathers holds true today: 'No one knows. No theory on this subject has ever been proposed that will bear even a brief critical investigation.'

Still, dusty as they are, the answers of the tireless theorists are more acceptable than the agnostic's doctrine of defeat. Swinburne in 1879 blew his withering blast—to nip all future sonnet-inquiries in the bud—with great gusto. And in 1883 the comfortable Max Koch encouraged every inquirer to see nothing in the sonnet-future but the poring dark. '*Ignoramus,*' intoned Herr Koch, '*ignorabimus.*' 'We do not know, and we never shall.' The agnostic is content to find 'the only impregnable answer' in eternal ignorance.

We have learned at least to ignore the agnostic. But how are we to make a positive start? In any search for Master William H——, this preliminary question stares one in the face. And the customary answer is familiar to all. The classic procedure is first to select one from among the possible candidates you have heard of. Next, to move heaven and earth for arguments which (as you hope) may serve to turn your 'possible' into a 'probable'. Yet common—even invariable—as this method is, it cannot be recommended. Significant features appear so utterly lacking, that your selection can be little better than a blind one, a lottery draw, a lucky dip.

There was a time when I tried it myself, in the thought that a greatly increased panel of 'possibles' might afford a more promising first choice. In 1936 an able reviewer strangely imagined that 'Every W. H. of the time, whether Master, Lord, or Knight, has been dragged into the discussion'. How far he was from the fact! For it should be obvious that no more than a tiny fraction of the 'possibles' has ever been considered. Since the Master William H—— of the Sonnets was certainly alive in 1609, it seemed to me that to examine the wills of gentlemen answering that description who died in the generation following might perhaps yield a clue. Reference to the indexes at Somerset House at once revealed (for the quarter-century beginning 1609) the testaments of about a hundred William H—— 'possibles' entered in the registers of the Prerogative Court of Canterbury alone.

When I had read through these hundred wills, to my mind one of the testators stood out as the man to mark. In him I fancied I had found a possible 'probable': William Heynes, Esquire, Shakespeare's junior by some two years and a half, a gentleman of London and Surrey. For he died early in 1611 *as an important and trusted agent of the Earl of Southampton*, having unluckily (and to his own great regret) gambled away large amounts of his patron's money. A Master William H——, close to the earl to whom Shakespeare inscribed both his *Venus and Adonis* and *The Rape of Lucrece*! Who more likely to have been the poet's young Friend?

Eagerness to learn more about him cost me long hunting through the archives of England in Chancery Lane. But however much biographical circumstance I found—and I turned up a surprising amount—unhappily no item of it drew Master William Heynes any closer to the story of the Sonnets or to Shakespeare. Nothing for him therefore but to shrink back into obscurity, discarded like the rest.

A negative result, but to me a valuable one. For it convinced me that the 'obvious' method was wrong. Much like chess problems, in which—and this naturally is what makes them problems—the *obvious* first move is always wrong.

The prevailing view of the pursuit today is both dim and damp, and no wonder. George Sampson tells us to be sensible, and dismiss W. H., 'that embarrassing phantom'. And even those who do not deny that W. H. once existed as a man of flesh and blood regard every known method of hunting him as futile. But if *no* method will succeed, one asks, what hope of breaking the case is left? Answer, none at all, barring the most unlikely chance that first-hand evidence, contained perhaps in some unnoticed Elizabethan letter, might turn up to reveal the lost identity: a chance at this day of the world as negligible as it is remote.

And yet, though wiser men pronounce solution impossible, I cannot let the Mystery of W. H. alone. In emulation of Sherlock

13

Holmes, I find my thoughts irresistibly drawn to it *because* the experts flatly state there are no clues at all. 'W. H. either was, or was understood to be, the boy of the Sonnets himself,' wrote Professor Mackail, and added, 'the boy . . . is unidentified, and unidentifiable.' John Bailey declared it 'a mere waste of time' to try to identify the persons of the Sonnets, 'because no material exists for identifying them.' We might be back in *A Study in Scarlet*: '"There is no clue," said Gregson. "None at all," chimed in Lestrade.'

At a distance of nearly eighty years, the methods of Lestrade and Gregson seem to us almost prehistoric. Yet will even the latest implements for scientific man-hunting run down the man we are looking for?

We cannot hope that an electronic computer might reveal the identity of W. H. Could anything conceivable do it but knowledge of the Elizabethans themselves? Certainly anyone who has suffered the toils and rebuffs involved in running down wanted men in the circles of Marlowe and Shakespeare is unlikely to share the popular notion that the true identity of Master William H——is 'anybody's guess'. Would he be brought to agree that an enthusiastic amateur might stumble on the truth by a happy accident? Or be persuaded that some great brain, untravelled in the Elizabethans, their language, their ways, and their habits of thought, might solve the problem by the application of critical acumen? This formidable case calls for something less spectacular, something more like the routine work of the Criminal Investigation Department at New Scotland Yard.

Considerations such as these bring us back to restate our problem. In the front rank of internationally Wanted Men stands the unknown Friend of Shakespeare, who disappeared upwards of three centuries ago. Down to the present moment he has eluded every one of his pursuers with ease.

Even in a man-hunt so intent and protracted as this, however, one may ask whether every well-tested detective means has as yet been tried. Might not some approach still exist, some unfollowed track—if only one could find it—which would lead to the quarry?

...our hand-written copies of this which I have seen, the
...ting most explanations later scribbled in may serve as a
... It gives the following twelve:

e all	Howard, Lord Admiral.
?	Essex, Lieutenant General of England.
are	Secretary Cecil.
d	The Court of Wards, promised to Essex, given to Sir Robert Cecil.
n	Lord Cobham.
nce	Lieutenant of the Ordnance. [*Essex was Master of this office; his enemy Sir George Carew was Lieutenant.*]
ou	Sir George Carew.
	Carey, Lord Hunsdon.
d	Sir Robert Cecil crooked.
	Lord Grey of Wilton.
	Sir Robert Cecil.
t's	Sir Robert Cecil.

...welve, together with the dirty word *politicians*, you will
...uld be enough to set Master Secretary's men hunting for
...r. But of course these are not all. Without any hope of
...g the allusions to that noble *Eagle* Essex and those vile
...ish *buzzards* his opponents evident to any eye in 1599
...ple, is not 22 *will apish*—pronounced 'will oppish,[1]—
...*Willoughby*, Southampton's enemy?) on further study
...add the four following:

Essex; his motto, *Virtutum Basis Constantia* (*Constancy, the Base of Virtues*).

sc. of Essex; his other motto, from Cicero, *Virtutis Comes Invidia* (*Envy* [*is*] *Virtue's Attendant*).

upon Sir John *Stanhope*. Backed by his cousin Burghley, in 1596 Stanhope had defeated Essex's candidate Sir Henry Unton for the Treasurership of the Chamber.

---

[1] Shakespeare rimes *apish—foppish*. *Lear* 1.4.182.

This heartening thought turns me once more on to the trail of Master William H——, now cold for centuries. And it is seconded by another. The Case of the Embarrassing Phantom is not the first or the only real-life case which has been said to present 'no clues at all'.

II

THE INCREDIBLE CLUE

WHAT problem ever had its few data so chaotically muddled, so densely overlaid with fantasy in the name of investigation as this of Master W. H.? You may well ask. And you may try reading some of the jungle-growth of guesswork. Without a doubt it will 'so entangle your head a thousand ways, yea, and lead you to such intricate matter, that when you have all done, you shall be little or nothing at all the wiser, but rather the contrary, even fraught with a thousand fond opinions and blind conceits'.

Even if (to change the metaphor) we ignored all but a protruding tenth part of that hulking iceberg of theory, we should still conclude with Sherlock Holmes that here 'We are suffering from a plethora of surmise, conjecture, and hypothesis'. So stuffed are we with this plenitude, that we lose sight of an obvious fact, namely: Shakespeare's original readers were entirely free of our modern disease, that of making a mystery of the matter. To them, the identity which is lost to us was ordinary common knowledge. As that clear-headed historian Peter Cunningham reminds us, 'Mr. W. H. was well enough known in his own day. *What is enigmatical to us was no obscurity then.*' And if it is asked, Who then has turned the poet's fair Friend into a mystery? the answer must be, No one but beauty's perennial enemy, wicked Time.

In passing, to illustrate the evident truth of Cunningham's piece of common sense, a set of verses by a contemporary of Shakespeare's offers itself. To help persuade anyone who might suppose our modern minds fully equipped to catch the reference obvious to an Elizabethan eye, here (in our spelling) are these bitterly allusive lines 'scattered abroad' to the man in the street by Essex's inflamed faction, during his disgrace, in December 1599. What Elizabethan matter is more familiar to us than Essex's story? Everybody knows it. Lytton Strachey is only one of the many

who have told us all about it.
hits can we readily check off

1 *Admire all! W*
2 *Honour in gener*
3 *Secret are ever t*
4 *Through whose*

5 *A ward in worth*
6 *By virtue's wrac*
7 *Pride, spite, and*
8 *Instead of virtue*

9 *No Cob am I th*
10 *Or frame my ton*
11 *God's ordinance*
12 *Let no man smile*

13 *Care you that list*
14 *By crooked ways*
15 *Nor will I stand*
16 *Where such impie*

17 *But basely clothëa*
18 *Unto the Court I'*
19 *Where, though I*
20 *A Cub is good eno*

21 *Whose malice swe*
22 *Will frame his wil*
23 *Or make a choice*
24 *And by ridiculous*

25 *There may I see w*
26 *The politicians of*
27 *That rob art's glor*
28 *Dipp'd in water fr*

29 *These buzzards imp*
30 *To wrong true nobl*
31 *Factious actions no*
32 *They that see nothi*

Of the
one prese
score-car

1 *Adm*
2 *gener*
3 *Secre*
5 *A wa*

9 Cob
11 *ordir*

13 *Care*
13 *care*
14 *croo*
17 *gray*
20 *Cub*
27 *rob*

Thes
agree, s
the aut
exhaust
and th
(for ex
Ambro
I shou

6 *vir*
8 *vi*
12 *vi*
10 *en*

15 *st*

What is left of our confidence that we know all about Essex? In short, what Time has rendered either quite invisible to our modern eyes, or at best dimly glimpsed dubieties demanding research, in 1599 was all too dangerously plain.

Who among us likes to face the discomfortable fact that Shakespeare's original readers were continually getting obvious meanings from his words which we cannot see? To suppose that the identity of the poet's Friend *fair, kind, and true* was hidden from those sonnet-readers is just as reasonable as to assume that this broadcast libel puzzled them because it puzzles us.

So far indeed from any 'hermeticism or hieroglyphicalness' (*sic*) recently imagined as pervading Shakespeare's Sonnets, 'as though he were trying to ensure that no reader should be able to discover from them the identity of the person addressed', the evident truth is the very opposite. For in Sonnet 78 Shakespeare himself complains that his poems have addressed that person only too pointedly and unmistakably. The trouble is that his frequent lyrics on the theme of his fair Friend, circulated in hand-written copies, have proved too successful. As a result, 'alien pens' imitating his manner now get themselves a hearing by addressing rival verses to that familiar figure:

78

So oft have I invok'd thee for my Muse
And found such fair assistance in my verse,
As every alien pen hath got my use
And under thee their poesy disperse.

In view of this obviously public knowledge, it is amusing to hear latter-day efforts to share it sometimes deplored as 'attempts to invade Shakespeare's privacy'. Privacy? On the contrary, Shakespeare made his friendship and his Friend as public as possible:

80 *O, how I faint when I of you do write,*
    Knowing a better spirit doth use your name,
    And in the praise thereof spends all his might,
    To make me tongue-tied, speaking of your fame.

100 *Return, forgetful Muse . . .*
     Give my love fame faster than time wastes life . . .

We can be sure of one thing. Master William H——, if he is ever found, will certainly turn out to have made a conspicuous figure in his springtime of life.

The fact that this familiar identity is lost to us should surprise no one. There are countless other circumstances well known to the Elizabethans which we don't know. But our vital question puts itself: Could this particular lost fact be one which might still be recovered? If we dare to hope that it may be, and we set aside the common illusory gambit of 'guessing a possible', where shall we look for a clue?

Before casting about, we must cement acquaintance with every available detail of description. Let us go back to the beginning and once more set down the few fragments gleaned from the published *Sonnets*:

NAME	William H——.	Shakespeare's social su-
RANK	Gentleman or Esquire.	perior, able to *honour* the poet *with public kindness*.
AGE	A youth.	Younger than Shakespeare.
HAIR	Like *buds of marjoram*, meaning dark auburn or 'brown madder', and curling.	See the notes of authorities on Sonnet 99:7.
APPEARANCE	Of striking and well-known comeliness and grace.	
DOCUMENTS	Poems other than Shakespeare's sonnets were written about him.	

To consider the last item. One such poem, though it brings us no nearer to ascertaining his identity, appears to be *A Lover's Complaint*. Thorpe printed this poem with the *Sonnets* under Shakespeare's name. Some scholars accept it as Shakespeare's work, some are sceptical. I suspect that its author was one of those *alien pens* the poet complains of, which have *got my use And under thee their poesy disperse.*

For whoever it was that wrote it, Shakespeare or an 'alien', the items of description he gives reproduce those presented in the Sonnets. In this poem, as in the Sonnets, the subject is a youth strikingly comely (here accused of seduction) whose 'browny locks did hang in crooked [*i.e.* curving] curls'. And so beautiful is he that 'Each eye that saw him did enchant the mind' a parallel to the beauty drawn in Sonnets 5 and 20—

> *The lovely gaze where every eye doth dwell*
> *Which steals men's eyes and women's souls amazeth.*

Similarly, as a prince of hearts 'whose real[1] habitude [that is, whose *royal nature*] gave life and grace', he 'did in the general bosom reign', saying '[I] Kept hearts in liveries, but mine own was free, And reigned commanding in his monarchy', recalling Sonnets 70 and 63—

> *thou alone kingdoms of hearts shouldst owe.*
> *all those beauties whereof now he's King . . .*

A Lover's Complaint reminds us further that a young gentleman celebrated for his beauty must (like the Earl of Essex, but to a lesser degree) have been a favourite subject of portraiture. The passage 'Many there were that did his picture get To serve their eyes' takes us back to Sonnet 47 and Shakespeare's delight in gazing upon his own treasured portrait of the youth:

> *With my love's picture then my eye doth feast.*

---

[1] *I.e.*, royal. 'The qween held a real Christmasse' (Capgrave); 'He edified the reall palace' (Hellowes); 'demanded of him how he durst attempt her [Queen Elizabeth's] real presence' (Richard Topcliffe); 'reall features [of Charles I] fit to make a King' (Henry Tubbe); 'the . . . real Crown' (William Strode).

And in Sonnet 16 he goes farther. Here Shakespeare points out the supreme artist who painted the picture. He tells us that no less a brush produced this *painted counterfeit* of his Friend than

this time's pencil

—that is to say, the unquestioned *master-limner of the age*. Has it ever been noticed that for Shakespeare's readers this could certainly be no other than the peerless *Nicholas Hilliard?* In praising the master, John Donne spoke for the age:

> *a hand, or eye*
> *By* Hilliard *drawne, is worth an history*
> *By a worse painter made.*

And Sidney's poet-friend Sir Arthur Gorges, when he must find a limner of supernatural powers, able to paint beauty's perfection, confidently invokes *Hilliard*.[1]

Now among the works of Hilliard's 'fine pencil' surviving today, we ask ourselves, is there no example preserved of his painting of the famously beautiful youth cherished by Shakespeare? And on setting his greatest known portrait-miniature, the unidentified *Youth leaning against a tree among roses (circa* 1588)

---

[1] Erect thy flight on high with Eagle's wings,
Surmount the force of Eol's fleeting band,
Strive still beyond the power of mortal things,
Until amidst the lofty heavens thou stand.
With Argus' eyes there view the shapes divine,
Observe their beauties, stature, form, and grace;
And that thou mayst my Mistress well define,
Of all their choice compound one perfect face.
For lively colours reap the freshest flowers
That in Eliza's blessed fields do grow,
And temper them with moisture of those showers
That on my cheeks despair hath caused to flow.
Then by those patterns taken from the sky,
Hilliard, depaint the face for which I die.

Sonnet 75, quoted (but with spelling modernized) from *The Poems of Sir Arthur Gorges* (1953), 73. The editor, Professor Helen Sandison, points out that this is a version of one of Ronsard's *Amours*, beginning *Hausse ton vol* . . .

—see Frontispiece—alongside the Sonnets, who can exclude the arresting possibility that here we have it? Few works of Elizabethan art are prized so highly as this. Authority pronounces it 'by general consent one of the prime masterpieces of English painting'.[1] And expert opinion holds that this picture 'might have been painted as an illustration to any of the sonnet-sequences of the time'.[2]

Yet one must admit that it illustrates none of them so closely, aptly, and vividly as it does Shakespeare's sequence. Indeed if Hilliard had added to it a name beginning with the initials W and H, it would long since have been claimed as a painting of Shakespeare's hero. For in this portrait by *this time's pencil*, and in no other piece of contemporary limning, we have the sonnets-picture painted to the life: the fair gentle youth with the warm brown curls, amid white roses for True Affection: the embodiment of beauty and truth, the *fair, kind, and true* of Sonnet 105. *True* is *constant*. Of this picture Mr John Pope-Hennessy notes that the tree is the symbol of constancy.[3] Here, as in the Sonnets, nothing is lacking but 'the magic of the name'.

But is this well-known masterpiece '*by* Hilliard *drawne*' indeed *beauty's pattern to succeeding men*—Shakespeare's celebrated fair Friend? Without question it may be. And it is not impossible that further evidence might show it to be. For in this picture— whose painted Latin legend reveals it as an *impresa* or 'heroical device'—more meaning is undoubtedly presented both in the phrase from Lucan *Dat poenas laudata fides*[4] and in its symbolism of subject, composition, pose, and colours, than meets the modern eye. Upon investigation we may hope in the sequel to be enabled to read significant items of its testimony.

Even by a lure so strong as this, however, we cannot now be

---

[1] Carl Winter, *Elizabethan Miniatures* (King Penguin), 10. See his Plate VII, and the frontispiece to Dr Erna Auerbach's *Nicholas Hilliard* (Routledge and Kegan Paul).
[2] Victoria and Albert Museum, *Guide to the Galleries* (1957), 104.
[3] *The Burlington Magazine* 83 (October 1943), 259.
[4] The source was first spotted by Miss Carolyn Merion.

drawn aside from the track, our search for some clue to the lost identity of Master W. H. Again, the first thing we face is the awkward question, Where shall we look for it? Certainly not in the mountainous heap of books devoted to the problem. That includes everything imaginable except a clue. And if we turn to the Shakespearean professionals for advice, Churton Collins will only reply very fairly for them all, 'If certainty about [the Sonnets] can ever be arrived at, it can only be attained by evidence of which as yet we have not even an inkling.'

Small encouragement; yet in this quarter we could hardly expect to secure the counsel we need—the practical hint distilled from generations of experience in the art of tracing the wanted man. But if on the other hand we apply at Scotland Yard to the C.I.D., the case is altered. This is what we get:

> The criminal always takes something to the scene of the crime and leaves it there, or else he takes something from the scene and keeps it: it is really as simple as that.[1]

Simple, and suggestive too. Will it work for us? Passing the second alternative as inapplicable to our problem, we ruminate the first: *always takes something to the scene . . . and leaves it there.*

The scene is the Sonnets. Now what was the something which W. H. took to that scene, and which he left there? Clearly, he took to it nothing he *could* leave but the distinctive impression of himself: his distinguishing quality, his *idea*. And departing, he left it there, drawn by the poet with features so unmistakable to contemporary eyes that (as we have seen) he was readily recognized:

> *So oft have I invok'd thee for my Muse . . .*
> *As every alien pen hath got my use*
> *And under thee their poesy disperse.*

Since these lines of Sonnet 78 show the fact of this ready and public recognition undeniable, we cannot escape the conclusion:

---

[1] Ex-Deputy Commander William Rawlings, *A Case for the Yard* (John Long, London, 1961), 64.

The Sonnets present some plainly identifying feature, some peculiar attribute of Master W. H.'s description, invisible to the unaided modern eye.

This thought flings down the very challenge carved on the poet's monument: *Read, if thou canst.* Well, can we? It also recalls the shrewd axiom Heminges and Condell tossed to the readers of their Folio Shakespeare, 'The fate of all books depends upon your capacities.' Are our capacities up to this one? Moreover, it lends an unpalatable irony to Edgar Allan Poe's thesis, *Every work of art contains within itself all that is necessary for its comprehension.* For if it does, but Oblivion has made a part of that 'all' invisible to our eyes, obviously we *cannot* comprehend until added knowledge concerning that part brings it up like an image latent in a photographic plate.

No longer are we at a loss, for the direction is clear—*Search the writings.* Our work with the Sonnets is cut out, to detect that descriptive trait unsuspected and crucial, that *individual attribute,* which for the original reader would plainly point out the poet's friend, set him off from every other handsome young gentleman, make his identity unmistakable. Although no scrutiny in a century and a half of searching has caught this unique essential, somewhere in these poems it must be lying in full view, unseen. It is there that we must (as they say in the Metropolitan Force) *give our eyes a chance.* And in going over that much-trodden ground, if habit compels us to look at the Sonnets once more as we have always looked, we shall infallibly miss it again. Rather, shaking off prepossessions, we must bring as open a mind as we can to examine familiar terms, habitually taken as metaphors, for some actual matter topical for the Elizabethan reader: something in some unsuspected way literal for him. And if this process presents things strange or even incredible? Meet them with the maxims from George Peele in *The Old Wives' Tale*:

> *Be not afeard of every stranger;*
> *Start not aside at every danger;*
> *Things that seem are not the same . . .*

25

that is, *Things are not what they appear to be,* or *What seems a metaphor is something more than a metaphor.*

Our first move, then, must be to assemble for scrutiny the various metaphors or allusions which Shakespeare's Friend, and his relationship with him, beget in the poet's mind. Then to set down and compare their respective Elizabethan *applications.* Among all the painful probing for the Friend's identity, and all the intent scanning of Shakespeare's imagery, has such a muster ever been made? To neglect pointers so obviously offered would however be an oversight not easy to explain away. Surely when brought together and compared, might they not prove able to cast fresh light, both on each other and on the central problem?

To begin at once, therefore, with what we are given:

1. SUN 33 1 *Full many a glorious morning have I seen*
            2 *Flatter the mountain-tops with sovereign eye . . .*
            9 *Even so my sun one early morn did shine*
           10 *With all-triumphant splendour on my brow . . .*
           14 *Suns of the world may stain when heaven's sun staineth.*

And in the next Sonnet, 34, the Friend is again 'the sun'. It is well known that, following a general Renaissance practice drawn from antiquity,[1] *kings* commonly figured as earthly 'suns' in the works of Shakespeare and his contemporaries.[2]

---

[1] See H. P. L'Orange, *Studies on the Iconography of Cosmic Kingship in the Ancient World,* 1953.

[2] *Lucr.* 1013:   Poor grooms are sightless night, kings glorious day

Rich. II 3.2.50:   see us rising in our throne, the East
Hen. V 1.2.278:   But I will rise there with so full a glory
                          That I will dazzle all the eyes of France
Cymb. 5.5.475:   radiant Cymbeline, Which shines here in the West
Hen. VIII 3.2.414:   Seek the King. That sun, I pray, may never set
Chapman, *Consp. of
  Byron* 1.1.163:   [to Henri III] thou, Sun
Sidney, *Arcadia:*   [dirge for a dead king]: Farewell, O Sun

2. A GOD *110* 12 *A god in love, to whom I am confin'd.*

'Gods on earth' was proverbially used of *kings* as far back as Menander,[1] and is frequent in Shakespeare.[2]

3. OCEAN 80   5   *But since your worth (wide as the Ocean is)*
            6   *The humble as the proudest sail doth bear . . .*
            8   *On your broad main . . .*
          10   *. . . upon your soundless deep . . .*

'Ocean' or 'sea' as a figure for *king* is often found in Shakespeare and his fellow-writers.[3]

Drayton, *Matilda*:	Kings. They be the suns
Ralegh, *12th Book*	
(*Cynthia*):	[of Queen Elizabeth] if she were not the sun
Aske, *Elizabetha*	
Triumphans, 1588:	the Sun, Elizabeth our Queen
Spenser, *F.Q.* 6.10.28:	Sun of the world . . . Great *Gloriana*
Sorrowes Joy, 1603:	[of Queen Elizabeth] Our sun eclipst did set
Jonson, *Masque of*	
Blackness, 1608:	[King James's Britain] Rul'd by a *Sun*

[1] H. P. L'Orange, *Apotheosis in Ancient Portraiture*, 1947.

[2] *Lucr.* 601:	Thou seem'st not what thou art, a god, a king
Pericles 1.1.103:	Kings are earth's gods
Love's L.L. 1.1.223:	[to King] My soul's earth's god
Rich. II 5.3.134:	[to King] A god on earth thou art
Jul. Caes. 1.2.116:	[of Caes.] And this man Is now become a god
Sir Th. More 104:	[of King] calls him a god on earth
Nashe (ed. McK.) 1.286:	Kings are Gods on earth
Fuller, *Holy State*	
4.21.334:	The King. He is a mortal God
[3] *Lucr.* 652:	Thou art, quoth she, a sea, a sovereign king;
	And lo, there falls into thy boundless flood
	Black lust, dishonour, shame . . .
3 Hen. VI 5.4.25:	And what is [King] Edward but a ruthless sea
John 5.4.57:	Even to our ocean, to our great King John
2 Hen. IV 5.2.129:	The tide of blood in me [Prince, now King]
	. . . shall mingle with the state of floods
	And flow henceforth in formal majesty
Merch. of V. 5.1.94:	A substitute shines brightly as a king,
	Until a king be by, and then his state
	Empties itself, as doth an inland brook
	Into the main of waters

27

Here, then, we have Shakespeare typifying his Friend variously as a *sun*, a *god*, an *ocean* or a *sea*: three familiar metaphors which he and his contemporaries use to represent a sovereign prince or king. *The Elvetham Entertainment* (1591) brings all three together, describing Queen Elizabeth as 'like the Sunne for shew, to Gods for vertue . . . More rich then seas'. And the sonnet painted upon her 'Ditchley' portrait again exhibits the three: 'Sonn', 'power divine', and 'boundles ocean'.[1] Whatever may be meant by it here in the Sonnets, the Shakespearean and Elizabethan element common to the three is certainly *king*, and the metaphors exhibit a consistency of reference. In looking farther we must ask, Is this mere chance? Or will this established 'royal' reference be maintained elsewhere in the Sonnets?

Pursuing the question, we find more figures showing the same sense:

37　6　*Or any of these all, or all, or more,*
　　7　*Entitled in thy parts, do crownèd sit*

69　1　*Those parts of thee that the world's eye doth view* . . .
　　5　*Thy outward thus with outward praise is crown'd*

114　1　. . . *my mind, being crown'd with you*[2]

Anon., *Selimus*, 190:　Is he a prince? . . . he is a sea
Chr. Brooke,
　Ghost of Ric. III:　In my vast sea their streams of joy were drown'd
Daniel, *Civil Wars*,　As stately Thames . . . Glides on . . . Unto the
　2.7,8:　　　　　　　　Ocean . . .
　　　　　　　　　　　So float the mighty with their following train
　　　　　　　　　　　Unto the all-receiving Bolingbroke
Chapman, *Consp. of*　I'll pour an endless flood into a sea
　Byron 3.2.170:　　Raging beneath me, which shall intimate
　　　　　　　　　　　My ceaseless service drunk up by the King
Idem, 4.1.30:　　　And being a sea, be sparing of his streams
[of Henri IV]

[1] Roy C. Strong, *Portraits of Queen Elizabeth I* (1963), 75–76. These passages, with those already quoted from Spenser, Aske, and Ralegh, dispose of the uninformed notion that the Virgin Queen was always Cynthia or the Moon with all the poets.

[2] *3 Hen. VI* 1.1.102: our title to the crown　3.3.145 your title to the
　　　　　　　　　　　crown　4.7.46 our title to the crown
　Rich. III 1.4.78:　Princes have but their titles for their glories

In the introductory group of sonnets, the poet repeatedly urges his Friend to marry and beget offspring:

2 10 . . . this fair child . . .
  12 Proving his beauty by succession thine

6 14 . . . and make worms thine heir

9 3 Ah, if thou issueless shalt hap to die

13 8 When your sweet issue your sweet form should bear

We note that the terms Shakespeare uses here—*succession, heir, issue*—he elsewhere applies to the paramount problems of royalty.[1] Further (like the issueless Queen 'maried to the

---

Rich. II 1.1.24:	Add an immortal title to your crown
Hen. V 1.2.68:	Make claim and title to the crown
Hen. VIII 1.2.144:	How grounded he his title to the crown
Selden, *Laws of England*, 1.47:	The Emperor could entitle the Pope to no power here
John 3.3.96:	[of the Prince] all his gracious parts
Jul. Caes. 3.2.56:	Let him be Caesar. Caesar's better parts shall be crown'd in Brutus
Hen. VIII 2.4.140:	[of Q. Katherine] thy parts Sovereign and pious else, could speak thee out The queen
Marston, *Sophonisba* 2.3:	howsoe'er a monarch feigns his parts
Davies of Heref., *Microcosmos* 2:	[Q. Eliz.] had in her a world of princely parts
Chapman, *Bussy* 1.2.17:	[Q. Eliz.] So full of majesty and royal parts
Daniel, *Civil Wars* 2.115:	what admirable parts . . . In this brave Prince
Faithf. Friends 2.2:	her A king shall crown with his affection
[1] *3 Hen. VI* 2.1.119:	Touching King Henry's oath and your succession
Rich. II 2.1.199:	How art thou a king But by fair sequence and succession
Haml. 3.2.356:	You have the voice of the king himself for your succession in Denmark
Wint. Tale 4.4.440:	We'll bar thee from succession
„ 3.3.136:	The king shall live without an heir

29

Realme'), his Friend dying a bachelor without issue will leave *the world* his *widow*, contrasted by the poet with every *private widow* —that is, the widow of 'a private man' as distinguished from a ruler, a king:

> 9 5 *The world will be thy widow and still weep*
> *That thou no form of thee hast left behind,*
> *When every private widow well may keep*
> *By children's eyes her husband's shape in mind.*[1]

Again in Sonnet 14 Shakespeare presents his friend as a prince. Here the poet professes himself a judicial astrologer, but one who employs uncommon means of prediction. Admitting that he cannot foretell *princes' fortunes* by the usual course of consulting the heavens, he maintains that he *can* do it by the art he learned

---

Hen. VIII 2.4.194:	My kingdom, Well worthy the best heir
Wint. Tale 5.1.46:	Care not for issue; The crown will find an heir
„ „ 5.1.174:	[*King.*] the heavens ... Have left me issueless
Hen. VIII 1.2.133:	That if the king Should without issue die
Heywood, *If you know not me*:	She's next successive, should your Majesty Die issueless

[1] Shakespeare, *Epitaph on a Bachelor*: When God was pleas'd (the world unwilling yet) Elias James to Nature paid his debt

1 Hen. VI 5.4.136:	Must he [King Charles] Retain but privilege of a private man
Tit. Andr. 4.4.75:	When I [Emperor] have walkëd like a private man
Hen. V 4.1.253:	What infinite heart's-ease Must kings neglect that private men enjoy
Hen. V 4.1.210:	... that a poor and a private displeasure can do against a monarch
Marlowe, *Edw. II* 1994–95:	The griefs of private men are soon allay'd But not of kings
Webster 'An Excellent Actor' (1615):	this day one plays a Monarch, the next a private person
Daniel, *Trag. of Cleopatra*, 393:	Princes like lions never will be tamed: A private man may yield
J. Davies of Heref., *Wit's Pilg.* 35:	For Kings ... Oft live alone ... But private men
Shirley, *Court Secret* 4.3:	Private men meet the force of common stings, But none can feel the weight of kings but kings.

from those stars, his friend's eyes.[1] And to prove it he proceeds
to prophesy about (the prince) his friend:

> 14 1   *Not from the stars do I my judgment pluck,*
>   *And yet me thinks I have astronomy; ...*
>   5   *Nor can I ...*
>   7   *... say with princes if it shall go well*
>   *By oft predict that I in heaven find;*
>   *But from thine eyes my knowledge I derive,*
>   *And, constant stars, in them I read such art*
>   *As truth and beauty shall together thrive*
>   *If from thyself to store thou wouldst convert;*
>   *Or else of thee this I prognosticate:*
>   *Thy end is truth's and beauty's doom and date.*

Or, to put it in another way, one may ask what conceivable
relevance or point is there in his confessing inability to foretell
the fortunes of *princes* in the usual manner, by the firmament,
unless the friend of whom by his special art he *does* prognosticate
is a prince?

Certainly nothing could be more explicit than Shakespeare's
expressions in the following:

> 57   6   *... my sovereign*
>
> 87 13 *Thus have I had thee as a dream doth flatter—*
>   14 *In sleep a king, but waking no such matter.*

Sleep, like his younger brother Death, makes all men equal: and
the sleeping poet dreamt that he was his friend's *equal*—that is, *a
king.*[2]

---

[1] Compare Sidney as a similar astrologer:
>   *... proof makes me sure,*
> *Who oft fore-judge my after-following race,*
> *By only those two stars in Stella's face.*
>   *Astrophel and Stella 26.12–14.*

[2] Chapman, *Hymnus in*   *... dreams ...*
   Noctem: Some taking forms of princes, to persuade
                 Of men deject, we are their equals made

  Lo. Herbert of Cher-   Sleep, which when it doth seize us, souls go play,
  bury, *To his Mis-*   And make Man equal as he was first day.
  tress ... Picture:

Sustained and unmistakable, this language of Shakespeare's lends no support to the common theory that his youthful Friend might be some nobleman or other. For it is obvious that his chosen terms point not to nobility, but to *royalty*. And as if to clinch it, what he sets before us in the following is *not* the powers of a peer, but those peculiar to a king: power *to grant charters of privilege* and *letters patent*, power *to pardon* crimes—in short, the exclusively *royal prerogative*:

> 87   5   *thy granting*
>   8   *my patent*

> 58   9   *your charter is so strong*
>   *That you yourself may privilege your time*
>   *To what you will; to you it doth belong*
>   *Yourself to pardon of self-doing crime.*[1]

And in these passages following we need no reminder that it was to the king, and to no mortal but the king, that his dutiful subjects and vassals offered *oblations*; similarly, that it was only to the monarch or ruling magistrate that *embassies* were directed:

> 125   10   *And take thou my oblation, poor but free*

> 45   5   *For when these quicker elements are gone*
>   *In tender embassy of love to thee*

---

[1] *Rich. II* 2.1.202:   call in the letters patents that he hath

MS. Harl. 6797 f. 63:   *The King's Prerogative.* The King may give, alter, take, forbid, enable

Exposition . . . Terms . . . Law (1579) 161:   Privileges are liberties . . . granted . . . by the Queen's great charter

Reg. Privy Council of Scotland (1547) 1.78:   Our Sovereign Lady privileges and grants to them

Lucr. 621:   To privilege dishonour in thy [the King's] name

MS. Sloane 4021 f. 149:   *The King's Power of Pardon.* The King is the fountain of mercy

Act 27 Hen. VIII, 24.1:   No person . . . shall have any power . . . to pardon . . . felonies . . . but . . . the King's Highness

Rich. II 5.3.116, 118:   Say 'pardon', king . . . No word like 'pardon' for kings' mouths so meet

Hen. VIII 1.2.104:   letters of the king's grace and pardon

1   *Lord of my love, to whom in vassalage*
      Thy merit hath my duty strongly knit,
      To thee I send this written ambassage
      To witness duty, not to show my wit;
      Duty so great . . .

58   4   *Being your vassal*[1]

Two further terms strike the eye—*largess* and *bounty*. Of the
first it is significant to note that in his other works Shakespeare
applies *largess* only to the gifts or donatives of *kings*:

4   5   *why dost thou abuse*
         The bounteous largess given thee to give?[2]

---

[1] Blount, *Law Dict.*:   *Oblata.* Gifts or Oblations made to the King
                                    by any of his Subjects.
    Giuseppi, *Guide* . . .   *Oblata* or *Fine Rolls* . . . sums . . . offered to
      Public Records, 1.26:   King by way of oblations.
    Bacon, *Letter to Q. Eliz.*: making to your Majesty my poor oblation
      „   *Adv. of Learning*:   To the King. I thought it more respective to
                                    make choice of some oblation
    Trial . . . Bishops (1689): To your illustrious Highness therefore the
                                    Oblation of these Sheets . . . is most justly
                                    due
    John 1.1.6:   *King.* Silence, good mother: hear the embassy
    Kyd, *1 Jeron.* 2.4.70:   But has the king partook your embassy
    Marlowe, *1 Tamb.* 725:   Now send ambassage to thy neighbour kings
    2 Hen. VI 1.3.161:   As I in duty love my king
    Haml. 2.2.261:   I hold my duty . . . to my gracious king
    Ralegh, *Pet. to Queen*
      (1618):   I your humblest vassal
    Wither, *Philarete* :   To yield Vassalage, or Duty . . . to the Queen
[2] *Rich. II* 1.4.44:   And for our coffers, with too great a court
                                    And liberal largess, are grown somewhat light
    Hen. V 4. Prol. 43–44:   A largess universal, like the sun,
    [of the King]   His liberal eye doth give to every one
    Macb. 2.1.14:   [The king] hath been in unusual pleasure,
                                    And sent forth great largess to your offices
    Kyd, *Sol. & Pers.* 4.1.64:   *Soliman.* I'll . . . straight reward thee with a
                                    bounteous largess
    Marlowe, *Edw. II* 1364:   *Edw.* Soldiers, a largess

C

As for *bounty*, the poet's attribution of this grace to kings, while not exclusive, is characteristic:

53　9　*Speak of the spring, and foison of the year:*
　　　　The one doth shadow of your beauty show,
　　　　The other as your bounty doth appear

11　12　*Which bounteous gift* [of Nature's] *thou shouldst*
　　　　in bounty cherish[1]

In the same way we recognize *grace*, *state*, and *glory* typically in Shakespeare's kings:

28　9　*thou . . . dost him grace*

78　12　*And arts with thy sweet graces gracèd be*

79　2　*My verse alone had all thy gentle grace*

62　5　*Methinks no face so gracious is as mine* [because 'I' am 'you']

96　12　*. . . use the strength of all thy state*

37　12　*I . . . by a part of all thy glory live*[2]

---

[1] *Macb.* 4.3.91, 93: The king-becoming graces, As . . . bounty
Rich. II 4.1.300: I thank thee, king, For thy great bounty
Lear 1.1.54: That we our largest bounty may extend
Cymb. 5.5.97–98: And ask of Cymbeline what boon thou wilt,
Fitting my bounty and thy state, I'll give it
Hen. VIII 3.2.184: King. That, as my hand has open'd bounty to you
Lover's Comp. 41: Or monarch's hands that let not bounty fall
Jonson, *Gyp. Met.* 1462: [The King's] Pages *Bounty* and *Grace*
[2] *Two. Gent.* 1.3.8: daily gracèd by the emperor
1 Hen. IV 1.2.19: God save thy Grace
Hen. V 1.1.22: The king is full of grace and fair regard
　„　2 Prol. 28: this grace of kings
　„　5 Prol. 30: our gracious empress
Rich. III 4.4.205: royal and gracious
Lucr. 666 [to King]: thy thoughts, low vassals to thy state
2 Hen. IV 5.2.99: And, as you are a king, speak in your state
Hen. V 1.2.273: I will keep my state, Be like a king
Rich. II 3.2.163: Scoffing his state and grinning at his pomp
Rich. II 4.1.192: King. You may my glories and my state depose
John 2.1.350: Ha, majesty! how high thy glory towers
Rich. III 1.3.203: [to King] Outlive thy glory
Pericles 2.4.6 [of King]: in the height and pride of all his glory

Although the rival poet who has followed Shakespeare in praising the Friend is already graced with learning—his poetry 'attired in the majesty of art'[1] the Friend's royal eyes have added *grace*:

> 78 12 . . . *Arts with thy sweet graces gracëd be.*

The royal reference both in this *grace* and in Shakespeare's *honouring* the Friend—

> 25 4 *I . . . joy in that I honour most*
>
> 125 2 *With my extern the outward honouring*

—is echoed in Thomas Campion's lines:

> Challenge then a Sov'raignes place:
> Say I honour thee when I love thee;
> Let me call thy kindnesse grace.[2]

Finally, like the *sovereign* of Sonnet 57, we have already noted the no less explicit *king* and *kingdoms*:

> 70 14 . . . *thou alone kingdoms of hearts shouldst owe.*
>
> 63 6 . . . *all those beauties whereof now he's King* . . .

As a result of this search—which is far from exhaustive—it will I think be agreed that the question of consistency of reference is answered. Clearly, these consenting terms, which appear in no fewer than twenty-eight of the Sonnets, cannot be dismissed as scattered surface-ornament. They are intrinsic. What is more, they intensify each other. By direct address, by varied metaphor, and by multifarious allusion, the description of the Friend communicated is always one: *monarch, sovereign prince, king*. And even a modern reader with no knowledge of the Elizabethans is not so ignorant as to confuse a *King* with a subject, whether the subject be an Earl or a Churl. The poet's

---

[1] Jonson, *Every Man in his Humour* 5.3.325.
[2] *Third Booke of Ayres* (1617), XIX.

harping on the same string is so insistent as to make one ask why it has not arrested attention. No doubt everyone has regarded this 'king'-sense as formal hyperbole and nothing more. Any literal meaning looks quite incredible—a rank impossibility. But before we go farther, caution warns us not to study our poet in isolation.

Now if with Shakespeare's metaphors in mind we examine a dozen other Elizabethan sonnet-sequences, we find a significant contrast. It is common knowledge that of all these collections none is written, like Shakespeare's main sequence, to a man. No other sonneteer celebrates a 'king'. And although in these other poems the woman addressed is at times figured as a royalty or a divinity—*queen, sovereign, empress, sun, goddess, saint*—, the difference is marked. Shakespeare's 'royal' figures and allusions are not, like these others, occasional. They appear throughout, and so consistent in their variety as strongly to suggest a peculiar, a particular reference. From these poems of his, circulated in hand-written copies, as we have noted in quoting Sonnet 78, his Friend was widely recognized.

The sporadic *queens* and *goddesses* of the others, however, are purely conventional. So formal indeed as to offer no shadow of a clue to the subject's identity. Consequently, if one of these poets wishes his reader to recognize the lady, he has to add more. Thus Drayton must reveal that his *Idea* is 'queen' of the stream Ankor in Arden (Polesworth, Warwickshire)—a localization which points to Anne Goodere, Lady Rainsford. And Sidney must assert that *Fame Doth even grow rich, naming my Stella's name* if he is to identify his 'princess' as Penelope Lady Rich.

To pause here for a moment and take stock. It must be admitted that up to this point the investigation, however promising it may look to me, has not impressed the born sceptic in the least. He does not hesitate to dismiss this approach as another example of wishful thinking: mere moonshine in the water. His crushing argument runs, 'If Shakespeare (like Drayton and Sidney) had here furnished a clue to his subject's identity, would not scholars have picked it up long ago? Since no one has found such a clue in the Sonnets, obviously there is none.' The very voice of Gregson and Lestrade.

But this is not the first time I have had to resist the sceptic. And I resist him now. I feel that the redoubling and variety of these well-aimed strokes of Shakespeare's, all falling on one mark, show intention. They have given me a hunch that here, awaiting us, is untouched and unsuspected matter solider than moonshine. Something tells me that the quarry may even turn out to be, as Damon Runyon would say, 'more than somewhat'. Scorn not the hunch. Or, rather, don't be afraid of the hunch. Back it, play it, and test it. For this we have high detective authority:

Hunches by themselves should never be relied on, but often they provide an opening angle on an apparently insoluble problem which can afterwards be solved by reason and deduction. I owed my greatest triumph . . . to a hunch in the first place.[1]

My hunch gathers strength from Sonnet 125. For it opens,

> *Were 't aught to me I bore the canopy,*
> *With my extern the [thy] outward honouring . . . ?*[2]

and continues in line 9,

> *No, let me be obsequious in thy heart,*

meaning, 'Would it be anything to me if I bore the canopy [over thee], outwardly honouring thy external appearance? . . . No; let my devotion attend thy heart'—recalling the protestation of Sonnet 46,

> *. . . mine eye's due is thy outward part,*
> *And my heart's right thy inward love of heart.*

For I cannot follow those who would take Shakespeare here as vapouring about some figurative 'canopy of verse' he might help to carry, under which his friend is publicly honoured, any more than I can take for an airy figment the poet's cherished treasure,

---

[1] Lt.-Col. Oreste Pinto, *Friend or Foe?* (1953), 96.
[2] The plausible emendation *thy* was suggested by Howard Staunton in *The Athenaeum*, 14 March 1874, p. 357.

the *painted counterfeit* of his Friend produced by *this time's pencil*. Without question, this *counterfeit* was a tangible portrait, and limned by *the age's unmatchable Nicholas Hilliard*. In like manner I see no ground for assuming that *the canopy* of Sonnet 125 was not a material canopy. Nor do I doubt for a moment that the eight-foot spears or staves supporting the corners of it over Master William H—— were carried by four officers: of which honouring squad of bare-headed spear-bearers William Shakespeare confesses he does not care to be one.

To accept *the canopy* as a canopy, however, lands us once more in the seemingly incredible. For when we look under carried canopies, we find none but princes, royalties. On turning to the dictionaries—Italian, Spanish, French—for authority, we have 'Palio ... *Used also for a Princes Canopie, or cloth of state*' (Florio); 'Palio: ... *a canopie to beare ouer a prince*' (Percivale); 'Poille: *The square Canopy that's borne over the Sacrament, or a Sovereign Prince, in solemn Processions, or passages of State*' (Cotgrave). As for peers, an earl might have a fixed cloth of estate *in his house*, but he was *not* privileged to walk abroad under it.[1] It is only 'to kings,' as Shakespeare wrote, that 'a rich embroider'd canopy' gives shade.

A few extracts will serve to bring the exclusiveness of the carried canopy freshly before us.

Over King Edward IV, on the day of his Coronation, the Barons of the Cinque Ports bore a canopy of cloth of gold upon 4 gilt lances or spears, and at each corner of the said canopy, a bell hanging, of silver gilt.

The Barons of the town of Rye claimed 'the canopy that had been carried over the King [Richard III] . . . with four spears and four silver bells.'[2]

---

[1] Dukes, Marquesses, and Earls were permitted *fixed* cloths of estate in their houses. Those of Dukes, with a pendant hanging within half a yard of the ground; those of Marquesses 'must hang a yard above the ground'. And '*An Earle* may have in his house a Cloath of Estate which shalbe fringed round about without any pendant.' B.M. MS. Harl. 2154, f. 308.

[2] Historical MSS. Comm., *First Report*, App. 496, 544.

Also from *Henry VIII* 4.1, the crowning of Queen Anne Bullen:

THE ORDER OF THE CORONATION . . .

8. A *Canopy*, borne by four of the *Cinque-Ports*,
    under it, the Queen . . .

1. Gent. They that bear
    The Cloth of Honour over her are four Barons
    Of the Cinque-Ports.

2. Gent. Those men are happy . . .

'Then shee under her canapy departed to her chamber; and at the
entry of her chamber, shee gave the canapie, with bels and all, to the
barons of the ports according to their claime, with great thanks.'[1]

And next, the report of Queen Elizabeth's entry into King's
College Chapel, Cambridge, 1564:

At the said [North] Church Doore foure of the eldest Doctors [in
their Gowns of Scarlet] carried a Canopy over her Majestie to her
Travis.[2]

Later, Stephen Powle saw the Emperor, Rudolph II, on 20 July
1581:

This day alsoe I did see a *Cannope* of State that was carried by .4. of
the principall of Strasbourg . . . over his head to defende him from the
beames of the sonne and to sette foorth an imperiall majestie. The
Cannopie was of yellow damaske with armes of the Empire gilded there-
on.[3]

And an English reporter summed up Henri IV's new Queen
Maria de' Medici after her landing at Marseilles (1600) in these
words:

. . . and but for an old damaske canopie, which was carried over her
by 4 townesmen, she would not have bene taken for a Queen of
France.[4]

---

[1] Marriage and Coronation of Anne Boleyn, 1552–53, pr. Nichols, *Prog.
Elizabeth* (1788), i.
[2] F. Peck, *Desiderata Curiosa* II. vii. 35.
[3] Bodl. MS. Tanner 309, f. 151ᵛ.
[4] P.R.O., S.P. 101/9/264.

Be not afeard of every stranger. We need that watchword now, for in Shakespeare's Friend we find ourselves confronted with a king of strangers, a Prince of the Unknown. Here in Sonnet 125 no reader acquainted with the Elizabethans can relegate him as a monarch to a poet's private imagining. We meet him in public, announced by trumpets, guarded by his gentlemen-pensioners, his glittering courtiers trooping before him as he paces forth in solemn state under a royal canopy, a 'pillared shade'. And this while Elizabeth Tudor rules sole sovereign of England. What do Gloriana's loving Londoners say to that? Is this *imperium in imperio*? Can one England brook a double reign? The thing looks unbelievable, and dark indeed.

In retrospect, we remember that Shakespeare's references, applying exclusively to a *king*, rule out of consideration not only both Southampton and Pembroke, but every nobleman. And Sonnet 125 clinches it. Anyone with a respectable knowledge of the Elizabethans is aware that no peer less than a vicegerent or viceroy was permitted to walk abroad under a carried canopy or cloth of state. The only viceroy in England was God's vicegerent Elizabeth; and her blazing anger at Leicester's unauthorized assumption of state as 'Governor' in Holland is unforgettable. Peers therefore eliminated as impossible, we are left with Shakespeare's *sovereign*, however improbable he looks.

But Sherlock Holmes to the rescue: 'How often have I said to you that when you have eliminated the impossible, whatever remains, *however improbable*, must be the truth?' And Feste too can find us a bracing word: 'I say there is no darkness but ignorance, in which thou art more puzzled than the Egyptians in their fog.' Well, if it is no more than ignorance, men before now have found their way out of its murky vaults. And long ago we learned to trust, with Don Quixote, that Fortune leaves always one door open whereby to come at a remedy.

Things that seem are not the same. It is time to apply our proverb to the problem. From Shakespeare's repeated and concurring testimony his Friend certainly *seems*, like Queen Elizabeth, a sovereign. Yet clearly he is *not the same*, the anointed ruler of England. What, then, is he sovereign of? What manner of prince is he? We are forced to the conclusion: he can only be an English subject, allowed by the Queen to be honoured as a king-by-courtesy—a sovereign *pro tempore*.

A Prince for a Time . . . Could this be the first thread of a clue leading to the wanted man, Master William H——?

Now to look back. We seem to have found that this fair gentleman-Friend—separated by his rank from full companionship with Shakespeare, who by misfortune stood no higher than a plebeian player—was some kind of temporary King.

A finding as novel as it is strange. We hold it in suspense. Is there anything ulterior to the Sonnets to substantiate it? Then, as we look at it from every side, sudden realization comes like a wave: *we have heard this before.* This very thing is what Shakespeare's friend John Davies of Hereford *mentioned in 1610 as a matter of common knowledge*, in writing

> To our English Terence, Mr. Will.
> Shake-speare.

> Some say (good *Will*) which I, in sport, do sing,
> Had'st thou not plaid some Kingly parts in sport,
> Thou hadst bin a companion for a *King* . . .[1]

Here we have it. Published evidence that in 1610 it was well known not only (*a*) that the *separable spite*[2] of social disparity which frustrated the poet's friendship was the *public means*—[3] *i.e.* Shakespeare's occupation as an actor (*Had'st thou not plaid*)—but also (*b*) that the Friend was a King.

Independent corroboration of our conclusion by Londoners of 1610 is a long step forward. And the next move is clear—a hunt for Kings.

---

[1] *The Scourge of Folly*, entered 8 October 1610.
[2] *Though in our lives a separable spite.* (Sonnet 36.)
[3] *That did not better for my life provide*
Than public means which public manners breeds. (Sonnet 111.)

III

A SHADOW-KING

KING. No word more auspicious for good hunting could be found. For we recall that *King* stands as the first key in the most marvellous feat of literary detection of the last century—the Decipherment of the Trilingual Cuneiform Inscriptions of ancient Persia. That problem did not look formidable; it looked utterly hopeless. What unheard-of languages were these? And what form of writing? Here was no lucky Rosetta Stone, on which a known tongue furnished the Egyptologist with a running key to the unlocking of the two unknown. *All three were unknown.*

It was Friedrich Münter who first guessed that in this welter of wedge-shaped characters a certain recurring group might represent the word for *King*. His guess proved to be the entering crack made by acumen in that vast wall of mystery. Decades of even more brilliant work by scholars of genius had to follow, prosecuted in the face of prevailing scepticism, before the three lost languages could be read. But they were read. In the annals of detective achievement against incredible odds there is no more heroic story.[1] And it began with *King*.

Like the cuneiform, the language of Shakespeare's Sonnets has been pronounced inscrutable. 'This autobiography is written by a foreign man in a foreign tongue, which can never be translated.' So Mr T. S. Eliot in 1927. Doctrine forbidding enough, but most welcome to the amateur explicator. For if nobody knows what the words mean, your explicator is free to say they mean whatever he chooses; or—to put it more elegantly—free to wallow in the loose joys of licentious interpretation.

But the Sonnets of Shakespeare were unquestionably understood by his audience of readers, a public largely composed, as

---

[1] See A. J. Booth, *The Discovery and Decipherment of the Trilingual Cuneiform Inscriptions,* 1902.

42

Patrick Cruttwell reminds us, of 'actual individuals personally known to himself'. Also they were unquestionably addressed to a well-known youthful Friend. If we should discover who and what that Friend was, together with some of the once-known circumstances surrounding the writing of these poems, might not the poet begin to show less outlandish? Might not his 'foreign language' begin to yield some of the rich meaning it once offered its readers? In any event, we can but try and see—and *King* presents an opening.

John Davies of Hereford's mention of Shakespeare's King rivets our attention upon that amiable writing-master and his volumes of verse. On the bare chance of learning something more of what he meant by 'King', we are prepared to sift everything he wrote. But as we open the first volume, we see that his editor Dr Grosart has luckily spared us the trouble. With no suspicion that Shakespeare's King was the Friend of the Sonnets, Dr Grosart picked out the following fascinating reminiscence:[1]

> I knew a man, unworthy as I am,　　　　[*as modest in rank as I*
> And yet too worthy for a counterfeit,　　　[*an impostor*
> Made once a *king*: who though it were in *game*,
> Yet was it there where Lords and Ladies met,
> Who honour'd him as he had been the same,
> And no subjective duty did forget;
> 　　When to himself he smil'd, and said 'Lo, here
> 　　I have for naught what Kings do buy so dear.'

> No odds there was in show (and but in show　[*No difference*
> Kings are too often honour'd) save that *he*
> Was but twelve gamesome *days* to king it so,
> And *kings*, more *years* of sovereign misery.
> His reign was short and sweet, theirs long in woe.
> He after liv'd; they, with or for theirs, die.
> 　　He had a taste of reign, with power to leave;
> 　　They cannot taste, but life must take or give. . . .

---

[1] From 'Speculum Proditori' in *A Select Second Husband for Sir Thomas Overbury's Wife* (1616) in *Works* (ed. Grosart, 1878) II. *i.* 18*b*. For convenience I give it in modern spelling.

He sat in state that mirth and love did stay;   [support
They sit in state that hate oft undermines.
He without fear had some to take assay;   [tasters to the king
But they have such for fear of sudden fines.   [deaths
He poison'd some (to play as Kings might play),
But 't was with sugar and perfumèd wines.
    He went with guards, yet stabbing fearèd not:
    They go with guards, yet fear the stab or shot.

He could devise with Ladies, if he could   [converse
Devise with Ladies, without all suspect.
If they do so, they do not as they should,
For 't will be said their honours they neglect.
He could command, and have all as he would;
But their commands oft have not that effect.
    Then who had better Reigns, judge all of sense,
    Either a King indeed, or in pretence?

This King is not Shakespeare's Friend; but could one ask a more pleasing introduction to the select group to which he belonged? As Jasper Mayne (adapting Petronius) observed, 'Poets and Kings are not born every day'—even Kings in pretence. Like W. H., this friend of Davies's was a 'Master', a plain gentleman as he was himself. Again like W. H., he was singled out and chosen to rule as King for a Time. Davies tells us that his subjects included real English lords and ladies, who paid him duty and honour and waited upon his pleasure. The circumstance that his reign was 'but twelve gamesome days' long reveals him as a Christmas Prince or Lord of Misrule, ruling or misruling for the Twelve Days, doubtless in the house of his noble master. According to Stow, in earlier times these reigns often lasted as long as three months—from the end of October to the beginning of February:

In the feast of Christmas, there was in the king's house . . . a Lord of Misrule . . . and the like had ye in the house of every noble man. . . . These Lords beginning their rule on All Hallow Eve, continued the

same till the morrow after . . . Candlemas Day. In all which space
there were fine and subtle disguisings, masks, and mummeries.[1]

And we find this 'long reign' tradition occasionally revived in
Elizabeth's days by the conservative Inns of Court.

Needless to say, we have here no hastily improvised frolic, but
a deep-rooted popular custom going back to pagan antiquity: the
genial winter feast of freedom, liberty, or 'the world turned upside
down'. 'Christmas succeeds the Saturnalia', as John Selden remarks. The festival's aim was to make Time 'run back and fetch
the age of gold'—to bring again the happy reign of the mythical
Italian King Saturn, in the world's young days of truth, love,
mirth, dancing, plenty, peace, and eternal spring.

Properly to overturn the world in which Age rules, your
Saturnalian or Winter Prince should be a youth or a child. In the
cathedral churches this principle produced the *Episcopus Puero-
rum* or Boy Bishop at Lincoln, Salisbury, and St Paul's, among
others. Queen Mary Tudor in 1555 twice received the Child
Bishop of St Paul's at St James's—on St Nicholas and on Innocents' Day (Childermas), which marked respectively the beginning and the end of his three weeks' reign.

While I do not find the rule of choosing tender youth as the
Christmas Prince always observed, whether in the houses of
noblemen, the university colleges, or the Inns of Court, it was
clearly followed in the case of W. H., Shakespeare's sovereign, the
lovely boy.

Naturally the most conspicuous of the Princes—and no doubt
the only ones in Shakespeare's day stately enough to walk abroad
honoured with a carried canopy—were those who at times
reigned in great magnificence at one or other of the crowded and
wealthy Inns of Court. These four societies or colleges, 'the
noblest nurseries of humanity and liberty in the kingdom', as Ben
Jonson styled them, formed the Third and most socially select and
desirable University of England. More 'collegiate' in those days

---

[1] *A Survey of London* (1603, ed. Kingsford 1908, 1.97), spelling modernized.

than they have ever been since, they housed the great majority of their gowned students, who dined together in Hall below the high table of Benchers and Ancients. Thronged with the nation's élite —scholars, wits, gallants—they made the capital city's intellectual centre. At this period the Inns of Court still prepared gentlemen not only for bar, bench, and parliament, and for county careers in the Queen's commission of the peace, but for office in the royal household and diplomatic service abroad as well. For in addition to the law—and the handling of a case 'to promote the faculty of ready speaking'—the arts and exercises studied by the young patricians included modern languages, fencing, tennis, music, and especially dancing—for masks and revels—with occasional production of 'stately shows', comedies, and tragedies.

We cannot consider these latter activities amusements for relaxation from the hard study of the law. To do so would be to disregard both the close application exacted by the excellence aimed at, and the original purpose of the Inns as defined by the fifteenth-century Sir John Fortescue:

The Students . . . did not only study the laws . . . but did further learn to dance, to sing, to play on instruments . . . using such exercises as they did which were brought up in the King's court. So that these houses, being nurseries or seminaries of the court, took their denomination of the end wherefore they were instituted, and so called the Inns of Court.[1]

Theirs was thus preparation in manners, arts, and accomplishments to fit them for the royal court, held to be 'the universal school of all the world', at least in the days *When reign'd our glorious dear Elizabeth, The nurse of learning and the blessëd arts.* Its best aspect is described by Thomas Storer with much truth along with the expected hyperbole:

The prince's court is mansion of the wise,
   Figure of heav'n, faire fountaine of delights,
Theatre of honor, earthly paradise,
   Sodaine advauncer, sphere of purest lights . . .[2]

[1] Qu. Francis Thynne, B.M. MS. Cott. Faust. E. V., f. 44. Spelling modernized.

[2] *The Life and Death of Thomas Wolsey, Cardinall* (1599), 9.

46

Accordingly, when one or other of the Inns felt able to stand the great expense incident to setting up a Winter Prince, they strove to produce so far as they could an image, a 'shadow' or counterfeit presentment of the Queen's court, along with the splendour of its elaborate ceremonial. A familiar instance is offered by the Inner Temple's triumph of 1561–62, when Lord Robert Dudley reigned there as Pallaphilos (*i.e.* Loving Friend of Pallas-Queen Elizabeth), Prince of Sophie (Wisdom), founding the Honorable Order of Pegasus (the Inner Temple's coat of arms) in the name of his mistress Pallas.

Of the pomp of service adorning the state supper of Pallaphilos, the herald Gerard Legh[1] testifies, 'I have seen the service of great princes, in solemn seasons of triumph, yet the order hereof was not inferior to any.' After the placing of the noble guests ('ambassadors of sundry princes'), Legh reports the seating of the Prince's numerous great officers—beginning with the Lord Steward, the Treasurer, and the Keeper of Pallas' Seal—at the various tables, all most nobly served and attended. 'At every course the trumpets blew the courageous blast of deadly war', and the intervals were filled with delicious music.

From the high table before the second course, the king of heralds proclaimed the Prince's royal style: 'The mighty Pallaphilos, Prince of Sophie, High Constable Marshal of the Knights Templars, Patron of the Honourable Order of Pegasus', cried 'A largess!' and received the Prince's praise with the reward of a rich chain of gold. When the tables were taken up, Prince Pallaphilos 'rose, and a while stood under the place of honour, where his achievement (of arms, with crest, mantlings, etc.) was beautifully embroidered, and devised (conversed) of sundry matters with the ambassadors of foreign nations (that is, the other Inns of Court).' The 'place of honour' was the 'state' or fixed canopy over the Prince presiding in Hall.

In some respects these 'pageant reigns' at the Inns of Court may be compared with the Basoche of the Parisian law-clerks, an

---

[1] *The Accedens of Armory*, 1562.

institution which had flourished continuously since early in the fifteenth century. 'The Basoche . . . was formed as a miniature kingdom. . . . It even had its own system of coinage. There was a king, a chancellor, a High Court of Justice. . . .'[1]

The mock trials staged by these law-clerks developed readily into acted farces. 'And so, very early the Basochiens began to include comic plays in their public shows, such as the May Day parade. Their reputation as play actors grew and . . . more and more they were summoned [to court] to entertain distinguished visitors.'[2] Similarly, for entertaining such visitors in London, we remember that in 1600–1 Don Virginio Orsino on his brief visit was regaled by Queen Elizabeth with Shakespeare's professionals in a swiftly prepared, seasonable, and topical *Twelfth Night*; and according to John Chamberlain, the Orsino 'should have been [feasted] . . . by Gray's Inn, that made preparation of shows to entertain him, but he made such haste away that they were disappointed'. Mock trials also formed an inevitable feature of the sports at the Inns of Court; and again like the Basoche, Gray's Inn had its own Saturnalian coinage, known as 'Gray's Inn pieces'.

The differences, however, are great. First, because of the contrast between the social structures of France and England. The Basochiens belonged to a class which did not mingle with the *noblesse*. Membership in the Inns of Court, by contrast, was limited to gentry (whether future barristers or judges or not) and nobility, preparing to serve in the governing of the land. And unlike the Roi de la Basoche, the Inns of Court Princes were inaugurated only infrequently, since the cost of the rich costume and decoration deemed necessary for their public 'riding' or show and their elaborate mask or device of revels for the Court was almost prohibitive. Moreover, the patrician English youth offered not farces, but on occasion comedy and tragedy at Elizabeth's court, a court 'gay, decent, and superb', and a model of order in

---

[1] Howard G. Harvey, *The Theatre of the Basoche* (1941), 18.
[2] *Ibid.*, 23.

comparison with the French. Also they specialized and excelled in dancing, to the point of contributing thereby to the development of the mask as an art-form.

Doubtless to foster a healthy spirit of rivalry—so familiar between the two Universities from which most of the young gentlemen came, without degrees, at the age of eighteen or so, the four law-societies divided into two groups. Gray's Inn and the Inner Temple were linked in 'ancient friendship', while the Middle Temple and Lincoln's Inn similarly professed themselves lovingly leagued as 'confederates'.

On the memorable occasions when a sovereign was chosen, his title at Gray's Inn was *Prince of Purpoole*, from the ancient manor of Portpool on which the Inn was built;[1] at the Middle Temple, *Prince d'Amour* or Love; while at the Inner Temple he seems to have been styled *Emperor*, and at Lincoln's Inn, *Prince de la Grange*.

One of the oldest folk-customs of the Christmas Lord was to adopt a personal badge or cognizance, in the usual manner of royalty and nobility, to be worn by his retinue on the left sleeve. And on his progress round the neighbourhood to raise funds to furnish the revels, the badge was awarded to each contributor. A custom still familiar today to every man in the street who contributes a coin to a 'good cause', and has a poppy or other emblem pinned on him in return.

Similarly, the sovereign's badge or cognizance formed an essential feature of the Inns of Court Prince. Here it was usually the badge of the Order of Knighthood which he founded, on the model of the Most Noble Order of the Garter. At the Middle Temple the Prince d'Amour always led the Most Ancient Order of the Quiver—full of Love's arrows—the badge of 'Affection's men at arms'. At Gray's Inn the manner, however, was to gain variety by drawing the symbol of the Order from the family arms of the gentleman elected Prince of Purpoole: *e.g.* the Heroical

---

[1] The name is preserved today—Portpool Lane, east out of Gray's Inn Road.

Order of the Helmet, from the three helmets in the coat of Mr Henry Helmes, and the Heroical Order of the Crescent, from the silver crescents borne by Mr Thomas Perient. And when they devised a mask for presentation at court, its theme embodied Knights of the Order engaged in a chivalric enterprise symbolically appropriate to it.

I suppose we are lucky to have first-hand chronicles surviving of the glorious reigns of as many as two of these late-Elizabethan Princes, one ruling at Gray's Inn, the other at the Middle Temple, and but three years apart. So fascinating are their details, and told with such high spirits, that one longs for more. The importance of having at least two consists in their corroborating and checking each other, revealing common features which were no doubt traditional.

One example of this has a special interest. For the first account, *Gesta Grayorum*—the anonymous history (printed 1688) of the reign 1594–95 of Henry [Helmes], Prince of Purpoole—included one 'grand night' (Innocents' Day, 28 December) when Shakespeare played them a comedy:

The Ambassador [of the Inner Temple came to Gray's Inn Hall] about nine of the clock at night . . . there arose such a disordered tumult and crowd upon the stage, that there was no opportunity to effect that which was intended. . . . The Lord Ambassador and his train thought that they were not so kindly entertained as was before expected, and thereupon would not stay any longer at that time, but [departed] in a sort [*i.e.* in a body], discontented and displeased. . . . A Comedy of Errors . . . was played by the players. So that the night was begun, and continued to the end, in nothing but confusion and errors; whereupon it was ever afterwards called *The Night of Errors*.

This discourtesy to the friendly Templerians, and their walking out affronted, has often been supposed a genuine *contretemps* marring the general mirth. But no such matter. A simulated 'falling-out of faithful friends' formed a necessary prologue to the renewing of love between the two societies. The 'renewing' furnished the theme for a subsequent dramatic show, presenting

50

their mutual love and amity. Three years later this identical programme of disorder and lovers' quarrel, with the indignant departure of invited allies, is reported from the Kingdom of Love at the Middle Temple under Richard [Martin], Prince d'Amour:

Upon Thursday night the Linconians intended to see the Prince's Court, and so did all the town, which bred such disorder that the Prince could not receive them according to their worthiness, nor his own desire. Upon this, Milorsius Stradilax [*i.e.* his Clerk of the Council, John Hoskins the wit] practised factiously against the Prince, and earnestly stirred up enmity betwixt him and the Linconians. [Two days afterwards] the Linconians were entertained with a banquet by our Prince, and our league was renewed.[1]

Other features obviously customary included the general pardon granted by the Prince on inauguration (with many curious criminals sternly excepted), creation of Knights of the Order, mock trials, and (at Gray's Inn) the Prince's hearing the various advice of his councillors (given with much eloquence, learning, and wit) on the course of royal life most advantageous for him to pursue, for achieving happiness or eternity of fame.

Besides the special feasts in Hall, followed by a show, a play, or a mask, and general dancing, at which the Prince entertained England's greatest lords and ladies, with many other courtiers, he customarily made at least two public 'ridings' in great state. On the first he went into the City to dine by invitation with the Lord Mayor of London, and on the second to present a mask or a play at Court.

In the City, the numbers and splendour of Henry Prince of Purpoole's mounted court were so great and rich that the thronging citizens took him for a *bona fide* foreign royalty on a state visit. And when Richard Prince d'Amour proceeded on Twelfth Night to Whitehall,

there went to the Court 11 Knights and 11 Squires, 9 Maskers, 9 Torchbearers; their setting forth was with a peal of ordnance; a noise

---

[1] 'Noctes Templariae', *The Memoirs of Sir Benjamin Rudyard* (ed. J. A. Manning, 1841), 16.

of trumpets always sounding before them; the heralds next; after, 2 Squires and 2 Knights; the Knights for their upper parts in bright armour, their hose of cloth of gold and cloth of silver, the Squires in jerkins laced with gold and silver, and their hose as fair; all upon great horses, all richly furnished.

Then came the Maskers by couples [also mounted], on velvet foot-cloths, in their short cloaks and doublets, and these of cloth of gold and silver of the several colours, representing 9 several Passions [of Love]; to every Masker a Torchbearer on a footcloth, carrying his device, besides 100 torches borne by servants. Never any Prince in this king-dom, or the like, made so glorious, so rich a show.

When they came to Court, the Knights brake every man his lance and two swords [at the indoor combat called 'barriers']: the 9 Maskers, like Passions, issued out of a Heart. All was fortunately performed, and received great commendations.

The Middle Temple was evidently determined not to be out-shone by Gray's Inn for all the latter's wealth, greater numbers, and enviable reputation for drama and device. This was indeed a lavish pomp of glory by land for the Prince d'Amour, but the effort had to be made, since three years earlier Henry Prince of Purpoole's reign had included a triumph at sea, inspired by the Queen's presence at her Palace of Greenwich.

Having led his valiant Grayans of the Helmet to fabulous and far-off victory against the Tartars in aid of the Tsar of Russia, from the poop of his flagship *Ark of Vanity* our homing Henry raised Greenwich. And after his navy had handsomely fired a salute to the Queen, and he had sent up to her Majesty a letter of excuse, the high and mighty Prince received at the Palace water stairs at the hands of one of her great officers her gracious answer, 'That if the letter had not excused his passing by, he should have done homage before he had gone away, although he had been a greater Prince than he was; yet [she said] she liked well his gallant shows that were made at his triumphant return, and that if he should come at Shrovetide, he and his followers should have en-tertainment according to his dignity.' Then advancing up London River, the Prince's fleet arrived at Tower Wharf 'where, by her Majesty's commandment, he was welcomed with a volley of great ordnance'.

From thence, just like a substantial monarch of England, Henry the most victorious shadow-king rode westward in triumph through London, acclaimed by crowding Cockneys, though

> some stood mute, as they amaz'd had been
> To see a Court and Princely noble band
> Come marching on,

and greeted at St Paul's by a loyal address in Latin from its ancient School, delivered on behalf of his assembled fellows by a chosen boy. And how familiar to all was this Prince's badge of the heroical Helmet appears by the graceful allusion to it at the oration's close:

> ... most sovereign Prince of Portpool. ... I hardly dare hope that you, who bear so exalted a personage, and your company of courtiers, after great victories won on land and sea, should pause in the solemnity of a most stately triumph for a boy's address.
>
> Yet through the affability always most praised in the greatest princes, may I be permitted to offer to your Highness passing by, the goodwill of our School and this congratulation of mine, such as it is, on your return from Russia so famous and triumphant? ... Do you not see that the whole City, as though plucked out of their houses, are thronging to congratulate so great a Prince? ... Upon whose favour and countenance, think you, are all eyes directed? ... What do we desire? What do we wish? ...
>
> Go forward, therefore; go with the best auspices, most renowned Prince: return to your Palace of Portpool, that Oracle of the Graii. ... You meditate invading the Spaniard. ... How easily will your sword, now dripping with the blood of the Tartars ... blunt the edges of all others ..!
>
> Meanwhile our Muses will both applaud your victories past and pray the ancient Pallas of the Graii that she may set her own helmet upon you—a second Agamemnon, who have many Achilles and Ulysses for your companions—, protect you with her shield, and

(your foes routed and scattered) with her spear preserve you for ever.

Graciously thanking and rewarding the loyal and learned St Paul's, his Highness proceeded home, to put in train the elaborate preparations for the great Shroving at Greenwich. When the time came, Prince Henry and his Knights of the Helmet brought their mask to Court, and entertained the Queen with *Proteus and the Rock Adamantine*. This magnetic Rock was huge enough to conceal the Prince and his gallant warriors imprisoned within it by Proteus. That mutable sea-god tyrannically refused to enlarge them until they solved the problem he had propounded. But when the Squire proved to Proteus that the learned Prince of Purpoole had solved it, he was obliged to open the Rock. And out came the splendidly costumed Maskers, the Sovereign and Knights of the Helmet, to perform their gracefully elaborate figures—after which each Knight chose a lady of the Court for general dancing.

To crown the festive night, at the chivalric 'fighting at barriers', in which some of the greatest lords competed, the youthful Prince acquitted himself so signally that the Queen awarded him the prize, together with most appreciative and gracious thanks for the excellence of the Grayans' entertainment of her.

And so ended the shadow-reign of Prince Henry, who, entertained by Shakespeare in a comedy, himself entertained Queen Elizabeth in a dramatic mask. When he laid down the sceptre of Purpoole, we know of no poet who 'royalized his acts' or 'eternized his facts In lasting registers of memory'. But his eloquent chronicler did much; and he brought the glorious story to a close with a bow—a deep and graceful reverence to the Queen as both Sun and Sea:

But now our Principality is determined; which although it shined very bright . . . yet, at the royal presence of her Majesty, it appeared as an obscurëd shadow: in this not unlike unto the morning-star, which looketh very cheerfully in the world, so long as the Sun looketh not on it; or as the great rivers, that triumph in the multitude of their waters, until they come unto the Sea.

From a monarch of such quality as the Prince of Purpoole to our common modern notion of 'a mock king in a pageant'—what a far cry! Only ignorance could imagine these Elizabethan shadow-princes to be mere walking or dancing dummies dressed by a court tailor, after the fashion of Plutarch's Aridæus, who

had never but the bare name onely of a King, like as in a dumbe-shew upon a stage, making a countenance onely with a guard of partizans and halberds about him, without speaking one word; and so he was a ridiculous pageant and laughing stocke among his nobles and peeres, who . . . led him as they list.[1]

And it would be equal folly to give the term 'mock' as used of them a crude connotation of horseplay, rag, or unmannerly burlesque. To *mock* was to present and to maintain as close an imitation of the real thing as possible. These sovereigns had not only to play host to the greatest lords and ministers of the Crown, but at Court to converse with the Queen like visiting royalties. Grace and dignity of manner and of speech had to rise to the most exacting standard:

Giovanni. I have seen a Counterfeit
With such a Majesty compose himself,
He thought himself a Prince; could frown as scornfully,
And give his hand out to great Lords to kiss,
With as much grace, as all the Royall bloud
Had muster'd in his veins.
Lucio. Some Monarch
Of Innes a Court in *England* sure.[2]

Here was a task of long-sustained 'personation' or acting which few could perform—the King was held to be the most difficult of all rôles—and it was seriously undertaken. Edmund Gayton indeed reports a sad case when but a single night of such acting

---

[1] *Plutarch's Morals* (tr. Holland 1603), 393.
[2] Shirley, *The Sisters* 2.2.

by an amateur (who put the greatest professional stage-kings in the shade) had serious after-effects:

A Gentleman importun'd, at a fire-night in the publike Hall, to accept the high and mightie place of a mock-Emperour, which was duely conferred upon him, by seven mock-Electors at the same time, with much wit and Ceremony; The Emperour ascended his chair of state, which was plac'd upon the highest table in the Hall, and at his instalment, all Pomp, Reverence, and signes of homage were used by the whole company: Insomuch that our Emperour (having a spice of self-conceit before, was soundly peppered now) for he was instantly Metamorphoz'd into the stateliest, gravest and commanding soule that ever eye beheld. *Taylor* acting *Arbaces* [in Beaumont and Fletcher's *A King and No King*], or *Swanston D'Amboys* [in Chapman's *Bussy*], were shadowes to him; his face, his look, his voice, and all his garb was alter'd. Alexander upon his Elephant was not so high; and so close did this imaginary honour stick to his fancy, that for many yeares he could not shake off this One nights assumed deportments . . .[1]

To recall the reigns of such Inns of Court monarchs seems to enhance the possibility that Shakespeare's King may have ruled as one of them. And we realize that no untitled gentleman could have been chosen for so high and exacting a rôle through favouritism, or at random. For the responsibility was great. His Inn's 'credit' or reputation with the Court and in London was affected by his public success or failure in taking state upon him and monarchizing 'as beseems so great a Prince', under the critical eye of the most expert judge of 'princelike majesty' in the world— Queen Elizabeth. Without question, even in those concentrations of the flower of England's gentry, the character and gifts of the youths or men so distinguished by election could only have been of the rarest quality.

Workaday kingdoms commonly must accept the ruler born to them, no matter what his nature, person, talents, and aptitudes may be. How rare the liberty of these Saturnalian common-wealths—freedom to make choice among their citizens of the man most fit to be their Prince. What were the qualities desired? Well,

---

[1] *Pleasant Notes upon Don Quixot* (1654), 24–25.

first of all, a very practical one. If not rich, he must be at least wealthy enough to bear the costly charge of the royal apparel. That requisite somewhat reduced the ranks of the possibles. Further, the punies or newly admitted first-year youths could be passed over, since a few weeks was not time enough for them to have proved their quality, or to have become sufficiently known.

The candidates remaining were measured against a mental list of the 'fair parts' of an ideal prince: youth, beauty, a tall well-shaped body; 'presence', princely carriage or 'port', and excellence in dancing; general popularity, the gift of leading; intelligence, learning; fairness, friendliness, dignity with courteous affability, a pleasing voice, persuasive eloquence, graceful wit. Leadership and persuasiveness were both needed, to hold a large court together and 'to take away discontentments in inequality of employments'. And we should never forget the additional requirement at Gray's Inn: the possession of a family coat of arms adaptable as a device for an heroical Order of Knighthood.

If it was beyond hope to locate a youthful paragon adorned with all these endowments and charms, yet among a couple of hundred of England's élite one might be found offering at least a respectable number of princely parts. Of the rulers actually elected, two of the contemporary descriptions are tantalizingly brief. At Gray's Inn, 1594, Mr Henry Helmes 'was thought to be accomplished with all good parts, fit for so great a dignity, and was also a very proper man of personage, and very active in dancing and revelling'. For the Middle Temple's Kingdom of Love, 1635, Mr Richard Vivian 'not onely in respect of his great estate but likewise by reason of his other excellent endowmentes & great abilityes of nature . . . was thought to be a fitt Gentleman to take upon himselfe the place & dignity of a Prince that might rule & governe within the precinctes of the Middle Temple for & during the Christmas then following'. Vivian agreed to undertake the part, and 'as a Prince both in state & charge to deporte & demeane himself'.[1]

---

[1] P.R.O., Req. 2/534 Pt. II, *Martyn v. Vivian*.

The life-stories of Helmes, Vivian, and Thomas Perient (Gray's Inn 1614) show points in common. All three experienced very young 'the determinate glory of an earthly prince', for on election each was just out of his punyship or novitiate, beginning his second year, still a youth. All three were knighted (and Vivian baronetted), but in later life made no notable mark.

Richard Martin as Love or Prince d'Amour offers an interesting exception. He was elected at the mature age of twenty-seven, and had been admitted to the Middle Temple ten years before. Always a leading spirit, in his fourth and fifth years he took part in the forbidden 'Lord of Candlemas' riot of misrule, suffering four months' expulsion for the second offence. In 1598 his chronicler Rudyard highly commends Martin's leadership in governing his Kingdom: 'The Prince himself descended into all particular charges and regards, and departed with much of his majesty to gain somewhat of every man's love, and to assure his court of a good report of strangers' entertainment.' And he goes on to describe him:

The Prince was . . . of a chearful and gracious countenance . . . tall bodyed and well proportioned, of a sweete and faire conversation to every man that kept his distance. Fortune never taught him to temper his wit. . . . Of a noble and high spirit . . . so wise, that he knew how to make use of his owne subjects, and that to theyr owne contentment; so eloquent in ordinary speech, by extraordinary practice, . . . that . . . studdy could not mend it. He was very fortunate and discreet in the love of women; a greater lover and complainer of company, having more judgment to mislike then power to forbeare.

Martin made a distinguished career in the law. Barrister, Reader, Member of Parliament, Recorder of London. And he won the hearts of the great and the learned as irresistibly as he had charmed the subjects of his Kingdom of Love. As the most attractive orator to be found, chosen by London in 1603 to welcome the new King to his capital, he so delighted James with his speech of greeting that the King became Martin's admiring friend. Fuller testifies, 'He had an excellent pen, and was accounted one of the highest wits of an age and of his nation.' And John Aubrey, 'He was a very handsome man, a graceful speaker, facetious, and well-beloved.' Ben Jonson, John Selden, and the poet Sir John Davys are numbered among the many who admired his mind and loved his company.

Small wonder then that Martin's name was *Love* both before and long after that brief blaze of public glory in 1597–98. His bosom-friend Davys in one of his Gulling Sonnets (probably before 1594) calls him both *love* and *Cupid*. And a quarter-century later, on his untimely death by smallpox in 1618, his sorrowing friend Hugh Holland hails him as *love of princes*.[1]

To see Richard Prince d'Amour allusively addressed as *love* is enough to arrest any eye open to the King of the Sonnets. For it reminds one instantly that Shakespeare likewise calls his sovereign *love*.[2] What if this should prove to be a similar allusion or title, a like personification? Merely to capitalize the word stimulates the thought:

22   9   *O therefore, Love, be of thyself so wary*

51   12   *But Love for love shall thus excuse my jade*

82   9   *And do so, Love;*

89   5   *Thou canst not, Love, disgrace me half so ill*

93   2   *so Love's face*

       3   *May still seem Love to me though alter'd new*

Then thou alone kingdoms of hearts shouldst owe. Can this be Shakespeare's way of saying with Spenser 'Love is Lord of all the world by right'? However that may be, we have here hit upon something not to be lightly discarded. If we hold it in mind, it is possible that recovery of some yet unknown fact about Shakespeare's King might suddenly activate it or set it alight.

---

[1] *Princeps amorum, principum necnon amor.*

[2] This is the term which to some minds unfamiliar with sixteenth-century language has suggested a sordid and mistaken suspicion about the Friend. To observe it applied by men to the heterosexual Martin, 'very fortunate and discreet in the love of women' should be corrective enough.

It is a possibility of this kind which makes our search enthralling. The new light struck instantly throws into view something never seen before. And at this point in our pursuit I must now report such an unexpected flash, and the revelation which followed. It came as a result of thinking about these shadow-princes of the Inns of Court. And the spark which set it off was—however inappropriate it sounds—the word *shadow*.

'Shadows we are, and shadows we pursue.' It is with this elegiac quotation that Sir Edmund Chambers[1] abandons a fruitless search for books and papers left by Shakespeare at his death. The thought has a sad beauty. But are substantial books and papers properly *shadows*? Perhaps we shall find less melancholy if we pursue true shadows: that is, some meanings of the Elizabethan word *shadow*. For two of its fascinating senses bear directly upon the object of our present search.

The first we have already had—a *representation*, a *semblance*, an *impersonation*. Thus actors on the stage are *shadows*:

> The best [players] in this kind are but shadows
> If we shadows [we players] have offended
> Life's but a walking shadow, a poor player
> You are no men, but maskers: Shapes, shadows[2]

It is similarly applied to *kings in semblance*—

> So many of his shadows thou hast met
> And not the very king

> What were it to be shadow of a king? A vanity; to wear a
> shadowed crown.[3]

---

[1] *William Shakespeare* (1930), 2.180, slightly altered from Edmund Burke (*Speech on Declining the Poll*, 1780): '. . . what shadows we are, and what shadows we pursue.'

[2] *Mids. N. D.* 5.1.213, 430; *Macb.* 5.5.25; Fletcher and Massinger, *Elder Brother* 4.1.1.

[3] *1 Hen. IV* 5.4.30; Middleton, *Wisdom of Solomon paraphrased* (1597), ix. 7.

or *kings without power*:

> But Henry now shall wear the English crown
> And be true king indeed, thou but the shadow

> But what are kings, when regiment is gone,
> But perfect shadows . . .?

> Who is it that can tell me what I am?
> —Lear's shadow.[1]

So much for the first meaning, which applies to human beings. The second describes a material object which gives shade or shelter. This *shadow* could be quite small—part of a woman's bonnet or head-dress:

> Shadowes . . . that women use to weare on their foreheads . . .[2]

larger, as a parasol or umbrella,

> Ombraire: *An umbrello, or shadow.* (Cotgrave.)
> (*Enter* Fancie [like a Queen], Concupiscence *going backward before, carrying an Umbrella over her* . . .)[3]

> Simon Shadow! Yea, marry, let me have him to sit under[4]

> With a great Sombrero or shadow over their heads . . . as broad as a great cart wheele[5]

larger still—

> The Testerne [canopy] or the shadow over the bed[6]

or very large:

> a shadowe or cover over the saide Stadge[7]

---

[1] *3 Hen. VI* 4.3.50; Marlowe, *Edw. II* 2012; *Lear* 1.4.251.
[2] Florio's Dictionary, s.v. *Velaregli.*
[3] Strode, *The Floating Island* 5.2.
[4] *2 Hen. IV* 3.2.132.
[5] Hakluyt, *Voyages* (1598), 2.258.
[6] T. M., *The Blacke Booke* (1604), sig. D1.
[7] Fortune Theatre, 1600. *Henslowe Papers* (ed. Greg, 1907), 5.

Now, bearing in mind two particular shadows—*a king in semblance* and *a canopy*—let us turn to the famous Elizabethan 'Poeme of Dauncing' entitled *ORCHESTRA*, and printed 1596. Its author John (afterwards Sir John) Davys of the Middle Temple dedicated it to Richard Martin,

> . . . first mover and sole cause of it,
> Mine-owne-selves better halfe, my deerest frend

—the very Love or Prince d'Amour we have just been following. And in the poem he pictures 'Love my King' inspiring Antinous with arguments to persuade the Queen of 'Dauncings vertue, and nobilitie'. At the close he invokes Martin (swallow, martin) both as his bird of poetic inspiration and his beloved ruler:

130

> . . . the Swallow, whose swift Muse doth range
> Through rare *Idæas*, and inventions strange,
> And ever doth enjoy her joyfull spring,
> And sweeter then the Nightingale doth sing.

131

> O that I might that singing Swallow heare
> To whom I owe my service and my love . . .

But just before this, he vainly longs for the enviable gifts of the famous poets past and present—Homer, Virgil, Chaucer, Spenser, Daniel:

128

> O that I had *Homers* aboundant vaine,
> I would heereof another *Ilias* make,
> Or els the man of *Mantuas* charmèd braine
> In whose large throat great *Jove* the thunder spake.
> O that I could old *Gefferies* Muse awake,
>   Or borrow *Colins* fayre heroike stile,
>   Or smooth my rimes with *Delias* servants file.

62

Next to these he envies another living poet:

> O could I sweet Companion, sing like you,
> Which of a shadow, under a shadow sing . . .

These two lines exploded the flash. Here is an enviable poet, and here are our two *shadows*; and we ask, What living poet deserves to rank next after Spenser and Daniel? What living poet pictured himself as a *Companion*? What living poet sang *of a shadow, under a shadow*?

To my mind, one poet—and only one—answers all three requirements: William Shakespeare. Shakespeare the player-poet of the Sonnets, those lyrics 'full of high thought's invention', addressed in noble humility to a Friend above him:

> 37 *Whilst that this shadow doth such substance give*
> *That I in thy abundance am suffic'd*
> *And by a part of all thy glory live.*

'Generous in mind and mood' as Davies of Hereford knew him, but for his calling he would have been 'companion for a *King*'— his *sovereign* whose praise he sang: his *shadow*-king, walking in glory *under a shadow* or royal canopy.

For me the conclusion is inescapable. In this passage of his poem ORCHESTRA Davys is envying Shakespeare as the poet of the Sonnets. And he wrote this praise *before his poem was entered at Stationers' Hall, 25 June 1594*. The Sonnets therefore were circulated in hand-written copies *before that date*.

In these celebrities of the Inns of Court we have read of notable mock princes, famous shadow-kings. But Shakespeare's *sovereign* —the *shadow, under a shadow*, reigning before June 1594—is still to find. If Master William H— indeed belonged to the select handful which included Henry Helmes (*Helmet*) 1594–95, Richard Martin (*Quiver* of *Love*) 1597–98, and Thomas Perient (*Crescent*) 1614–15, just when did he reign? Answer, he reigned at the time when Shakespeare began to eternize him in the

Sonnets. But when was that? For lack of evidence there is no sort of agreement among scholars about that date, beyond some preference 'on stylistic grounds' for 'the middle and late 1590s'.

Yet the date is crucial. And the period within which the poet's Friend could be addressed as *my lovely boy* and *my sovereign* must be both brief and precise. In Sonnet 104 only three years have passed *Since first I saw you fresh which yet are green*. Which three historical years before June 1594 were these?

Given two unknowns, the date of the poetic address and the identity of the person addressed, in our problem the first must be solved before we can attack the second. If we can find out when Shakespeare wrote his Sonnets, we shall know within what years to look for his missing Prince.

IV

THE TIME *WHEN?*

'THE question when the sonnets were written . . . is the most important of all the unanswerable questions they pose.' Such was the view of Hyder E. Rollins in 1944,[1] reporting that 'an average of the guesses' indicates the period as 1593–99.

A few years, however, after this unconditional surrender to the Sphinx, I found topical references in several of the later sonnets to universally known current events. These references all point to the period 1587–89[2] as the date of composition—more than seven years earlier than the usual conjecture. My inference, that Shakespeare had completed at least the first group (1–126) of his Sonnets at the age of twenty-five, was widely accepted both in the literary press and by leading writers, scholars, and critics. But as search continued in these intervening years has uncovered interesting corroboration of that conclusion, the reader may welcome a fresh setting-out of the essential matter with the new evidence.

First, then, it seems clear that anyone attempting to approximate the period at which Shakespeare wrote the Sonnets must consider at least three primary questions:

(a) *What was the normal, conventional, usual age at which Elizabethan poets wrote sonnets or love-lyrics?*

(b) *What indications of their author's age do Shakespeare's Sonnets present?*

(c) *Are there any topical references in his Sonnets which indicate their date?*

To take these in their order. Among all the familiar studies of sonnet-conventions, the elementary question 'Which of the Seven Ages of Elizabethan Man was the age for sonneteering?' is one

---

[1] Ed. *The Sonnets* (*Variorum Shakespeare*, 1944), 2.53, 73.

[2] *Shakespeare's Sonnets Dated and Other Essays* (1949); 'More Light on Shakespeare's Sonnets' *Shakespeare Quarterly* (April 1951).

seldom asked. Yet the authoritative answer, given by the Elizabethans themselves, is not far to seek. It is the Third Age, or Youth. The whining schoolboy grows immediately into the sighing lover with his woeful ballad.

'Then youth (our third age) Love's Queen, Venus sways.'[1]
May pricketh tender hearts their warbling notes to tune.

Youth is not only most prone to fall in love, but (as always) unquestioningly follows what is 'done' by its leading spirits. As Florio remarks early in 1591, 'more active gallants . . . blaze and blanche their passions with aeglogues, songs, and sonnets, in pitiful verse . . . and most for a fashion'. The sober contemporary view of this adolescent Petrarchizing has been well summed up: 'Verses were the kickshaws, the idle, if not pernicious employment of youth.'[2]

'Ther nedeth of this make none argument', as Chaucer would say. The proofs are too abundant. In 1578 Thomas Newton writes of William Hunnis,

In prime of youth thy pleasant Penne depaincted Sonets sweete
Delightfull to the greedy Eare, for youthful Humour meete.
Therein appeared thy pregnant wit, and store of fylëd Phraʒe
Enough t'astoune the doltish Drone, and lumpish Lout amaʒe.[3]

Thomas Kyd's Hieronymo confesses,

When I was yong, I gave my minde
And plide my selfe to fruitles Poetrie.

And as William Drummond tells us in a sonnet,

In my first years, and prime not yet at height,
When sweet conceits my wits did entertain . . .
I first began to read, then lov'd to write,
And so to praise a perfect red and white.

Such testimony is typical. On publishing his sonnet-sequence *Fidessa*, Bartholomew Griffin calls himself 'a young beginner'.

---

[1] John Davies of Hereford, *Microcosmos* (1602), 65.
[2] Gladys D. Willcock, *Shakespeare as Critic of Language* (1934), 7.
[3] Verses to Hunnis's *A Hyve Full of Hunnye*, 1578.

Sir William Alexander describes his own quatorzains as 'the first fancies of the Author's youth'. William Shakespeare calls his sonnets-quill 'my pupil pen'. Samuel Daniel, in accord with the epigraph he chose for his works, beginning *Ætas prima canat Veneres*—'Let the first age sing loves'—tells us that his *Delia* sonnets were 'the private passions of my youth'.

Further, Sir Philip Sidney set about his *Astrophel and Stella* when he was twenty-six. Constable at the same age was writing a series to Penelope Rich, and Watson published his *Passionate Centurie* at twenty-five. As for Donne's lyrics, Ben Jonson maintained that all the best of them were written 'ere he was twenty-five years old', and on the authority of his biographer Isaak Walton, Donne had produced most of them 'before the twentieth year of his age'. Barnabe Barnes completed his *Parthenophil* at twenty-one. Richard Barnfield's *Affectionate Shepherd* appeared when the author was twenty. William Browne had finished the first book of his *Britannia's Pastorals* before reaching twenty, and William Percy launched his *Coelia* at the age of nineteen.

Youth has ever been the time for lyric, and certainly the Elizabethan age of early maturity is no exception to the rule. In an age in which Death was so rife that (as Dr Thomas Wilson testifies in his *Arte of Rhetorique*, 1560) 'not one among a thousand commeth to three score yeares', no time was to be lost. Prince Edward at the age of seven could decline any Latin noun and conjugate any regular verb. At thirteen he was translating Cicero into Greek. Men entered the university at fourteen or younger,[1] often (like Shakespeare) married at eighteen, and as Shakespeare tells us, were old at forty. Sonnets were universally held to be among the aspirant's first steps to Parnassus.

Here we have the true circumstance and frame into which to set the composition of Shakespeare's Sonnets: the literary custom of his time, the common practice and fashion of his

---

[1] Ferdinando Lord Strange and his two younger brothers entered Oxford together, aged respectively twelve, eleven, and ten.

contemporaries. In this nest of singing birds, the average age for sonneteering is well under twenty-five: that is, Youth.

Yet in the face of this evident fact, what has our latter-day world done with 'mighty Shakespeare's nimble vein'—Shakespeare, easily the master of them all? And not only king of poets, but conspicuous for 'great quickness and invention'? '*Shakespeare*, that nimble *Mercury* thy brain'—'Shakespear. *His quill as quick as feather from the bow!*'—so enviably quick that Jonson, the slower-witted 'elaborate Ben', felt driven to growl, 'he needed the drag, the trigger in his wheel'?

Paradoxically enough, in modern times this same over-quick Shakespeare has been commonly represented for our credulity as the very opposite. For the textbooks all ask us to accept a Shakespeare strikingly *sluggish* when compared with his contemporaries. Lagging with his Sonnets, some say seven years, some even say fourteen years, behind the average of his generation. Offered a notion so repugnant to common sense and utterly contrary to all the evidence, any thinking reader will naturally ask, What are the grounds for such an idea? And the answer, when at last you manage to extract it, proves equally astonishing: Nothing whatever requires the Sonnets to be many years tardy *except the dates demanded by the respective ages of a couple of earls*—because these noble peers are alternatively fancied to be the youthful Friend whom Shakespeare addresses in his poems.

That is to say, in order to lend some colour of possibility to a biographical theory, which must have the Earl of Southampton, or the Earl of Pembroke, as the poet's 'lovely boy', theorists have postdated the Sonnets to suit: quite artlessly asking you to believe that the Mercury-quick Shakespeare was not merely *not* quick—he was notably backward. An outstanding case of arrested development. A kind of Dopey, trailing cheerfully along far behind all the rest of the Seven Dwarf sonneteers.

To bolster their Looking-Glass belief—in which the quick Shakespeare is reversed into a laggard follower of a fashion—the theorists point to the well-known spate of sonnet-printing in the mid-1590s, as though this revealed a great writing-vogue into which the retarded genius might have been belatedly caught up. But we have seen Florio reporting the fashion of sonneteering already in early 1591. What this access of sonnet-publication in the middle nineties does in fact show is *a new and large market of general readers*, a few years after the posthumous printing (1591) of Sidney's sonnets, which had already been 'spred abroade in written Coppies' for more than ten years.

The important sonnets of Shakespeare's immediate contemporaries and peers Daniel, Drayton, and Constable had similarly circulated in manuscript for years before the mid-1590s. Constable was writing sonnets in 1588 or 1589. Daniel's 'private passions', if we regard age twenty-five as the close of youth, came before 1588. And Drayton, on printing his *Idea* sonnets in 1594, when the plague-years ended, tells his readers that these poems of his had 'long slept in sable night'.

If one asks why all these ultimately printed were not promptly given to the press in the late 1580s, the answer must be the practical one: In those days there was no profitable sale for such wares. A clear hint of the unfavourable market in 1588 is given by James Aske, addressing 'the Gentle Reader' in that year:

But if any man write loving Songs, and amiable Sonnets, they, as foolish toyes nothing profitable, are of every one misliked.[1]

If therefore in and about 1588 the general public was not yet interested, small wonder that the foolish toys even of the best poets such as Shakespeare, Daniel, Constable, and Drayton were spread abroad, like Sidney's, only in written copies.

It is a striking change in the *reading public's* taste or fashion which the wave of sonnet-printing in the middle nineties reveals. For whatever reason, many more people now wanted to read these lyrics, as they had not done before. Just as they now wanted to read *plays*, as they had not done before. The figures of play-publication for the decade 1587–96 are significant. During the

---

[1] *Elizabetha Triumphans*, 1588.

first five years, 1587–91, the total number of plays published was 9. But for the next five years, 1592–96, the total leaped to 36.

Who would think of concluding from these figures that in the latter period—which comprised the two great plague-years, during which the closing of theatres destroyed managers' demands for new plays—four times as many plays were *written* as in the former? Yet this is just what the textbooks have done in the contemporary case of sonnets. Neglecting the leading writers' own testimony, they have mechanically equated sonnet-*writing* with sonnet-*printing*, deduced a 'sonneteering craze' for the mid-1590s, and shoved Shakespeare's sonnets into it.

They cannot have it both ways. If on the bare basis of *publication*-figures we are asked to believe in a great outburst of sonneteering in the middle nineties, we must on the like ground believe in a great explosion of play-writing at that same time: and of such a phenomenon there is no evidence at all. Let us remember that readers' fashions come and go, and cling to sense. Confuse writing with printing, and we shall not merely have Shakespeare sonneteering as a grandfather aged forty-five, but John Donne writing his lyrics two years after he had breathed his last. As for the spate of sonnet-publication, what could it conceivably have to do with Shakespeare's Sonnets? They were neither written in it, printed in it, nor in any way affected by it.

So much for the answer to our first question, *How old was the typical Elizabethan sonneteer?* And as a corollary, in the light both of the common practice of Shakespeare's fellows and of his own notorious characteristics as a writer, clearly the normal time to expect his 'pupil pen' to be finishing his sonnets is about 1589—that is, when he reached twenty-five—and *not* seven or fourteen years later.

Now for the second query, *What indications of their author's age do Shakespeare's Sonnets present?*

To set this question likewise in proper perspective, we should first inquire, What indications of their authors' age do the other sonnet-series present?

Perhaps the most striking and amusing feature which at once

meets the eye here is the conventional 'old man' pose characteristic of the young Elizabethan sonneteers. We find these youths bewailing in rime their old age, their ugliness, their decrepitude. You ask, Why in the world—? Well, it seems it was the fashion, first instituted by the passionate and doleful young Petrarch, 'head and prince of poets all'.

As with any established fashion, however novel, you don't question it; you follow it. One might as reasonably ask, Why beards? or, Why do our modern poets ape John Donne in writing about human bones? Answer, It's the style; and—pauca, there's enough. Within living memory the poets wrote about stars, not bones. Fashion again. They took as little genuine interest in astronomy as ours take in osteography.

And as the modern gentle reader accepts the proffered bone (always clean and white) without muttering 'Peace to thy bones', so it never even occurred to his Elizabethan counterpart to smile at the doleful Richard Barnfield, aged twenty, stylishly complaining

Winter hath snow'd upon my hoary head . . .

or at that passionate youth Samuel Daniel's lament,

Whilst age upon my wasted body steals . . .

or yet at the 'young beginner' Bartholomew Griffin, vowing

I'll pluck my silver hairs from out my head,
And wash away the wrinkles of my face . . .

For he accepted this paradoxical senility as sonneteers' legal tender, bearing the authentic stamp or mint-mark of the author's decrepit, white-haired, and wrinkled Petrarchan youth.

In brief, adoption of this preposterous pose is unmistakable *prima facie* evidence of a sonneteer's youth. For it is of course *only* to the young man—while his glands are still shouting to him 'O King, live for ever!' that it seems interesting or attractive, and quite safe, to advertise his weary life as in the sere and yellow, to proclaim that he totters on the brink of the grave. Let him but continue even a few years into middle life, crawl to maturity with

71

its uneasy intimations of real mortality, and that particular brand of make-believe will present him no charms at all.

But for him *now*, in prime of youth, the creeping clutch of Age is still far in the future: as unbelievable as it is unknown. *Now* he is both ready and willing, like the young Petrarch, to peer into his mirror and report wrinkles and decay. And like him, young Shakespeare with his pupil pen—except that he does it better— does the same; for he belongs with his fellows, soul of the age:

> 62 9 *But when my glass shows me myself indeed,*
> *Beated and chopp'd with tann'd antiquity . . .*

> 63 1   *as I am now,*
> *With Time's injurious hand crush'd and o'erworn . . .*

No one of Shakespeare's readers could make the elementary blunder too many of us moderns have made—that of taking this withered sonneteer, far stricken in years, for anything but a youth like the rest.

Shakespeare employs this fashionable 'old man' fiction not only in the poems to the 'lovely boy', but in those to the Dark Woman too. Here, however, in Sonnet 138 the stock pretence wears thin. So thin indeed that the young poet does not even bother to keep it up:

> *I do believe her, though I know she lies,*
> *That she might think me some untutor'd youth . . .*

For no matter how solemn his affirmation of senility, obviously none but a youth could be taken for an untutor'd youth.

In retrospect it is hard to understand why, with all our study, we have hitherto failed to realize with Samuel Butler that Shakespeare's adopting this unmistakably young man's Petrarchan pose of preposterous senility throughout his Sonnets is enough in itself to show that *he wrote them all while he was young*. The dusty dogma of a mentally retarded or backward Shakespeare will not stand examination, however long it may continue to be repeated through the inertia of habit.

At the same time it must be agreed that his pervasive and

plainly expressed feeling of maturity and experience in relation to his younger Friend is no assumed pose, no *exercice de style*. How does this fact fit with our conclusion? If in 1586 when they grew acquainted we see Shakespeare well over twenty-two, and his 'lovely boy' barely eighteen, this feeling of relatively marked maturity in the poet is clearly both natural and understandable. At twenty-two, Shakespeare was the father of three children, and had been four years a married man. Take a comparison from our own observation, as Samuel Butler did on this very point. Who feels older than a married graduate-with-children, and to him who seems younger than the entering freshman? When he comes to middle life, such a few years' difference in age shrinks to a trifle. But at twenty-two, it is everything.

Now for our third question, *Are there any topical references in the Sonnets which indicate their date?* Here I shall not only present new evidence on the topicality of Sonnets 107, 123, and 124, but add notes on Sonnets 66 and 25—which were not handled in *Shakespeare's Sonnets Dated*.

I. The Mortal Moon

107

Not mine own fears, nor the prophetic soul
Of the wide world, dreaming on things to come,
Can yet the lease of my true love control,
Suppos'd as forfeit to a confin'd doom.
The mortal Moon hath her eclipse endur'd,
And the sad Augurs mock their own presage;
Incertainties now crown themselves assur'd,
And peace proclaims Olives of endless age.
Now with the drops of this most balmy time
My love looks fresh, and Death to me subscribes,
Since, spite of him, I'll live in this poor rime,
While he insults o'er dull and speechless tribes;
*   And thou in this shalt find thy monument*
*   When tyrants' crests and tombs of brass are spent.*

73

This is the chief 'dating sonnet', and it has been called the most difficult of all. And here I think we shall find that the world has been led down a false trail by assuming that *the mortal Moon* means Queen Elizabeth, and that *hath her eclipse endur'd* means either that she is dead, or that she has survived a dangerous crisis in her life.

To read it as 'the Queen is dead' would place this sonnet in 1603. Beyond the unnatural callousness of writing '*the* Moon' instead of '*our* Moon', there are other serious objections to this interpretation. For the Elizabethan vogue of sonnet-writing, 1603 is far too late. It is also far too late in Shakespeare's career, as we have seen, for the sonnets of a beginner, wielding a *pupil pen*. Most critics have therefore taken the second meaning—that *the mortal Moon* is the living Queen.

But this theory will not stand the test of the times. All the English poets write of their beloved Queen in terms approaching adoration. She is a goddess come to earth, a heaven-born Astræa. 'This is that Queen, as writers truly say, That God had markèd down to live for aye.' She is Diana. 'Time wears her not. . . . Mortality below her orb is plac'd.' Her word is *Ever the Same*. Her loyal subjects neither wish nor dare to remind her that she is mortal. 'We are afraid,' says John Donne, 'to speak to the great men of this world of their death, but nourish in them a vain imagination of immortality.' As Maurice Kyffin sings in the year before the Armada,

> *Far foreign lands bear witness of her name,*
> *Far surging seas have felt her warlike ships;*
> *Both seas and lands forth thunder out her fame,*
> *Through force of flow'ring acts, free from eclipse:*
> *Elizabeth's due praise shall never die,*
> *In earth, nor seas, nor in the starry sky.*[1]

Mortal, moreover, bears a meaning even more hideous, and one equally common in Shakespeare's works: *deadly, death-*

---

[1] *The Blessednes of Brytaine* (1587), B3. Spelling modernized.

dealing. 'Mortal poison', 'mortal murders', 'mortal butcher', 'mortal rage'. To fancy Shakespeare deliberately writing of his 'imperial Vot'ress' not only that she is *mortal*, but that she has been obscured by an eclipse, is to fancy him a fool.

If it cannot be Elizabeth, what then is this *mortal Moon?* For more than three centuries the answer has vainly stared us in the face. It is the *deadly Spanish Armada of 1588*—the mightiest sea-borne army the world had ever seen—which in its menacing moon-shaped formation[1] appeared in the English Channel, only to be shattered by the drum-fire of Elizabeth's heavy guns, and driven northward away before an irresistible gale in defeat, disaster, and eclipse.

The Spanishe fleete . . . beinge then thwarte of Gravelinge, then went into . . . a proportion of a half moone.
Sir William Winter, aboard *Vanguard*, 1 August 1588.

Hispanique . . . conglobati manserunt in forma semilunii.
'And the Spaniards . . . remained gathered on a cluster compass wise like the Moone.'
Emanuel van Meteran, *Historia Belgica*, c. xv. (Written 1589: cf. B.M. MS. Royal 18. A. lxvi, f. 26ᵛ.)

. . . their fleete was placed in battell araie, after the manner of a Moone cressant, being readie with her horns & hir inward circumference to receiue either all, or so manie of the English nauie, as should giue her the assault.
Petruccio Ubaldino, *A Discourse concerninge the Spanishe fleete. . . 1588*, 1590.

And sent first bullets, then a fleet of fire
. . . through the enemies moone,
That wan'd before it grew.
Ben Jonson on the Armada, *Prince Henries Barriers*, 1610.

---

[1] See Garrett Mattingly, *The Defeat of the Spanish Armada* (1959), 357.

... as clearely as wee have eclipsed the memorie of the Crescent in 88. (The Armado which came displayed in forme of the Moone Crescent.)

Anon., *The Passionate Remonstrance* (1641), 31.

... a horned Moone of huge and mighty shippes. ... But all is vaine: for the breath of the Lords mouth hath dimmed the brightnesse of her Moone, and scattered those proud shippes.

J[ames] L[ea], *The Birth, Purpose and mortall Wound of the Romish holie League*, 1589.

The mortal Moon hath her eclipse endur'd. Philip laboured to bring the Moon out from its eclipse in the year following, but the damage had been too great. At a conservative estimate, dead 8000, ships lost or useless 63, damage 1,400,000,000 *reales*. And that Shakespeare, like James Lea, is here in Sonnet 107 celebrating England's Great Deliverance through the eclipse suffered by the deadly 'Moone of huge and mighty shippes' now appears (as John Benson said of the Sonnets) 'serene, clear, and elegantly plain'.[1] And he is not alone: for upon her discomfiture of the Spanish Moon, Elizabeth's Groom of the Leash Edward Hellwis identifies her with the Sun-Woman of the Apocalypse (*Rev.* 12); for 'proceeding against all the enemies of Europe . . . with power to performe marvels at sea' she 'now at this instant . . . standeth clothed with the Sunne . . . and having the Moone . . . placed under her feete.'[2]

The year 1588 brought three eclipses—one of the sun and two of the moon—as well as the eclipse of *the mortal Moon*. What the universal world feared it would bring was the end of human life: the day of doom long prophesied for 1588:

> *Not mine own fears, nor the prophetic soul*
> *Of the wide world, dreaming on things to come,*
> *Can yet the lease of my true love control,*
> *Suppos'd as forfeit to a confin'd doom.*

---

[1] For Shakespeare's repetition of his metaphor of an eclipsed moon for a defeated fleet, in Antony's 'Alacke our Terrene [that is, Mediterranean] Moone is now Eclipst', see *Shakespeare's Sonnets Dated*, 7–10.

[2] *A Marvell Deciphered* (1589), B1ᵛ–B2.

The fate had been confined[1] or limited to 1588 for more than a century, ever since that 'most notorious prophesie' of 1475, attributed to Johann Müller of Königsberg (Regiomontanus), and taken up and repeated by Melanchthon:

Tausent fünffhundert achtzig acht,
Das ist das Jar das ich betracht:
Geht in dem die Welt nicht under,
So gschiet doch sonst grosz mercklich Wunder.

These apocalyptic rimes were expanded into Latin verses, of which this was one English version:

When from the Virgin Birth a thousand yeares
With full five hundred be compleat and told,
The Eightie Eighth a famous yeare appeares,
Which brings distresse more fatall then of old.
If not in this yeare all the wicked world
Do fall, and land with sea to nothing come;
Yet Empires must be topsie turvie hurl'd,
And extream grief shall be the common summe.

Regiomontanus was reprinted 1588 in Holland, with grim elaboration.[2] Ominous corroboration came from the astronomers, for

... conjunctions of *triplicities*
Of *Saturne*, *Jupiter*, and *Mars* aspecting
Are held most powerful *principalities*,
Greatest *alterations* effecting;[3]

and during 1588, in the 'fiery triplicity or trigon' (Aries, Leo, Sagittarius), on the 29th day of April would occur 'a conjunction of Saturn and Mars ... thereafter on the 15th day of October

---

[1] 'Heauens haue confinde all by some fatall houre'
And all are bounded by some fatall houre'
Poetical Works of Sir William Alexander, ed. Kastner and Charlton, I 1921), 317.
[2] *Een wonderlycke nieu profecije* ... 1588. The Hague, Royal Library, Pamphlet No. 855.
[3] John Norden, *Vicissitudo Rerum* (1600), B3ᵛ.

would happen a conjunction of Jupiter and Mars . . . and upon them cruel, terrible, and hitherto unheard-of things will ensue'.[1]

Even before the terrible year had opened, Death struck:

> *Sudden Death, much sickness and unknown diseases*
> *in many parts of England, 1587 & 1588.*

And those . . .
Such Plague, Disease, & Death most strange did feel and also bear: . . .
Some young, some old, some rich, some poor, and no degree excepted;
By one and one many were gone, and of their lives berefted.

> *Sickness in England called Death without Dread, 1588.*

And this was rightly called the Death long spoken of before;
Death without Dread, for so it was . . .[2]

And not only Death Unawares, but three baleful eclipses in one year! Alarm was so deep and general that John Harvey was ordered to write 'especially in abatement of the terrible threatenings, and menaces, peremptorily denounced against the kingdoms, and states of the world, this present famous yeere, 1588. supposed the *Greatwoonderfull,* and *Fatall* yeere of our Age'. Broadside ballads and books were printed 'Of the end of the world.'

Such were the universal fears and 'sad auguries' of 1588. And the arrogant Spaniards, 'Who by report through all the world, had won The name of conquest ere the fight begun,' assumed that the prophecy would be fulfilled by the fall of England under the blows of their military might. To advertise their purpose, and to strike cold terror into *los lutheranos,* they painted their England-bound men-of-war black, and flew great 'pennons tragicall' bearing 'sad ostents of death and dismall feare'. One such displayed a sun and moon, with a menacing legend in Spanish to this effect: *Yesterday the Full, but Today the Wane.*

---

[1] Georgius Ursinus, *Duo Prognostica Astrologica* (1580), B4; and cf. Rodolphus Graephius of Deventer, *Praedictio Astrologica* (1587), A3. And see Mattingly, *op. cit.,* 159–162.

[2] William Woodwall, *The Acts of Queen Elizabeth Allegorized* [finished *ca.* 1600]. Bodl. MS. Eng. hist. e. 198, ff. 110ᵛ–111ᵛ.

The mortal Moon came, was well beaten, and went into eclipse. As Queen Elizabeth saw it, the defeat began the eclipse of Philip:

I doubt no whit but that all this tyrannical, proud, and brainsick attempt will be the beginning, though not the end, of the ruin of that King. . . . He hath procured my greatest glory that meant my sorest wrack, and hath so dimmed the light of his sunshine, that who hath a will to obtain shame, let them keep his forces company.[1]

The Invincible Armada has suffered defeat: an event, wrote G. M. Trevelyan, 'which all Europe at once recognized as a turning point in history.' Instead of doom, 1588 brought to England, and to all Protestant Europe with her, the rejoicing dawn of certain deliverance. As Robert Humston preached on 22 September, 'God is now come to us . . . not in the sharm of the trump denouncing death, but in the sound of the trump proclaiming life.' In his *Continuation of the Blessednes of Brytain* (entered 17 October) Maurice Kyffin reports the Pharaoh-like doom of 'Spanish pomp':

> *This was the year wherein by fire and sword*
> *Our foes forethought to work this kingdom's wrack . . .*
>
> *Which hugie Fleet, full fraught with murd'ring minds*
> *Meaning massácre to our native soil,*
> *Being furnish'd forth with ships of sundry kinds*
> *To give the fall, receiv'd themselves the foil.*
>
> *The fatal year of fearful Eighty Eight,*
> *Forethreat'ning falls of empires, realms, and kings,*
> *Out-breathing bale to every earthly wight*
> *By pest'ring plagues and dreadful dreary things,*
>   *Is now nigh spent, and yet our realm and Queen,*
>   *Through God's great pow'r, secure in safety seen.*
>
> *Whereby appears, men's prophecies be vain,*
> *When God decreeth a contrary success . . .*[2]

---

[1] To James of Scotland. Rymer, *Foedera*, xvi. 18–19. Spelling modernized.

[2] Spelling modernized.

Here are the fears, the world-wide apprehension through prophecies of doom and death to all men, which Shakespeare mirrors in his opening quatrain. Then, proved false by the event, the grim predictions now look ridiculous.

> *The mortal Moon hath her eclipse endur'd,*
> *And the sad Augurs mock their own presage;*[1]

The world did *not* come to an end, but the sad presages did much harm, as Woodwall relates of 1588:

> What false Prophets in many a place which took on them to tell
> The year of Consummation, and when the world should fail,
> That insomuch the people were at their wits' end now brought,
> In list'ning what would hereupon ensue or else be wrought.

The modern historian likes to call the Armada fight the beginning of Elizabeth's formal hostilities with Philip, leaving us to think that Shakespeare's countrymen now knew they were at war. How totally different was the view of the man on the spot! For him, the victory of '88 brought not war, but the certain assurance of *peace* for England. Immediately upon the victory, Kyffin writes

> *To honour her with yearly fame's increase*
> *Who holds the helm of our long-lasting peace.*

There would be no invasion and butchery, such as the Low Countries suffered under Alva. No savage wars of religion, like those torturing France. Francis Bacon, looking back over Elizabeth's reign, saw the Armada beaten, 'while on the ground and territories of England, peace remained undisturbed and unshaken'.

> *Incertainties now crown themselves assur'd,*
> *And peace proclaims Olives of endless age.*

---

[1] We have mistakenly understood this *augurs* to mean 'prophets'. But as J. Q. Adams sensibly observed, 'Augurs are not likely to *laugh* at the failure of their own predictions.' In *Macbeth* 3.4.114, as Ernest Schanzer pointed out, *Augures, and understood relations* means 'predictions'. And anyhow, it is not the prophets, but their presages which are *sad*: 'Praesagia tristia' (Robert Johnston, on Regiomontanus and 1588, *Hist. Rer. Brit.*, p. 128); 'These sad presages' (Marlowe, *Lucan* I. 672); 'sad comet'; 'sad token'.

It would be hard to match these two lines for richly heaped meanings and connotations, of which we commonly catch but one—the olive signifying 'peace'. To begin with *crown*: a coronation ends uncertainty, and includes anointing with oil of *olive*. Again, Olive is not only 'peace', it is 'victory' (over the mortal Moon), and 'long life' (*endless age*).[1] Also, both a crowned ruler and peace are *proclaimed*; 'Live!' or 'O live!' is the universal shout of the Queen's loving subjects—'*live, live, and God preserve her!*' '*O live as do the stars, which live for ever!*' '*Live, Sovereign Lady, Live, Elizabeth!*'[2] And every proclamation ends *Vivat Regina Elizabetha!* In his works, Shakespeare employs *Olive* seven other times, in every case with its proper accent. Only in this Armada sonnet does he wrench it, making evident his play on *O live!* and *Olive*:

> And peace proclaims Olives of endless age.

Nashe shares the post-Armada sentiment with Shakespeare:

. . . the prayers of the Church of England fly up into heaven for her Majesty, and return again with Olive-branches in their mouths . . . to bring tidings of peace and long life unto her highness.[3]

> Now with the drops of this most balmy time
> My love looks fresh, and Death to me subscribes,
> Since, spite of him, I'll live in this poor rime,
> While he insults o'er dull and speechless tribes;

We may not take *this balmy time* in the modern sense of 'soft and gentle weather', since that use was unknown to the Elizabethans. What they understood by the phrase was *this time which restores life like the drops of balm*. Balm is the biblical Balm of Gilead or Balsam of Mecca, the prime life-restoring elixir. As Othello says, 'Drop tears as fast as the Arabian trees Their

---

[1] See J. Poole, *English Parnassus* (1657), 146; G. C. Capaccio, *Delle Imprese* (1592), 121ᵛ–123.

[2] J[ames] L[ea], *An Answer to the Untruths*, 1589; T. Bastard, *Chrestoleros*, 1598; Kyd, *Verses of Prayse and Ioye*, 1586.

[3] *The Returne of . . . Pasquil of England*, 1589. Spelling modernized.

med'cinable gum.' Books were written on the magical healing powers of the drops of balm. Shakespeare often mentions it: 'balm, Earth's sovereign salve', 'drop sweet balm in Priam's painted wound', 'balm to heal their wounds', 'Balm of hurt minds'. It is frequent in his fellow-authors: 'the drops of balsamum, that salveth the most dangerous sores' (Dr Thomas Lodge). 'The tree of life . . .

> From that first tree forth flow'd, as from a well,
> A trickling stream of balm, most sovereign . . .
> Life and long health that gracious ointment gave,
> And deadly wounds could heal, and rear again
> The senseless corse appointed for the grave.'
>
> (Spenser)

For *this balmy time*, Dekker exclaims, 'The time! O blessed time! Balm to our sorrow!'

Like the drops of life-giving balm, the blessed Time of Deliverance has rescued Shakespeare and his 'true love' or true-loving Friend from the universally apprehended Death.

> *And thou in this shalt find thy monument*
> *When tyrants' crests and tombs of brass are spent.*

Shakespeare's use of the word *tyrants* is enough in itself to rule out 1603 as a possible date for this sonnet. For it is evident that when James came in with his policy of peace with Spain, there were no longer any 'tyrants' in the western world for Englishmen to execrate. In 1603 the thought was obsolete. Of the two tyrants universally lashed in Elizabethan literature the one, the fighting Caesar-Pope Sixtus V, had died in 1590, and the other, the aggressive despot Philip II, in 1598. In the year after the Armada, however, the Lord Chancellor, Hatton, was denouncing them in Parliament respectively as 'that wolfish bloodsucker' and 'that insatiable tyrant'. For in that year they were both alive, and more than that, still dangerous. And like prudent tyrants, they were notoriously preparing grandiose mausoleums for themselves —the Pope in S. Maria Maggiore, and Philip in the Escorial— supplying plenty of point for Shakespeare's scornful line, *When tyrants' crests and tombs of brass are spent.* At Tilbury Camp Queen Elizabeth's word was 'Let tyrants fear.'[1]

Now that the Elizabethans have given us the indispensable background, we are better equipped to attempt a running comment on the thought of Sonnet 107, as follows:

The poet's fear, shared with the whole Protestant world, of cataclysm and death—the doomsday limited to 1588—, cannot end his Friend's, his True Love's lease of life. It is the foe's 'invincible'

---

[1] In her own time she was universally contrasted with these despots. And in our appraisal of her today (apart from those who have reasons of propaganda for casting odium on her memory), it should not be necessary to point out the ineptitude of applying to her the hostile term 'despot'. As Professor Joel Hurstfield said in his inaugural lecture, 'the term "Tudor despotism" has disappeared from our historical writing. The Tudors were not despots, and their subjects never believed themselves to be slaves'. The latter indeed saw themselves on the contrary blest with 'peace, health, wealth, and prosperity, with free liberty to sit at home under our vines and fig-trees, when other nations have been grievously tossed and troubled with wars and vexations, even to the loathsomeness of their lives' (John Carpenter, *A Preparative . . .*, 1597).

If *despot* were cleaned of its connotations of tyranny and restored to its original sense of *absolute ruler*, Shakespeare's countrymen would contrast their enviable constitution with the situation of the French under the despot Henri IV: 'The King of France is a most absolute monarch: because he not only makes peace and wars, calls and dissolves parliaments, pardoneth, naturalizeth, ennobleth whom he pleaseth, names the value of moneys, and presseth to the war, but even makes laws and imposeth taxes at his pleasure; and all this he doth alone' (Robert Dallington, *ca.* 1604).

Queen Elizabeth's contemporary character as a ruler is no secret: 'As it is a glory to England and a praise to her Majesty to rule with mercy . . . so it is a foul reproach for other Princes abroad . . . whilst they rule with tyranny' (James Sandford, *Houres of Recreation*, 1576); '. . . it is a great gift of God, instead of a tyrant, to be governed by a queen, instead of a cruel persecutor, to have a gentle ruler' (John Stockwood, *Sermon*, 1579); '. . . in the whole course of her glorious reign, it could never be said that either the poor were oppressed without remedy, or the guilty repressed without cause; bearing this engraven in her noble heart: that *justice without mercy were extreme injury*, and *pity without equity plain partiality*; and that *it is as great tyranny not to mitigate laws, as iniquity to break them*' (Lyly, *Euphues*, 1579). Nor can these views be discounted as prejudiced. The French ambassador de Maisse (who was critical, and in his report had no reason whatever to flatter) wrote: 'The Queen by nature loves justice, and is very tender-hearted.'

battle-crescent which has suffered disaster; proved false, the grim auguries stand as a mockery of their forebodings: threatened death is now 'ridiculous fear'. Danger of invasion and civil war has vanished —gone with the wind that wrecked the beaten Armada. Elizabeth's Englishmen find themselves joyfully gazing down far vistas of assured peace.

To minds hurt by cruel apprehension, the miraculous passing of Eighty Eight not only in safety but with England's Queen crowned with victorious olive, has come like drops of life-restoring balm. In this blessèd time of Deliverance, his True Love shows, as ever, young. Death, shorn of his terrors, now submits to the poet, whose verse is his passport to immortality. England's foes Philip and Sixtus are building ostentatious cenotaphs for themselves; but his Friend, the subject of his lines, will be remembered when those blazoned crests and tombs of the defeated tyrants are long gone into oblivion.

Recorded by his *pupil pen*, Sonnet 107 is young Shakespeare's poem on the Great Deliverance of the terrible Eighty Eight—the eclipse of *the mortal Moon*, of the insatiable tyrant's dream of world dominion, which he and his Friend have survived to see.

Its unmistakable tone, as well as its present tenses, mark it as 'occasional' verse—topical, written on the event. To argue that it might have been composed long afterwards, in retrospect, is as plausible as it would be to assert that Milton waited for seven years after the Piedmont massacres to write *Avenge, O Lord, thy slaughter'd saints*. As soon as we locate the spiritual landscape— the passing of Eighty Eight—in which it was written, Shakespeare's 'most difficult' sonnet becomes clear and plain. We see what events he has turned into ideas; and, for the first time, we understand. May not other sonnets that still seem puzzling or obscure behave in the same way?

II. THE RIDDLE OF THE NEW–OLD PYRAMIDS

123

No! Time, thou shalt not boast that I do change:
Thy pyramids built up with newer might
To me are nothing novel, nothing strange;

84

They are but dressings of a former sight.
Our dates are brief, and therefore we admire
What thou dost foist upon us that is old,
And rather make them born to our desire
Than think that we before have heard them told.
Thy registers and thee I both defy,
Not wond'ring at the present nor the past;
For thy records and what we see doth lie,
Made more or less by thy continual haste.
This I do vow, and this shall ever be:
I will be true, despite thy scythe and thee.

In this scornful address to Time, Shakespeare refuses to admire: 'Thy pyramids built up with newer might To me are nothing novel.' By these ostensibly novel old pyramids of Time's he obviously cannot mean structures as stupendous as the Great Pyramid of Gizeh, which the Elizabethans reckoned took 360,000 men working continuously for twenty years to build. Preposterous to suppose that monsters like that were set up 'with newer might' as 'novel' and 'strange' in Shakespeare's age. But what then *does* he mean?[1]

Now when a concrete term in Shakespeare offers a puzzle, the most promising method of attacking it has two steps. First, to find out what the word meant to his contemporaries. Second, to acquire some notion of its specific application here by studying any contemporaneous events involving the thing referred to.

If we think we 'know what *pyramid* means' we are surprised to find that to the Elizabethans it principally meant 'something tall and slim': a mast, a stake, a maypole, a pinnacle, a spire, an

---

[1] It is difficult to take seriously the Pembrokian theory, which—arguing for 1603—would see in Time's ancient pyramids (which Shakespeare refuses to admire) the ephemeral wooden pageantry nailed up in Soper Lane by the 'newer might' of the joiners for King James to ride under. Instead of being marvelled at as 'former sights' re-born, the wonder was (as John Chamberlain wrote) that the flimsy things stood up: 'Our pageants are prettily forward, but most of them are such small-timbered gentlemen that they cannot last long, and I doubt if the plague cease not the sooner they will rot and sink where they stand.'

obelisk, a pillar, a column—all these were 'pyramids'. Deriving the word from *pyr-*, they held it to mean 'flame-shaped'.[1] So dominant indeed was this sense of the word (in contrast to our usage), that when the traveller Edward Webbe (1590) wished to describe the Pyramids of Gizeh so as not to be misunderstood, he called them not 'pyramids' but *mountains*:

There [within six miles of the Gran Caer] are seven Mountains builded on the outside like unto the point of a Diamond.[2]

The Masts . . . Hollow Pyramides . . . a Pyramis (that is a pyked peece of Timber, sharpe at one end) . . . Taper: a Pyramid made of Wax . . . Alas poore May-poles . . . to cast your tall Piramides to ground . . . Egyptian Pyramis raised in fashion of a May-Pole . . . a Pyramis or steeple . . . the Pyramis or pinnacle of the temple . . . some pyramid . . . on whose mounting spire . . . a Piramide, a great spear . . . Spears . . . cloud-kissing pinnacled Pyramides . . . a Star-ypointing Pyramid . . . Pyramis, or Heaven-menacing Tower . . . a high Piramid . . . laid prostrate . . . the Pyramis or Pillar . . . a pale Pyramid pillar . . . that Column is a Pyramide . . . the Pyramid in London (*ca.* 1680, the Monument).

For Shakespeare, naturally, the same. In *Antony and Cleopatra* at 2.7.21, the pyramid is the Nilometer, an octagonal pillar; at 5.2.61, it is an obelisk; in *Macbeth* 4.1.57, pinnacle, tower, or spire; and in *Two Noble Kinsmen* 3.6.352, a 'Pillar'. He would call both Cleopatra's Needle and the Washington Monument 'pyramids'.

The *old* 'pyramids' were of course the Egyptian obelisks; and if we now read Shakespeare's line *Thy obelisks built up with newer might*, and at the same time recall Elizabethan news about building, at once a flood of light breaks in. For the mightiest builder in all the world in Shakespeare's time was the enterprising, 'almost ferociously severe, obstinate, autocratic' Pope Sixtus V, who reigned from 1585 to 1590, and 'died execrated by his own

---

[1] [Egypt] Hath there uprais'd, outreaching ev'ry cloud,
Many a gallant and star-threat'ning Tower;
Whose strange, sky-piercing, flame-resembling spires
This age distrusts, Antiquity admires.
   Richard Zouche, *The Dove* (1613), B8ᵛ. Spelling modernized.

[2] *Travels* (ed. Arber), 32.

subjects'.[1] As we have seen, he was England's enemy, the tyrant described in Parliament as 'that wolfish bloodsucker'. So many were his notable constructions that under his hand Rome rose from its ruins and 'forthwith doubled itself'. His most spectacular and world-famous achievement, however, was the re-erection (as 'monuments of religious magnificence') of four age-old 'ambitious obelisks, ostents of pride'. These had been brought from Egypt to Imperial Rome by the Caesars and—all but one—were long since thrown down, broken, and even buried many feet underground.

Mighty Sixtus, who regarded himself as one of the two most powerful temporal kings in the world, set up a great Egyptian obelisk in each of the years 1586, 1587, 1588, and 1589. They stand today where he stationed them. The hugest one in existence, which in 1588 he erected by S. Giovanni in Laterano, had been discovered the year before buried in the Circus Maximus, broken into three pieces. This giant of red granite had therefore to be 'born'—extracted from Mother Earth—and then literally 'built', requiring in its broken state more 'building' than the placing of an entire monolith on a pedestal.

But first in priority, as well as alone in its glory of having survived the centuries unbroken and erect, was the Vatican obelisk, familiarly known as St Peter's Needle, 'the largest entire obelisk out of Egypt, and the second in size in the world'. This is the one which Mephistophilis promises to show to Doctor Faustus—the 'high piramides which Julius Caesar brought from Affrica'. Weighing some 320 tons, it stood near the Basilica, deep in the mud and rubbish of what had once been the *spina* of the racetrack of Nero's Circus. The stupendous task of taking it down, moving it to its present commanding site, and re-erecting it on a splendid pedestal in 1586, was the first and most dramatic feat to bring universal fame to the Pope's brilliant engineer, Domenico Fontana.

---

[1] Pasquino's epitaph on him ran
> *Fu Nerone impio, crudele, e tristo,*
> *Ma molto più di lui fu Papa Sisto.*

'Nero was impious, cruel, and grim, But Sixtus far exceeded him.'

Flocks of important persons hastened to Rome from the corners of Europe to witness the marvellous operation. As the biographer of Sixtus tells us,

Contemporary letters, reports of the diplomats, the stage-plays . . . numberless verses celebrating the event, and even views of the city of Rome published for visitors, by the exaggerated size they give to the obelisk, all witness to the sympathetic interest Europe took in the successful accomplishment of an enterprise which the leading authorities of art and engineering (Michael Angelo and Antonio da Sangallo) had pronounced impossible. Strangers just off the ship ran to see the Needle.[1]

The re-discovery in the following year of the tallest obelisk ever quarried, together with its excavation and its building, completed in August 1588 as the *Obelisco Lateranense*, was a fresh 'sensation'. And in 1589 Pope Sixtus was once more in the news with a fourth obelisk, likewise dug up out of the Circus Maximus, which he erected in the Piazza della Madonna del Populo. This was his last: he died in August 1590.

Dressing these re-born former sights of pagan pride with Christian crosses and his coat of arms, Sixtus

wrote to inform the foreign powers, had medals struck, ordered the raising of the [Vatican] obelisk to be recorded in official chronicles; . . . and the institution of special indulgences for those who would in passing render obeisance to it was identical at San Giovanni in Laterano, Santa Maria Maggiore, and on the Piazza del Populo.[2]

And the Protestant poet, while exulting in the Catholic defeat of 1588, cannot fail to mention the Pope's notorious accomplishments: 'They had craftily erected trophies or ensigns (*signa*) of impious memorial, posted of old between the Lateran and the Amphitheatre.'[3] Whereas Sixtus's flattering poets, seeking 'high

---

[1] Baron J. A. de Hübner, *Sixte-Quint*, ii, 'The Needle.'
[2] J. A. F. Orbaan, *Sixtine Rome* (1910), 170, 264.
[3] 'Sustulerantque vafrê monumenti signa nefandi,
  Posta olim Lateranam aedem inter & Amphitheatrum.'
  N. Eleutherius, *Triumphalia de Victoriis Elizabethae* (1589), 18.

compare' for his pillar-lifting, naturally seized upon the god
Atlas, who was supposed to hold up the pillars of the universe:

Atlas . . . stays
The two steep columns that prop earth and heaven.

*To Sixtus Quintus, holy and true Atlas . . . To Him, who like Atlas
holds up Heaven . . . Who, a new Atlas, rules and holds up
Heaven . . . And holding up Heaven, this new Atlas.*[1] Here is the
newer might: O potenza di Sisto! And with *Tue . . . Piramidi,
Spettacolo à le genti,* and *rinasce,*[2] we have Shakespeare's *pyramids,
sight,* and *born.* But for a sonnet on the pyramids of Sixtus to
compare with Shakespeare's it is only fair to take the effort of the
best poet, Torquato Tasso; of which together with the original
I give my very inadequate version:

On the Obelisk
erected in the Piazza di San Giovanni Laterano.

The obelisk with records grav'd about,
Which Egypt's Kings did rear erect to heav'n,
From Nile Augustus took, from Pharos took,
To make it grace in Rome his Circus fair.
Broken, entomb'd it lay, long suffer'd scorn
Through rage of greedy Time. But now by thee
It re-unites, and rises to fair place,
The peer of any loftiness on earth.
A thousand, nay, five thousand years, hold high
The Cross of gold, the vanquisher of death,
That here below nought hide and cover it.
Like the first miracle, the greatest work
Is giving as 'twere life to a marvel dead;
And with new grace the old thou glorifi'st.[3]

---

[1] *Rime del Sig. Antonio Costantini et altre . . . in lode del Papa Sisto Quinto*
(1611), 31, 95, 86, 43.

[2] *Ibid.*, 101, 92, 9.

[3] Per l'Obelisco inalzato ne la piazza di San Giovanni Laterano.

L'obelisco di note impresso intorno,
Che de l'Egitto i Regi al Ciel drizzaro,

Now let us put Shakespeare's beside it:

> *No! Time, thou shalt not boast that I do change:*
> *Thy pyramids built up with newer might*
> *To me are nothing novel, nothing strange;*
> *They are but dressings of a former sight.*
> *Our dates are brief, and therefore we admire*
> *What thou dost foist upon us that is old,*
> *And rather make them born to our desire*
> *Than think that we before have heard them told.*
> *Thy registers and thee I both defy,*
> *Not wond'ring at the present nor the past;*
> *For thy records and what we see doth lie,*
> *Made more or less by thy continual haste.*
> *This I do vow, and this shall ever be:*
> *I will be true, despite thy scythe and thee.*

In a Europe at war, a great poet in each of the forces opposed looks at the new-old pyramid of the Pope. Each sees Time as a villain, each sees his records in hieroglyphs,[1] the rising or birth of the old, and its new dressing or adorning. But with a world of difference. Tasso writes in flattery of an autocrat whom everybody hates; Shakespeare in scorn of the fickleness of Time.

The topical force of Shakespeare's 'pyramids' for the period about 1589 is now evident. On re-reading the Sonnet with our

---

> Il tolse Augusto al Nilo, il tolse al Faro,
> Per farne Roma, e'l suo bel Cerchio adorno.
> Giacea rotto, sepolto, longo scorno
> Sostenea dal furor del tempo avaro;
> Hor per te si rintegra, e sorge al paro
> D'ogni terrena altezza al bel soggiorno.
> Così mille anni inalzi, e mille lustri
> La Croce d'oro, onde la morte è vinta,
> Acciò nulla quà giù l'asconda, e copra.
> Com' del miracol primo è maggior opra
> Dar quasi vita à maraviglia estinta,
> E nova gratia, onde l'antica illustri.

Op. cit., 106.

[1] 'Historical events ... recorded ... on obelisks.' G. Rawlinson, *A Manual of Ancient History* (1869), 3.

eyes opened to the background of the world news, we can now offer a comprehensible summary, somewhat as follows:

Standing firm himself, the poet scorns the tricks of Time. He declines to join the childish world in its admiration at a nine days' wonder which it regards as a 'strange novelty'. Everybody's talking about the pyramids brought forth—as if produced for their special delight—from the womb of earth by the hated autocrat of Rome and his engineer. The poet is not impressed. After all, these obelisks, while newly set up, and dressed with his armorial bearings and Christian crosses by Sixtus, are in fact no new invention, but some 3000 years old, and we had heard about them from historians. Though now palmed off as a novelty on an ignorant world gaping for curiosities, their austere shafts, bearing Time's registers in royal hieroglyphs, were common sights ages ago.

But the poet puts no trust either in Time or in his deceptive memorials. Time's restless pace often destroys his own records, thus making them less. Just now, on the other hand, he has had some lost and forgotten ones dug up, thus making them more. Fickle and unreliable as he thus shows himself, who will believe him? The poet will remain unchanged and a true friend in spite of all that Time the deceiver and destroyer can do.

Notorious events as reported to the Elizabethan world have shown us approximately how Shakespeare's contemporaries would understand the allusions in this sonnet. So far from being metaphorical, intricate, and cloudy (as they seemed to our ignorance) they were concrete, topical, and clear. We can easily see now what was conveyed by *pyramids, newer might, novel, dressings of a former sight, admire what thou dost foist upon us that is old,* and *thy registers.*

As for the date of this sonnet, I place it late in 1588.or in 1589. Since *pyramids* is in the plural, it cannot have been composed before 1587, when the *second* obelisk (S. Maria Maggiore) was set up. Moreover, the first two were bare stone: only the third and fourth (1588 and 1589) bore Time's *records* incised in hieroglyphs. The topicality of the term *novel*, meaning new, the latest thing;

91

the phrase *not wondering at the present*; the admired 'birth' of the excavated pyramids of 1588 and 1589 to the satisfaction of a sensation-hungry age in which (as Tom Nashe writes in 1589) 'men haste unto novelties, and run to see new things'; and the present tense of *what thou dost foist upon us*—all these indicate that the Sonnet was written while the obelisks were still being set up: while, in short, they were 'news'. Death put an end to *la potenza di Sisto* in August 1590; thereupon the *newer might* of *this new Atlas* was a thing of the past, and Time's old pyramids, so recently revived and dressed up amid Sistine ostentation and papal puffs, were no longer either novel or news.

III. THE BLOW OF THRALLED DISCONTENT

Having found that the topicalities of Sonnet 107—*the mortal Moon*, and of Sonnet 123—the *pyramids* lead us to refer them both pretty closely to the year 1589, let us now turn to the Sonnet which immediately follows the *pyramids*, and scrutinize its political allusions to the fortunes of princes—one assassinated, another surviving all plotted attempts:

124

If my dear love were but the child of state,
It might for Fortune's bastard be unfather'd,
As subject to time's love or to time's hate,
Weeds among weeds, or flowers with flowers gather'd.
No, it was builded far from accident;
It suffers not in smiling pomp, nor falls
Under the blow of thrallèd discontent,
Whereto th'inviting time our fashion calls:
It fears not Policy, that heretic
Which works on leases of short-numb'red hours,
But all alone stands hugely politic,
That it nor grows with heat nor drowns with show'rs.
   To this I witness call the fools of time,
   Which die for goodness, who have liv'd for crime.

Here we find Shakespeare first contrasting the strong, sure structure of his love for his Friend with the pitiful insecurity of some prince, some heir of majesty or child of state[1] subject to 'accident', who 'suffers in smiling pomp' and 'falls under the blow of thralled discontent'.

Very little familiarity with the momentous events of Shakespeare's times is required to recognize the ruler he is thinking of. A prince who, suffering shameful deprivation of his royal power, had with smiles dissembled his fierce resentment. A prince who, after waiting his time, deftly murdering his two capital enemies and reporting his deliverance to his politic Queen Mother, himself fell under the blow of an assassin who thought him a tyrant. This 'Fortune's bastard', this victim of the 'time's[2] hate', is the *Gallica proles* or Gaulish child Henri de Valois, King Henri III of France, favourite child of Catherine de' Medici, and sometime suitor for Elizabeth's hand.

The first great *accident* (line 5) or misfortune that befell him was Paris's famous Day of Barricades, 12 May 1588, which the Venetian ambassador in Madrid called '*l'accidente di Francia contra quel povero Re*'—the accident of France against that poor King. On that day the people of Paris showed the *time's hate* by rising against their King in support of his enemies the Duke of Guise and the Holy Leaguers, backed by Pope Sixtus and Philip of Spain. Escaping immediate deposition by a hair's breadth, Henri managed to get away. He was obliged, however, to convoke the hostile States General, which sat at Blois throughout the autumn after the Armada scorning him as a do-nothing king, and preparing to make their 'Caesar', the Duke of Guise, master of the throne.

---

[1] And in thy throne a foreign state shall sit (Sidney, *Arcadia* Bk. 1); All mortal Princes and imperial States (Spenser, *Hymn of Heavenly Beauty*, 88); The chief Estates and Princes here below (Nixon, *The Christian Navy*, 1602); that Prince, that State . . . that thinks Power or Policy a Rampart (Donne, *Sermon* 24 February 1625); How like you this wild counsel, mighty states? (*K. John* 2.1.395).

[2] I take Shakespeare's phrase to mean 'the love or hate of the time—the age, the "times".' To capitalize the word here and in Sonnet 70 ('*woo'd of time*') is to forget the character of Time. That *sluttish, bloody, devouring, thievish tyrant* would never *love* or *woo* anybody, even if he were capable of it.

Elizabeth's ambassador to Henri, Sir Edward Stafford, describes for his Queen how her former suitor *suffered in smiling pomp* and hid his hate in affability. Stafford writes that though Henri 'was enforced to sett a faire face on the matter, and wisely to dissemble,' he 'laye hoovering in the winde to take the Duke and his fellow-conspirators at an advantage, when he might safelie . . . be revenged upon their cursed bodies'. Hearing that Guise intended to kill him on the approaching Christmas Eve, 1588, 'yett did the King make outward semblance as if he had suspected nothing', but sat up all night scheming how to end his suffering by taking arms against a sea of troubles. Morning found him resolved to prevent his own murder 'if he could, by hazarding to kill the Duke the next daie'.[1]

In an earlier dispatch Stafford had sent off the first news of Henri's successful murder of the Duke, with his belief—later confirmed—that Guise's brother, the Cardinal of Lorraine, was also killed: Guise, he reports,

was slaine by 8 of the *quarante cinq* who were there appointed for the same purpose; who executed theire charge so promptly as after he was entred into the said antechamber, hee never spake word untill he was dead. The King beeing assured that hee was dead, and having seene him on the ground, hee went to his mother and told her, Madame I am now come to tell you that I am King without companion, and that the Duke of Guise, th'enemy of all my proceedings, is dispatched. Whereunto shee answered that hee had given a great blowe . . .[2]

For his English theatre audience, Christopher Marlowe developed this scene of Henri viewing his dead enemy:

Captaine. My Lord, see where the Guise is slaine.
King. Ah this sweet sight is phisick to my soule . . .
 I nere was King of France untill this houre:
 This is the traitor that hath spent my golde
 In making forraine warres and civile broiles.

---

[1] B.M. MS. Harley 4888, ff. 9–25.
[2] B.M. MS. Cotton Galba D3, f. 321.

> Did he not draw a sorte of English priestes
> From Doway to the Seminary at Remes,
> To hatch forth treason gainst their naturall Queene?
> Did he not cause the King of Spaines huge fleete
> To threaten England and to menace me? . . .
> Tush, to be short, he meant to make me Munke,
> Or els to murder me, and so be King . . .
> Nere was there King of France so yoakt as I.
>   *The Massacre at Paris.*

Or as James Lea reports it to his readers in 1589,

> Because he suffered long, you thought that he would beare . . .
> Because he would not be of *Romish League* and trade
> You thought to cut him off, you thought him to betray;
> Which deede your *Guize* must do, and make the King away.
> But *Guize* hath his reward, and in his guise is slaine: . . .
> The bloodie *Guize* hath bloodie end, most justly to his hire,
> The bloodiest man that *France* ere bred . . .[1]

A few months after this 'great blow', in August 1589 came the news that 'Blood hath bought blood and blowes have answer'd blowes.' As a contemporary partisan historian tells it,

a divellish Monke, an excrement of hell, a *Jacobin* by profession, *James Clement* . . . vowes (said he) to kill the Tyrant, and to deliver the Cittie beseeged by *Sennacherib*. . . . The King bends his eare, but instead of hearing what he expected, this wretch drawes a knife out of his sleeve made of purpose, thrusts his Majesty into the botome of the belly, and there leaves the knife in the wound.

Or, as Marlowe has it,

> *King.* Ile read them Frier, and then Ile answere thee.
> *Frier. Sancte Iacobus,* now have mercye upon me.
> *He stabs the King with a knife as he readeth the letter . . .*
>
>> Confesse and be hanged man, In English some saie,
>> Confesse and be stabde, nowe In Fraunce Friers plaie.[2]

---

[1] *The Birth, Purpose, and mortall Wound of the Romish holie League* (1589), B3ᵛ.

[2] *De Caede et Interitu . . . Henrici Tertii . . .,* 1589.

This brings us back to Shakespeare's line, *falls Under the blow of thrallèd discontent*; and we can now consider the 1589 background of the Sonnet as a whole.

News of political assassinations has come thick and fast across the Channel to England. Not long ago Henri of France murdered the uncles of Mary Queen of Scots, the Duke of Guise and the Cardinal of Lorraine. Now we hear that a disgruntled friar, a partisan of the League, has murdered the King. 'Slaying is the word; it is a deed in fashion.' 'Let's turne Traytors awhile, this time rewards offences.' With the persistent efforts to assassinate Queen Elizabeth before our eyes, we may well fear lest English traitors take to king-killing in the French style, *whereto th'inviting time our fashion calls*.

Shakespeare's metaphor contrasts the readily plucked Flower or Weed with the strongly rooted majestic Tree. That unfortunate flower or weed King Henri had once been Pope Sixtus's favourite child; but when the lines were drawn between him and the Holy League, Sixtus turned on him with hatred. And when Clément's dagger had cut him down, Sixtus declared a Roman holiday of rejoicing, and gleefully preached his Consistory a sermon extolling the assassin as another Judith or Eleazar.

> The Pope as king of kings hath power from hye
> To plant, and to roote out successively:
> Why fell the king of *France* in wofull case?
> Because the Pope did plant him of his grace.[1]

Shakespeare's love—in contrast with that poor child of state, the weed untimely cropped by the assassin—stands like that great tree[2] Queen Elizabeth, which, *Semper Eadem*, Ever the Same,

---

[1] T. Bastard, *Chrestoleros* (1598), 26.
[2] Great trees—cedar, oak—inevitably connoted *kings*:
'the Prophets . . . resemble and compare Emperours, kings, princes, and potentates . . . unto high trees, as Cedars . . .'
Lemnius, *An Herbal for the Bible* (1587), 250.
The lofty Cedar, Royall *Cymbeline*, Personates thee   *Cymb.* 5.5.453.

> *all alone stands hugely politic,*
> *That it nor grows with heat nor drowns with show'rs.*

Your majesty they account the Oke, the tree of *Jupiter*, whose root is so deeplie fastened, that treacherie, though shee undermine to the centre, cannot finde the windings . . .

Lyly (ed. Bond), 1. 425.

England . . . shadowed with a Cedar against heate.

William Covell, Polimanteia, 1595.

His love, which *fears not Policy, that heretic*[1] *Which works on leases of short-numb'red hours*, stands like the Queen, untouched by the many attempts on her life,

> . . . that the prompter of their practises
> Might see the firmenesse of her diademes:
> Not mov'd by *weapons* or by *pollicies*.

Any crafty assaults upon his love are to be scorned. They are as futile and fatuous as the short-laid, Jesuit-inspired plot of young 'Babbington with all his companie', stigmatized by English

---

> I cut the cedar Pompey, and I'll fell
> This huge oak Cæsar too.   Fletcher, *False One* 4.3.159.
>
>   I, that did helpe
> To fell the loftie Cedar of the world,
> *Germanicus*; that, at one stroke, cut downe
> *Drusus*, that upright Elme . . .   Jonson, *Sejanus* 5.241 f.
>
> The King stands only now betwixt, and is
> Just like a single tree, that hinders all the Prospect:
> 'T is but the cutting down of him, and we . . .
> Suckling, Aglaura 2.1.
>
> So fals that stately cedar . . .
> Epitaph upon King Charles, B.M. MS. Addl. 28839 f. 44.

[1] There was never any Hereticks which maintained treason but the Papists. Henry Smith, *The betraying of Christ* (Sermon, *ca.* 1591).

If the pope and *Spaine* with their hereticall confederates fill the narrowe seas with Vessels. . . . Greene, *Spanish Masquerado*, 1589.

John Barthlet, *Pedegrewe of Heretiques* (the Church of Rome), 1566.

writers at the time as 'these witlesse youths', 'sencelesse sottes', 'fond youths', and 'Yoong English Fooles':

> *Babington* and all his *Complices*, who were condemned for their attempt to have raised warre in the Realme, and to have murdered the Queene, and to have set up the Queene of Scots, all which the said *Babington* and all his complices voluntarily confessed and were condemned and executed, onely for those their great treasons: and yet divers of them at the place of their execution did in like manner (as these Priests and Jesuites use to do) make confession of their Catholike faith, with offer to dye for the same.[1]

> *To this I witness call the fools of time,*
> *Which die for goodness, who have liv'd for crime.*

To the folly of attempting a *blow of thrallèd discontent* against a prince as strong as his love, Shakespeare calls to witness the English fools of the inviting time, who die 'for their religion', having lived to murder their Queen.

'The great poet,' remarks Mr T. S. Eliot, 'in writing himself, writes his time.' And in Sonnet 124 Shakespeare makes affirmation of the strength of his love voice the joy of every true-born Englishman in the preservation of his Queen from all the treacherous attempts on her life.

IV. Art Made Tongue-tied by Authority

66

Tir'd with all these, for restful death I cry:
As, to behold desert a beggar born,
And needy nothing trimm'd in jollity,
And purest faith unhappily forsworn,
And gilded honour shamefully misplac'd,
And maiden virtue rudely strumpeted,
And right perfection wrongfully disgrac'd,
And strength by limping sway disablèd,
And art made tongue-tied by authority,

---

[1] *The Copie of a Letter Sent out of England* (1588), 12.

> *And Folly (Doctor-like) controlling skill,*
> *And simple truth miscall'd simplicity,*
> *And captive good attending captain ill.*
> *Tir'd with all these, from these would I be gone,*
> *Save that, to die, I leave my Love alone.*

Several critics—Sir Edmund Chambers among them—have been struck by a special feature of this catalogue of the world's repulsive injustices. Most of the damnable wrongs in the list, as might be expected, are hardy perennials still flourishing today, and would find a place in any jeremiad. But a more Elizabethan note is sharply sounded in the two-line passage running

> *And art made tongue-tied by authority,*
> *And Folly (Doctor-like) controlling skill.*

This is recognized to be the outburst of an able literary artisan galled by the arbitrary prohibitions of an officious and stupid censor. Significantly, a single line proves sufficient for each of the other evils. But tired especially by this one, the poet emphasizes it from a slightly different angle by repetition.

Concerning the Elizabethan control of stage and press we have learned that there were two periods of particularly active censorship. The longer and more intense one began in 1586 and tapered off in 1593, *passing its peak about 1589*. The other was a much briefer revival in 1599. The authority was wielded by the bishops. In practice, they delegated most of the immediate control to clerical deputies, many of them Doctors of Divinity or Doctors of Theology:

> *Folly (Doctor-like) controlling skill.*

The bearing of the sustained period of active censorship on the date of this sonnet cannot be overlooked. Evidently, the passage can hardly be a product of the middle nineties, when censorship was relaxed. But we can understand that the heavy-handed and growing interference which took hold in 1586 might well in time harass a working actor and playwright into resentment and disgust. The Elizabethan Englishman was, however, no slave-born

99

Muscovite, and could at least voice his indignation in the lines

> And art made tongue-tied by authority,
> And Folly (Doctor-like) controlling skill.

In sum, if this was written about 1589 we can see point in the protest. But if we attempt to assign the Sonnets to the middle nineties, none.

V. THE FAMOUS WARRIOR FORGOT

25

> Let those who are in favour with their stars
> Of public honour and proud titles boast,
> Whilst I, whom fortune of such triumph bars,
> Unlook'd for, joy in that I honour most.
> Great princes' favourites their fair leaves spread
> But as the marigold at the sun's eye;
> And in themselves their pride lies buriëd,
> For at a frown they in their glory die.
> The painful warrior famousëd for worth [fight],
> After a thousand victories once foil'd,
> Is from the book of honour rasëd forth [quite],
> And all the rest forgot for which he toil'd.
> Then happy I, that love and am beloved
> Where I may not remove nor be removed.

Fortunate for once in the misfortune of his humble birth, Shakespeare here contrasts his security and happiness in a love requited with the misery of the great who fall from favour with either prince or people.

His first examples are *Great princes' favourites*, and with him we might readily recall Leicester, Hatton, Ralegh—who's in, who's out—the great ones that ebb and flow by the moon. No particular disgrace of some one of them is singled out. But with his second example the case is altered. Here it is one man, and that man *The painful warrior famousëd for fight*. While always dramatic, the falls of princes' favourites are not unexpected. Quite otherwise, however, with the veteran commander crowned with victories manifold, who upon one reverse is turned away into disgrace and neglect. Here is a startling and shameful evidence of man's ingratitude, comparable in our day to the rejection of Winston Churchill soon after he had saved his country.

To our question *Who was that rejected hero?* the answer is, This peculiar event exactly mirrored by Shakespeare happened once, and only once, in the reign of Elizabeth. To begin with, let us ask ourselves, What Elizabethan commanders were famous and ever victorious? Sir John Norris, yes, and Sir Francis Vere. But just as he does today, easily first in every mind stood England's glory, 'the matchless paragon of war', the all-conquering Dragon whose name struck relentless terror to the Spanish enemy in both worlds, Sir Francis Drake.

After his countless triumphs, the latest of which was gained over the greatest army ever entrusted to the sea, in the spring of 1589 Drake set out with Norris to attack King Philip's home-strength in Spain and Portugal:

> *You follow Drake by Sea, the Scourge of Spayne,*
> *The dreadfull Dragon, terror to your foes,*
> *Victorious in his returne from Inde,*
> *In all his high attempts unvanquishëd.*

Though sped by these wingëd words of George Peele's, and in the upshot highly damaging to the enemy, the expedition was dogged by ill luck, bagged no great booty, and was treated at home as a failure. On his return, Drake's supreme services and his record were not remembered. Greeted with disgrace, he went into retirement: the famous warrior, all his past forgot, quite rasëd from the book of honour.

Nothing short of complete concentration on an erroneous date for the Sonnets could have blinded our eyes to the force of Shakespeare's instinctive response to the challenge of this unique event. For no thought, as we know from his works, cut more deeply into his generous mind than *ingratitude*. Even an ungrateful England naturally found it could not do without Drake, and he was later called back. But the year of his—or, rather, England's—disgrace was 1589.

Now for a summary—to recollect in brief what has passed before us in these poems. The scene is the year 1589.

107. Through Shakespeare's eyes we have marvelled at our Great Deliverance, not only from the deadly threat of the Armada, but even from the universal death foretold for that fatal year 1588.

123. News of rebuilt old pyramids, that specious and repeated novelty of the hostile Pope of Rome, fails to impress us.

124. In August, hot news from France of the fall of Henri III, Catherine de' Medici's poor 'child of state', under the assassin's blow, makes us thank God, both for Queen Elizabeth's strength and for preserving her royal Majesty from the like.

66. Times so tense as ours may call for some sort of censorship, but as imposed these three years it has proved both clumsy and tiresome.

25. This same summer, on his return from Portugal, we are shocked to see England's renowned champion, valour's noble mirror, sea-taming, sail-wing'd Drake, rejected by his own.

What do these discoveries reveal about the date of the rest of the Sonnets? In the 1609 arrangement (which, as we shall find, was Shakespeare's own) the first three we have studied all stand near the close of the 'first series' of 126 Sonnets. And most of the proposed rearrangements keep them there. The indication is that Shakespeare completed this main group of his Sonnets by 1589.

The grand point which now rises to dwarf all else is the new knowledge—since the Sonnets unquestionably embody some of his highest poetry—that Shakespeare's power had reached maturity by the time he was no more than twenty-five years old. Yet strictly speaking he was not far from 'a beginner'. That he is quite literal in writing in Sonnet 16 of his 'pupil pen' is beyond question. As for his reaching maturity in youth, we may well be warned against passing hasty judgment on the world's most incalculable genius, by the familiar examples of such lesser figures as Sidney, Donne, and Keats. No one is tempted to suggest that their mature work *could not* have been written in their twenties, for the effective reason that evidence is at hand to show that it *was*. Yet if John Keats had lived to be fifty-two, and we had no clue as to when he wrote those finest odes, some middle-aged critic would infallibly discover that their poetic texture and thought are obviously 'far too mature' for any youth of twenty-four.

And had Logan Pearsall Smith known the true date of the Sonnets, he would never have been forced by the mannered narrative poems, *Venus and Adonis* and *Lucrece*, to conclude that 'of all that wealth of poetic emotion seeking to find expression, that mass of brooding thought we are aware of in young poets like Shelley and Keats, there is no trace'. He would certainly have discovered a profusion of it in the Sonnets: which we may now study as an eloquent portrait of the artist as a young man, a young man expressing in his own person the very movements of the soul and the height of feeling which were later to appear in his plays.

What does this discovery do to 'Shakespeare chronology'? Certainly several of Shakespeare's early plays may well have preceded the completion of the Sonnets about 1589. Why not? Since we know nothing whatever about the dates of the earlier pieces, and the field for conjecture has been all too embarrassingly wide, a fixed point for the Sonnets may perhaps prove useful in our attempts to chronologize. Those who still imagine that Shakespeare had written nothing before Greene's outburst in 1592 (because no contemporary mention has survived) have forgotten the case of that other dramatist, Henry Porter. Of Porter we never heard a word—didn't even know he existed—before December 1596, when he appeared in Henslowe's book as a leading and popular playwright. Could anyone be so unaware of the difficulty of the dramatist's art as to argue (as some have done with Shakespeare A.D. 1592) that Porter had written no plays before the end of 1596, but leaped to the head of his profession on his first attempt at play-writing?

No one needs reminding that the earliest publication-date for anything of Shakespeare's is 1593. *Venus and Adonis* was un-questionably printed in that year, and no one puts it in a class with the Sonnets. But who can tell us when it was composed? The Shakespeare who could complete his Sonnets by the age of twenty-five might readily have turned out these unpolish'd lines at the age of twenty, and published them only under the pinch of a plague-year, when the theatres were closed, to raise some money. The poem of a twenty-year-old should please an Earl aged twenty. 'The younger sort takes much delight in Shakespeares Venus, & Adonis,' notes Gabriel Harvey, contrasting it with *Lucrece*, which is worthy of pleasing the wiser. The poet himself, in promising 'some graver labour,' regards *Venus and Adonis* not merely as an early work, but as *the first heir of my invention*—the earliest work of all.

Now to sum up. No particle of convincing evidence has ever been adduced to suggest a late date for the Sonnets. On the con-trary, the topicalities of a number of them now indicate decisively that the series was completed about 1589. In that year Shake-speare was twenty-five, not yet beyond the normal, customary, recognized age for an Elizabethan to write sonnets. And his employment throughout of the young poet's convention of 'old age' is clear testimony to his youth. We can rid our minds of the textbook's monstrosity—namely, that the Mercury-quick Shake-speare was mentally backward, lagging seven years or more be-hind the average of his generation. Shakespeare's Sonnets, the profound as well as the slight, are the work of a young man.

If for a moment we can shake off our sluggish modern notions of mental development, do we find here any occasion for surprise? Shakespeare's contemporary Montaigne considered that a man was at his prime at the age of twenty, and produced his best work before reaching thirty. What do we expect of Shakespeare, that rising star whose influence will strike the mind of Milton with wonder and astonishment? In the crowd of what in 1591 John Florio calls the 'more active gallants . . . devising how to blaze and blanche their passions with aeglogues, songs, and sonnets,' most, to be sure, trickling in the numbers that Petrarch flowed in, squeeze out very pitiful verses. But this is the mounting Elizabethan generation in which (Ben Jonson tells us) 'were all the wits born that could honour a language': the generation which Shakespeare, who was the soul of it, recognizes as *this growing age of time-bettering days*. And among its mature poets we are granted not only 'the miracle of our age', the rare Sir Philip, but also the more miraculous Shakespeare with his 'pupil pen', both young, and both able to make what the sagacious essayist Sir William Cornwallis—himself barely out of his teens—describes with such fervour:

This music of two strings is the most delightful harmony: for the world affords not a more admirable excellency then youth and judgement included in one substance. Both partes shew their richest treasure: the Soule judgement, the Bodie youth.

V

MY SOVEREIGN

BRIEFLY now to reconnoitre the position reached in our man-hunt. Scrutiny of the terms which Shakespeare applied to his beautiful young Friend allowed but one conclusion. Namely, this well-known Friend must have been recognized as some kind of King-by-courtesy, walking abroad shadowed by a royal canopy. Next, a recalling of Davies of Hereford's epigram to Shakespeare (Stationers' Register, 8 October 1610) reinforces that conclusion. It reports a current opinion: had not Shakespeare been a stage-player, he would have been a 'companion for a *King*'.

Thereupon we remembered some youthful sovereigns of Shakespeare's London who on occasion made impressive public appearances in great glory—the Inns of Court Princes: Henry Helmes, Richard Martin, Thomas Perient.

Shakespeare's Prince remains to be found. But the period in which the Sonnets were written unquestionably included the reign of William H——. More than that, John Davys's *shadow under a shadow* indicates a period before June 1594. To fix the date of the Sonnets would be to narrow the search.

Considerations advanced in the foregoing chapter all point to the years 1587–89 as the period of the Sonnets' composition. The present conclusion may be stated in a phrase: If Prince William H—— is discovered, he will certainly be found reigning between 1587 and 1589.

Now if (instead of being a scholar, tied to historical fact as I am) I were a carefree concocter of detective thrillers, I know the kind of fiction I should dream up here for my readers. Following an ideal formula, I should make triumph result from a brilliantly-conceived-and-carried-out plan of pursuing the missing Prince, somewhat as follows: I should picture the inspired detective locating a great collection of Elizabethan lawyers' notebooks in the Library of Lincoln's Inn—the richest law-library in England—manuscripts seldom consulted; securing an introduction from an indulgent barrister for permission to search them for 'Elizabethan legal antiquities'; hunting eagerly through their end-papers and margins for stray jottings of events connected with the life of the Inns of Court. For a long while, nothing; then, a few fragments, reviving hope. And now, luck—discovery of a notebook with memoranda of an Inn's mootings and boltings. Mounting excitement; and at last, noted in a corner, there it is, the precious quarry:

$\overline{\text{Md}}$ on Monday viij. Jan^{ij}
was y^e Prince M. W^m H—— of
oure fellowship inuited to
my L. Maiors wher he went in
greate state/

Such a tale as that would tell How Master William H—— Should Have Been Found: carrying to every reader the sound moral of intelligent planning and dogged work crowned with success. Sometimes I think I should rather like it to have happened like this. But it didn't.

By contrast, the true story is short and simple. Impossible to dress it in drama, or to mount through absorbing incidents to a climax. For it contains but one incident. Yet it arouses another kind of interest—interest of a rarer sort, and perhaps more significant.

The truth is that Shakespeare's Prince—when once I had his date and description—was not ingeniously or painfully pursued in a long exciting chase through obscure and musty manuscripts, and at length hunted down. He was simply *recognized*. Recognized sitting in full view, and in what everyone will allow is an obvious place. For his surname, coupled with his specific title as Prince, has since 1831—Wordsworth's time—stood printed in books widely read by people interested in the drama or in the law.[1]

It is hard to believe. For if so, everyone asks, Why was he not recognized long ago by some one of the numberless hunters on the trail of Shakespeare's Friend? The answer can only be that none of them had data in mind sufficient to make recognition possible. For the lowest number of items necessary is now seen to have been three. First, Shakespeare's Friend was no peer, but an untitled gentleman, really named Master William H——. Second, the Sonnets were written in the years 1587-89. And third, Master William H—— was also a Prince, reigning within that period.

Of all the seekers, relatively few have firmly believed the first, and acted on it. The second—the early date—has been grasped by one or two only, such as Samuel Butler, author of *Erewhon*; and Butler's best guess at Shakespeare's Friend was a humble naval rating named William Hughes, who ended up as a sea cook. As for the third—the Prince—I know of no one who has ever given the notion a second thought. This must explain why the discovery was reserved to our times, simple though it now seems. We recall Dr Watson: "'How absurdly simple!' I cried. 'Quite so!' said he, a little nettled. 'Every problem becomes very childish when once it is explained to you.'"

Luck therefore came to meet me only because these three notions had gained sufficient body and shape to be floating together somewhere in my head. Pasteur puts the experience into more formal words: *Chance favours only the prepared mind.*

One day, then—in search of a point quite unconnected with the Sonnets—I picked off my shelf one of the books which contain this great diamond always passed over as a pebble. The volume had long sat there unopened. It was Percival Vivian's

---

[1] J. P. Collier, *Hist. of Engl. Dram. Poetry* (1831), 1. 266-267.
R. R. Pearce, *A Hist. of the Inns of Court* (1848), 87.
R. J. Fletcher, *The Pension Book of Gray's Inn . . .* (1901), 78.
Malone Society Collections II (1909), 179.
Campion's Works, ed. P. Vivian (1909), xxix.

excellent edition (1909) of *Campion's Works*. That Elizabethan phoenix Thomas Campion the composer-poet, whose music sang the thought and feeling of his lines. What lyricist but Campion could couple his 'words and notes lovingly together'—make a true marriage of the arts? In him we shall find an intimate part of the story of W. H.

After throwing light on Campion's family, Vivian's Introduction then takes the gifted young poet from Cambridge on to his cluster of warm friendships at Gray's Inn, where he was admitted 27 April 1586. Absorbed in the story, I followed along to page xxix. Here Vivian prints the cast of a Gray's Inn comedy—produced 16 January 1587/8 in Hall before a gathering of England's greatest lords—a comedy in which Campion (listed next after 'The prologue') played 'Hidaspis yᵉ sonn'. And there, alone above the head of the list, as the Prince of Purpoole who presented the play to his noble guests, stood title and name—

Dominus de purpoole: Hatclyff

A footnote gave the name in full: *William Hatcliffe*, of Hatcliffe, Lincolnshire.

In that moment I knew that Shakespeare's Friend, lost for centuries, was found. Thorpe's Mr. W. H., 'the onlie begetter'; Shakespeare's *lovely boy, Will, my sovereign*; the high and mighty Prince of Purpoole or Gray's Inn 1587/8—all these were one, and that one no other than Master William Hatcliffe of Lincolnshire. Flooding in, the light of realization was dazzling but sustained: bringing conviction that to uncover further knowledge about him would but increase it, and reveal things in the Sonnets never seen since the age when he flourished as

the world's fresh ornament
And only herald to the gaudy spring.

Armed with his long-lost name I could now ransack the records for all recoverable details about Shakespeare's Friend, and present them in connected form. But questions vital to the reading of the Sonnets crowd for reply; and perhaps we should take one of the most pressing at once—namely, What was Hatcliffe's age? How do his actual years suit with the apparent statement in the opening lines of Sonnet 104—

> *To me, fair friend, you never can be old,*
> *For as you were when first your eye I eyed,*
> *Such seems your beauty still. Three winters cold*
> *Have from the forests shook three summers' pride,*
> *Three beauteous springs to yellow autumn turned*
> *In process of the seasons have I seen,*
> *Three April perfumes in three hot Junes burned,*
> *Since first I saw you fresh, which yet are green.*

This looks very much like a birthday poem inspired by the young Friend's coming-of-age: [*Although the day has come you now write man,*] *To me, fair friend, you never can be old.* Be that as it may, the poem is certainly written in autumn, for it reveals that the three years completed since Shakespeare first saw his Friend *began with a winter.* Also it stands among the latter Sonnets of the sequence, with those (107, 124) which date from 1589.

If then we ask, Does a date in Autumn 1589 suit with William Hatcliffe's coming-of-age? the answer is, Yes, perfectly. We shall find that he was baptized 6 September 1568. Consequently he attained the age of twenty-one in September 1589. Further, as we shall also find, he had come up to London and been admitted at Gray's Inn three years earlier, on 4 November 1586, six months later than Campion. If that was quite naturally when Shakespeare first saw him, *Three winters cold . . . Three beauteous springs to yellow autumn turned* would bring him to Autumn 1589 and his coming-of-age.

On entering the society of Gray's Inn, Hatcliffe was thus just eighteen years and two months old. And Shakespeare at this date was twenty-two and a half. If Shakespeare—nearly four years married, and father of three children—was thus still a youth, he would yet feel old and experienced in the company of a boy just turned eighteen. We need only recall once again the married university graduate's view of the freshman to realize how great at those ages the difference of more than four years seems to both.

And now to look into the 'extreme nook of the Kingdom' which nurtured this beautiful young Prince who both entertained England's greatest lords and won the heart of her highest poet:

> For Lincolnshire, whose borders with delight
> Still Trent, loud Humber, sea-green Amphitrite
> Do twine within their arms, whose fruitful soil
> Did give thee birth . . .[1]

We must travel north and east many long miles into Tennyson's country to reach it, where it lies on the seaward slope of the Lincoln Wolds near the great Humber estuary, facing the North Sea. For the family seat was the manor of Hatcliffe, 'a place happy in the sweetness of the air, and very delectable by the pleasant hills and dales'; and the Hatcliffes also possessed a town house seven miles off to the northeast, in the seaport of Great Grimsby, today the chief fishing-port of England.

Some will not fail to see a marvellous aptness—indeed Clio repeating herself—in this latter-day discovery of a fair young prince (celebrated in poetry) at Grimsby. For the oldest legend of the town, recorded on its seal, is told *circa* 1300 in a poem, *The Lay of Havelok the Dane*: the refugee lad, wondrous fair and strong, recognized as royalty by a miraculous light shining from his mouth in sleep.

The *lovely boy* from Lincolnshire came naturally by his good looks. As long ago as Henry III Robert of Gloucester's rime gives the prick and praise to *Everwike* [York] *of fairest wood: Lincoln of fairest men.* And as recently as 1885 the anthropologist reports of Lincolnshire, 'the Danish element is particularly strong. . . . They are a fair and handsome people, with regular features.'[2]

Physical beauty, though a prime essential for a Prince of Purpoole, was however but one requirement. He must also show

---

[1] Edward Bullingham, verses to James Yorke's *Union of Honour*, 1640.
[2] Dr John Beddoe, *The Races of Britain*, 252.

III

excellent grace in dancing, to lead the revels at Court; and Hatcliffe's Lincolnshire led all England, not only in the rhythmic
'round ringing' of bells, but also in dancing to the bagpipes:

> Who sees so pleasant plains, or knows of fairer scene?
> Whose swains in shepherd's gray, and girls in Lincoln green,
> Whilst some the rings of bells, and some the bagpipes ply,
> Dance many a merry Round, and many a Hydegy.[1]

At Healing near Grimsby the parish register bears a note dated
1589:

> That Charles Mowbray above named was in his time a delicate
> young gentleman and a courtier, an excellent dancer, so that Queen
> Elizabeth took notice of, and did him the honour once or twice to
> dance with him.[2]

Here was a neighbour for Will Hatcliffe's emulation.

To crown all, Good Queen Bess's glorious days were also
Lincolnshire's; for the shire then produced more great men for her
Majesty's service than any other county of England. Old Thomas
Fuller in his *Worthies* calls a distinguished roll of Elizabeth's men
of Lincoln:

1. Edward Clinton [Earl of Lincoln], Lord Admiral.
2. William Cecil, Lord Burghley [Lord Treasurer].
3. Sir Edmund Anderson, Lord Chief Justice.
4. John Whitgift [Archbishop of Canterbury, and a Grimsby man].
5. Peregrine Bertie [Lord Willoughby of Eresby], Lord General in
   France.
6. Thomas Wilson, Doctor of Law, and Secretary of State.

And he adds, 'Here I mention not Sir Thomas Heneage [Vice-
Chamberlain of the Household], at the same time a grand
favourite and Privy Councillor to Queen Elizabeth.' His

---

[1] Drayton, *Poly-olbion*, 25th Song. Fynes Moryson reports the proverb
'Lincolnshire Belles and Bag-pipes' *Itinerary* (1617), III. 1. 3, p. 54.
[2] *Notes and Queries*, 6.1.375.

reminder makes this extraordinary record of Elizabethan Lincolnshire still more astonishing:

> Thus sea and land, church and camp, sword and mace, gospel and law, were stored with prime officers out of this county. Nor must it be forgotten, though born in the same shire, they were utterly unrelated in kindred, and raised themselves independently (as to any mutual assistance) by God's blessing, the queen's favour, and their own deserts.

Two more leading names may possibly be added, from the arts. William Byrd, England's greatest composer, first appears at Lincoln Cathedral, and may well have been a native of the shire. And Thomas Heywood's latest biographer Arthur Clark finds evidence to think that the dramatist was born a clergyman's son at Ashby-cum-Fenby, only a couple of miles from Hatcliffe. Heywood was but a few years junior to Shakespeare's Friend, and if he knew this neighbouring squire's heir, there is more regret than ever that Heywood's Lives of the Poets has not survived. For if we had his Life of Shakespeare, we might very possibly find in it a personal reminiscence of William Hatcliffe.

With Lincolnshire so strong an interest at Court, it is no surprise to find court-drama catering for it. *Locrine*, for example (one of the plays mistakenly attributed to Shakespeare), shows the legendary Scythian or Hunnish invaders led by their King, Humber, on the Lincolnshire banks of the great river Abus:

> *Humber.* Thus are we come, victorious conquerors,
> Unto the flowing currents silver streames,
> Which, in memoriall of our victorie,
> Shall be agnominated by our name,
> And talkëd of by our posteritie. [3.2]

Here is irony, for the British Locrine then defeats Humber, whereupon the Scythian morosely drowns himself in the Abus. And so the change of its name to Humber commemorates not his victory, but his defeat and suicide. In similar fashion, Lyly's

Gallathea—produced at Court during Hatcliffe's reign as Prince of Purpoole—carries its audience to 'famous Lincolnshire':

Mariner. You are now in Lyncolnshire, where you can want no foule, if you can devise meanes to catch them: there be woods hard by, and at every myles ende houses. [1.4]

And also to the Humber, where Lyly personifies its great rushing tidal wave, the dangerous *eagre*, as a sea-monster sent by Neptune to fetch his tribute from the inhabitants—'the fairest':

Augur. To this Tree must the beautifullest be bounde untill the Monster *Agar* carrie her awaie; and if the Monster come not, then assure your selves that the fairest is concealed, and then your countrey shall be destroyed. [4.1]

In his brief blaze of glory as Prince of Purpoole William Hatcliffe shines as the last notable of his race[1]—the Hatcliffes, or *Hatliffes*, as we shall find that the name was commonly pronounced. He outlived his cousin William Hatcliffe, who maintained the old family tradition of administrative service in the royal household and died unmarried at Greenwich as 'Avener to the King's Majesty'—that is, as a chief officer of James's Stables, in charge of provender.[2]

His was an ancient lineage. As early as the Testa de Nevill or Book of Knights' Fees A.D. 1242, an Alan de Hadeclive held the estate at Hatcliffe.[3] How long the family had already been there is unknown; but the span from that Alan's birth to our William's death is more than four hundred years, the distance from Shakespeare's birth to the present day.

---

[1] Last, that is, if we except Vincent Hatliffe (1600–71), who was converted to Roman Catholicism and in the Society of Jesus assuming the name of John Spencer, became professor, missioner, superior, and author of controversial works. See John and J. A. Venn, *Alumni Cantabrigienses*, ii. 330.

[2] *Misc. Genealogica et Her.* (N.S.) iv. 218.

[3] In Haverstoe Wapentake, North Riding, Parts of Lindsey, co. Lincoln. *Testa de Nevill* (ed. 1923), 363, 1021, 1472. Eilert Ekwall finds the place-name about A.D. 1115, and gives its meaning as 'Headda's cliff or slope'. *Concise Oxford Dictionary of English Place-Names* (1947), 214a.

The Hatcliffes gained distinction chiefly in the fifteenth and sixteenth centuries, and the one who rose to prominence first rose highest: William Hatcliffe, Physician and Secretary to his Majesty. Two rival Kings of England—Lancaster and York—successively entrusted their health to him; and the second, appointing him councillor and secretary as well, charged him with the negotiation of treaties with foreign powers.

King's College Cambridge claims this William Hatcliffe as one of its two original scholars, named by King Henry VI in his patent founding the College, 12 February 1440/1.[1] He had been a Fellow of Peterhouse; went on at King's to graduate as Doctor of Medicine, and to immediate appointment as Physician to his patron King Henry. After the deposition of that unfortunate king, Dr Hatcliffe served his supplanter Edward IV until his own death at an advanced age in 1480. *The Dictionary of National Biography* gives the details of his long career in high diplomacy.

Others of the line also distinguished themselves as officers of the Crown. William Hatcliffe (d. 1518), as Clerk of the Marshalsey of the Household and Deputy Under-Treasurer of Ireland to Henry VII;[2] Edward Hatcliffe, appearing 1512 as Clerk of the Signet;[3] and Thomas Hatcliffe (d. 1540, the Prince of Purpoole's great-grandfather), Clerk of the Green Cloth or 'one of ye fowre masters of ye howsholde to oure soveraigne lord King Henry ye viij.'[4] And at Great Grimsby for various periods in the century Hatcliffes presided as Mayors of the Corporation. The first I find, William Hatcliffe of Hatcliffe, Esquire (d. 1530), appears as Mayor 1521 and 1525, and sat for the borough in Parliament, 1525–29.[5] At least two others are recorded as Mayors

---

[1] See John Saltmarsh, *King's College* (1958), 1.

[2] P.R.O., Misc. Bks. Exch. L.T.R. 208; B.M. MS. Royal 18C. xiv.

[3] B.M. MS. Stowe 146 ff. 18–20.

[4] Inscription on the fine sepulchral brass of 'Thomas Hatteclyff Esquyer ... Anne hys wyfe' in the ancient church of Addington, Surrey. Cf. B.M. MS. 32490, BB No. 35, f. 42. Anne (*née* Leigh) Hatcliffe as a widow married Thomas Horden; and surviving him also, was buried at Hatcliffe. See her will (P.C.C. 28 Tashe) dated 3 March and proved 10 March 1553/4.

[5] Dr George Oliver, *Gentleman's Magazine* XCIX (1829), 409.

—Christopher Hatcliffe 1582, and John Hatcliffe 1584, 1589, 1596, and 1597.

For the immediate background of Shakespeare's Friend we may begin with his grandfather, William Hatcliffe, Esquire. Great-grandfather Thomas, Henry VIII's Clerk of the Green Cloth, had clearly left his heir William among the very wealthy, as an ancient list reveals:

The names of all the Gentlemen being Inheritores within the Countye of Lincolne

Sir Rt Tirwhit 500 m[arks] . . . S^r Fr. Askeugh 500 m[arks] . . . Sir Ed Dimocke 500 m[arks] . . . Sir Wm Skipwith 400 marks . . . Sr Richard Thimbleby 300 m[arks] . . . Th. St Polle Ar[miger] 200^{li} . . . Thos. Missendun Ar 100^{li} . . . Wm Manby Ar 100^{li} . . .

Next after these, ninth in the list, stands

William Hattcliffe Ar[mi]ger maried
the daugh[ter] to Sr William Skipwith knight[1] } 100^{li}

Another testimony to the high standing of the Hatcliffes in the society of Elizabethan Lincolnshire is given by an heraldic manuscript[2] which ranks the contemporary gentry. In all, 219 Lincolnshire names are here given, with their coats of arms. Of these 219, *Hatcliffe of Hatcliffe* stands eighteenth in dignity; preceded only by five peers headed by the Earl of Lincoln, three knights, and names such as *Manby of Elsham, Hansard of Biscarthorp*, and *Skipwith of Ormsby*. We shall see that Shakespeare's Friend was a connection by marriages in his family not only with these last named, but with the highest of all, the Earl of Lincoln.

Our Hatcliffe's grandmother Anne was thus a daughter of the rich Sir William Skipwith of South Ormsby, making him a quarter-Skipwith. That marriage took place 1545; and six years later, 19 July 1551,[3] grandfather William died. The inscription on his incised stone in the floor of St Mary's Church at Hatcliffe,

---

[1] B.M. MS. Harl. 2145, f. 136.   [2] Ibid., 1452, f. 27.
[3] P.R.O. E150/586/10; C142/96/6.

almost illegible with age, confirms the date. He left three sons very young, William, 6, Thomas, 3, and George. The heir William died aged 12 or 13, in 1558 or 1559, leaving the second son, Thomas (future father of Shakespeare's Friend), as the new heir. Since Thomas (born 1548) was still a minor he was declared a ward of the Queen, his estate put into the hands of his mother as guardian.

In Michaelmas Term 1564, at the age of sixteen, he was matriculated at Cambridge as 'Thomas Hatlefe' a pensioner from Jesus College; and his brother 'George Hatlyffe' followed a year and a half after, also as a pensioner from Jesus.[1] The *pensioners* formed the middle and largest group of undergraduates. The term means those who paid for their own commons (board) and other expenses. (Compare *pension*, payment for board, lodging, and education.) We shall return to this subject later in more detail.

Like most of the gentlemen-students, Thomas and his brother took no degree. But he could not look forward as many of them did to the more select life of the Inns of Court. Some profit from a ward's wealthy marriage was one of the perquisites of a guardian; and in 1567, at the age of nineteen, Thomas went down from Cambridge and was married before the end of the year. The marriage which he made—or perhaps which was made for him— was an excellent one: Judith, a daughter of Sir Francis Ayscough (or Askew, brother of Anne Askew the famous Protestant martyr, burnt 1546) of South Kelsey, Lincolnshire, whom we have already met as one of the wealthiest magnates of the county. And here brother George was again able to follow him: he married Judith Ayscough Hatcliffe's sister Elizabeth Ayscough.

And it was at father-in-law Sir Francis's house in September 1568 that Thomas's son and heir Master W. H. was born, and christened William on September 6 at St Mary's Church, South Kelsey.[2] This church lies only some ten miles in a bee-line from

---

[1] Venn, loc. cit.
[2] A. R. Maddison, *Lincolnshire Pedigrees* (1903), ii. 472–473.

West Ashby, where Oscar Wilde in latter days visited his uncle the vicar. Here in Lincolnshire, Wilde had thus casually brought himself far closer to the real W. H. than his imagination could ever do in *The Portrait of Mr. W. H.*

I have found as yet no recorded trace of the doings of William Hatcliffe in his first fourteen years, between his baptism and his matriculation at Cambridge University. That he did not spend the most important of them at home or at a local school—Caistor, Louth, Grimsby—is however a certainty. A wealthy gentleman's child-heir who showed gifts of nature capable of development into 'princely parts' would be put very early to his book, his tongues, his music and dancing, under the best teachers obtainable, as well as to all exercises fit for gentlemen, such as fencing, vaulting, riding, and shooting. And following an excellent practice of the time, at the age of nine or ten he would be placed out in a household of higher rank: if possible, that of a peer.

In Hatcliffe's case, as he was half an Ayscough, the choice would be obvious, and one offering the rarest advantages. His childless aunt Anne was the Lady Anne Ayscough (Askew), daughter of Edward Fiennes de Clinton, 1st Earl of Lincoln, Lord Admiral, and as Lord Steward from 1581 to 1585, also chief of her Majesty's Household. Naturally the Earl of far-off Lincoln had a house more conveniently placed for his duties, in Surrey—a few miles from the Palace of Oatlands—at Pyrford, where he entertained the Queen in September 1582.

The Lady Anne and her husband were doubtless included in the Earl's household, for she had become a favoured courtier as early as Christmas 1580, when she presented Queen Elizabeth with a jewelled hair-pin—a New Year's gift symbolic both of Hope and of her father's office as Lord Admiral. The entry reads

Item, an ancker of gould, garnished with small sparkes of dyamonds, hanging at a bodkin of goulde enamyoled, with a small pearle pendante, Geven by the ladye Anne Askewe.[1]

---

[1] Nichols, *Progr. Elizabeth* (1788), ii.

Early training in the Earl's household would be an ideal one for the childless Lady Anne's beautiful small nephew Will Hatcliffe; especially near the royal court where the most influential included his countrymen Lord Burghley and the Queen's favourite courtier Sir Thomas Heneage: a Court where he could both find the best teachers in the kingdom and

> Hear sweet discourse, converse with noblemen,
> And be in eye of every exercise
> Worthy his youth and nobleness of birth.

Conjectural biography of this sort can be taken as not far from the truth. Certainly experience of this very kind was needed to produce the youth's mastery of the princely parts and graces which fitted him to be singled from out the scores of England's most accomplished young gentlemen at Gray's Inn to be their King.

Under the ever-present example of so learned a Queen, a few years' preparation at Oxford or Cambridge was held desirable even for young noblemen. And to understand the social structure of the undergraduate life young Hatcliffe was to enter, we must recall the three classes from the humblest to the highest, from *sizar* to *fellow-commoner*. For the poorer boys, the colleges helped to keep education open to the talents by offering some scholarships on the foundation, and places known at Cambridge as sizarships. *Sizars* received free their portions or 'sizes'—halfpenny loaves of bread and pints of ale—and in return performed services for their betters such as bed-making, water-fetching, and waiting at table. In the main, sizars were hard, ambitious students, their goal a full degree as Master of Arts, followed by a post as a schoolmaster, or a living as a parson, with chance of rising higher in the Church. Some mounted without leaving Cambridge. Dr John Hilles, for example, rose from sizar at Jesus to Master of St Catharine's and Vice-Chancellor of the University.

Above these were the *pensioners*, the large central bulk of each college: sons of gentry, of well-to-do yeomen-farmers or merchants, who paid their own way.

At the top stood the select few known as *fellow-commoners*, since in Hall they dined not with the pensioners, but more expensively (and with wine) at the high table, in conversation with the Fellows and the Master. Today this rank is virtually obsolete everywhere. A witness in 1750 informs us that at Cambridge 'it differs from what is called a gentleman-commoner at Oxford . . . in the greater privileges and licences indulged to the members of this order, who . . . are allowed to absent themselves at pleasure from the private lectures'.[1]

Under Elizabeth and James this small class was made up almost exclusively of noblemen's sons and the heirs of rich gentry. And from the moment of his admission as a freshman, a fellow-commoner outranked not only all the undergraduate sizars and pensioners in the University, but the Bachelors of Arts as well. This distinction vividly appears in the marshalling of the University in ascending order of dignity to receive King James at Cambridge in 1622:

The young Scholars were placed from Jesus College gate next the street unto Trinity College gates in this manner: the Freshmen, Sophmoors, and Sophisters all being in their capps; the Bachelors of Arts in their hoods and capps; next to them the Fellow-commoners in their capps; after them the Regents and Non-regents [Masters of Arts] in their hoods and capps; [then the Doctors;] the Proctors, Presidents, and Deans of the severall Colleges did walk up and down in the streets, to see every one in his degree to keepe his rank and place.[2]

On the King's earlier visit in 1615 the order of ranking had been exactly the same.[3]

If by the age of fourteen William Hatcliffe had by the favour of his childless aunt Lady Anne been brought up to consort with the highest in the land, doubtless both she and his father would see it as a step backward, were he to enter Jesus College a

---

[1] Qu. *O.E.D.*, s.v. Commoner *sb.* 6.
[2] Nichols, *Progr. James I* iv (1828), 1114–15.
[3] *Ibid.*, iii. 86.

pensioner as his father and his uncle George had done. If in looks, manners, grace of speech, and accomplishments of mind and body he was clearly a fellow-commoner's peer, a fellow-commoner he should be, regardless of expense. And so Master W. H. matriculated at Cambridge—in Michaelmas Term 1582, a fellow-commoner from Jesus College.[1]

In this same term the Master of Jesus, Dr John Bell, was elected Vice-Chancellor for a year; and thus as a freshman Hatcliffe found himself dining daily with the Head of the University. Among others whom he joined at the high table was the son of the Archbishop of Armagh, Ireland: the twenty-one-year-old Dudley Loftus, already in his third year as a fellow-commoner. And if Will Hatcliffe felt youthful as a freshman at fourteen, he could look down at the pensioners' tables and see a sophomore named Cotton, aged eleven—hardly yet the distinguished antiquary-and-manuscript-collector he was to become as Sir Robert Bruce Cotton, Bart. Another of Hatcliffe's contemporaries at Cambridge, 'Mother of Muses and great Nurse of Art', was Christopher Marlowe at Corpus Christi, son of a shoemaker and certainly a poetic genius. At St John's—the college of Lord Burghley, Chancellor of the University—Thomas Nashe entered this same Michaelmas 1582 as a lowly sizar, and afterwards grew to be a friend of Marlowe's, and famous as 'young Juvenal'. And Thomas Campion, the one poet who—besides Shakespeare —we know became Hatcliffe's dear friend, was already in his second year at Peterhouse under Dr Perne. Considerably senior to these youngsters was Robert Greene, B.A., already within a year of proceeding Master of Arts from Clare College.

With its walled and gated colleges like vats of youth in ferment, Cambridge could be no dreaming town. If the age-old hostility between Town and Gown could only occasionally be heated up, at least the ancient feud between Trinity and the Johnians kept things lively with Montague–Capulet street fights. And for the greater battles of university civil war, the colleges divided into

---

[1] Venn, *loc. cit.*

North and South, with Jesus College no doubt enlisted in the army of the North.

Few in any age could resist the beauty and charm of Jesus College, the one-time Benedictine nunnery, more retired than any other, quiet in its broad greens extending to the Cam. There is an air about it enough to make Jesus men consider themselves a race distinct and favoured. Its unique attractions made the college early famous. And in 1639, for example—when Jesus College was almost a century and a half old—Henry Peacham tells his readers what travellers looked for when they went out to view Cambridge:

especially the ruines of the Castle, built by *William* the *Conquerour*, Pythagoras' Schoole, and the Round Church sometimes a Synagogue of the *Iewes*, the Nunnery of Saint *Radegunde*, now converted into *Iesus* Colledge ...[1]

No mention of King's College Chapel; indeed the only other college named is Queens', and that solely for '*Erasmus* his Chamber and Study'.

Now it is just at this point in the story, where we have seen Shakespeare's Friend received into the college of his father and his uncle, to be for three long boyhood years identified as a 'Jesus man', that I would ask the reader to pause, and look with me again at the problem presented by the extended simile of Sonnet 143. This is one of the famous 'triangle' sonnets (Dark Woman, Lover's Friend, Lover)—the one by which in plain terms Shakespeare the Lover tells the Woman (who is pursuing his Friend, Will) that if afterwards she will only come back to him and be kind, he will let her have Will, his Friend. It is also the sonnet which exhibits that startling and puzzling plunge to a humble dooryard-simile: these persons of the love-triangle

---

[1] *The Progress of Meum and Tuum*, p. 14.

suddenly likened to a huswife (hussy), her fugitive fowl, and her
crying babe:

143

Lo, as a careful huswife runs to catch
One of her feather'd creatures broke away,
Sets down her babe, and makes all swift dispatch
In pursuit of the thing she would have stay;
Whilst her neglected child holds her in chase,
Cries to catch her whose busy care is bent
To follow that which flies before her face,
Not prizing her poor infant's discontent:
So runn'st thou after that which flies from thee,
Whilst I thy babe chase thee afar behind;
But if thou catch thy hope, turn back to me,
And play the mother's part, kiss me, be kind:
  So will I pray that thou mayst have thy Will,
  If thou turn back and my loud crying still.

Granting that this scene has a comic look, that a lover presenting himself as a crying babe can be only half serious, the real
puzzle is, what could possibly have suggested it? What mental
link could there be between the Friend and a 'feather'd creature'?
Or how is Will (Hatcliffe) recognizable to himself and others at
Gray's Inn as a cockerel? From *sovereign,* that seems a leap indeed.

But to walk from Jesus Gate down The Chimney, the long
walled path into Hatcliffe's college, is to be struck at once by its
rousing and unforgettable emblem: the *cock.* John Alcock,
Bishop of Ely, took the nunnery of Saint Radegund on its decay
near the close of the fifteenth century, founded Jesus College in
its augmented buildings, and brilliantly eternized his own name
there in symbol. His coat of arms tells it with three cocks' heads.
The College arms not only preserve them, but add a black cock
as the crest.

Further, as Dr Frederick Brittain in his absorbing story[1]
points out, Alcock's personal emblem or badge, a cock standing

---

[1] *A Short History of Jesus College Cambridge,* 1940.

on a ball or globe, presents 'a pun on the whole of the founder's surname, as the ball represents the earth—that is, *all*'. Twenty-eight of these 'all'-cocks shone in coloured glass in the Library windows, another stands in the Chapel over the Master's stall—a 'beautifully carved cock standing on a ball'—, and still another 'large cock, without a ball this time' stands over the original doorway 'which leads from the First Court to the cloister'.

Collegians, like regiments (The Old Contemptibles), or gangs (The Limbs of Limehouse), covet the distinction of a good nickname, and cling to it like limpets. That the men of Jesus find an enviable one ready-made is evident from the name of their most famous club, the Roosters.[1]

Now I have found no documentary evidence of the fact; but nothing could shake my conviction that in those old pugnacious days of street battles between North and South the men of Jesus—their regimental badge a cock—were traditionally known as the Cocks of the Game, the Fighting Cockerels, the Game Chickens, or something of the sort.

Here then is a theory to account for Sonnet 143, where the Sovereign of Purpoole—a veteran Jesus man while still a youth— is to be recognized by his old Cambridge comrades at Gray's Inn as a Cockerel. 'The king's a bawcock, and a heart of gold.' Far-fetched? Fanciful? When anyone uncovers a likelier source for that extraordinary simile, I will give this one up, but not a moment before.

For gentlemanly exercise (and incidentally for losing money by betting on the strokes), Alcock's college had its own walled-and-roofed court for the royal or real tennis, built 'in or next to the portion of the nunnery cloister which then existed in the third or "Pump" court'.[2] And in fencing, and especially in music and dancing, excellent private instruction was offered by leading teachers in the town. '*A young gentleman of the university* . . . His

---

[1] *A Short History of Jesus College Cambridge*, 1940, 47–48.
[2] Arthur Gray, *Jesus College* (1902), 96.

father sent him thither because he heard that there were the best fencing and dancing-schools.'[1] These extras were devotedly followed by the young gentlemen who could afford them, in particular those who looked forward to the dancing society of the Inns of Court.

Few but specialist readers would guess at another extra-academic subject which absorbed the attention of gentlemen-students: noble Heraldry—the history, description, and significance of gentle families' coats and crests. 'A knowledge of heraldry was deemed in the sixteenth century a necessary part of a gentleman's education.'[2] Something of what they felt about it may be gathered from the following contemporary lines addressed to William Penson, Lancaster Herald, entitled *An Eulogy of Honour*:

> You that of kings, of princes, and great lords
> Their high descents and fair allies records;
> That hold the register of former time
> For all the noble houses in our clime,
> Preserves their names alive, though they be dead,
> And their high honours still unburiëd;
> That know to rank great lords and noble knights
> At tilts, at tourneys; and in funeral rites
> Their honour'd arms and ensigns do set forth
> Join'd with the symbols of their high-born worth;
> That keeps their fair coat-armours perfect still,
> Free from the grave; and with an herald's quill
> Can from dead ancestry cause to revive
> Their nobleness, and make them seem alive,
> As if you would give immortality . . .[3]

As Earle further observes of *A young gentleman of the university*, 'His main loytering is at the library, where he studies arms and books of honour, and turns a gentleman critick in pedigrees'. In

---

[1] Earle, *Microcosmographic*, 1628.
[2] Oswald Barron, 'Heraldry' in *Shakespeare's England* (1916), 2.77.
[3] Composed by —— Morley. Bodl. MS. Tanner 236. Spelling modernized.

this the youths had the high example of their University's Chancellor, Lord Burghley, the greatest minister of the Crown. Somehow, despite the incredible mass of detailed work he packed into his days, Burghley found time for deep study of heraldry and genealogy, not only English but Continental too, as his papers surviving witness.

Heraldry's importance to him and to Elizabethan society appears in the princely mansion he built for himself, Theobalds, as described when Queen Elizabeth came to visit him there in 1583:

Inner Court . . . Over the Gate, a Gallery painted with the Armes of the Noblemen and Gentlemen of England in Trees.[1]

And of course in Lord Burghley's gallery among the coats of his fellow-gentry of Lincolnshire stood the escutcheon of *Hatcliffe of Hatcliffe*.[2]

What was that escutcheon? We shall find that it proved to be in a very real sense the Luck of Will Hatcliffe. Already we are familiar with outstanding features of his rare good fortune. Nature had granted him exceptional beauty and gifts of mind and character. By birth he was distinguished as the wealthy heir of an ancient line—and his aunt the daughter of the Queen's Lord Admiral and Lord Steward. At Cambridge as a fellow-commoner he ranked with the nobility. To all this we now add another, his hereditary coat of arms—the form and significance of which proved to be a great means in achieving his future honour and glory.

Its technical description—*Azure, three quatrefoils pierced and slipped argent, 2 & 1*'—does not convey much to modern and uninstructed eyes. If we recall that the four-leaved clover brings luck, we begin to glimpse something. But for full illumination we need to turn to 'the prime authority in Shakespeare's era',[3]

---

[1] Nichols, *Progr. Elizabeth* (1788) ii. (*sub* 27 May 1583).
[2] B.M. MS. Harley 1436, f. 122; and 2145, f. 4ᵛ.
[3] Barron, *loc. cit.*

that best-selling vade-mecum Gerard Legh's *The Accedens of Armory* (editions 1562, 1568, 1576, 1591, 1597, 1612). Opening a copy of 1576 to page 95, we find sketched a shield like Hatcliffe's —except that the four-petalled forms are gold, not silver like his. And here is the description:

The field Azure, iij. Caterfoyls Or, Slipped argent. This though it be termed a foyle, yet it is a flower by the name of the primrose. This of all other flowers bringeth good tidings unto man, that the Spring of the yere, is at hand. The flower likewise especially when the leaves thereof bee but to the nomber of fower, beinge founde, is the rather with a certaintie taken from the grounde, and the more estemed, because as it is commonly called a trewe love, so it importeth a manner good lucke unto the first finder thereof.

On an earlier page Legh had given 'Quater foyles, otherwise called, prime Roses'.

When we come to find Hatcliffe known in London by his heraldic flower—the 'True Love' or the 'prime Rose', 'that of all other flowers bringeth good tidings that the Spring . . . is at hand', it becomes clear that Shakespeare was not puzzling his readers, when in poetry he called him *Love*, *True Love*, *beauty's Rose*, my *Rose*, and the *only herald to the gaudy spring*. But we shall return to this in a later chapter, and must not anticipate its discoveries-by-recognition too soon.

The academic subjects studied by Will Hatcliffe, Tom Campion, Kit Marlowe, and the rest at the University were few. The curriculum offered a grounding useful for both pulpit and bar, beginning in the first year with rhetoric (directed by logic and ethics), and proceeding in the second and third years with dialectics. Lectures furnished instruction and example, but the essential practice was gained in the frequent and required disputation or 'wrangle', and the declamation: all, naturally, in Latin.

Thus, what we might call 'debating' and 'oratory'—which are no longer the subjects of formal study—in those days were central, as the exercises and tests of proficiency in learning. For a livelier glimpse of it we may follow Henry Peacham's characters, who

desired to see the common Schooles, and desired to heare the Disputations and wranglings of Sophisters; with some of whom, after they had acquainted themselves, they learned all the rules of Arguing, with the Nature of Syllogismes, and every Fallacie, whereby they enabled themselves, for reasoning *pro* & *con* in all places, and upon every occasion; and were now become able to entangle any Adversary or Opposite in Logicall limetwigs. Now ... being furnished with Latine and Logick, enough for the practise of the Law, they take their leaves, and to *London* forward by *Trompington* they goe.[1]

Most of the gentlemen-students did not proceed to a degree, holding firmly to the conviction that 'the greatest clerks [scholars] are not the wisest men', and realizing with Lord Burghley—who was himself a first-class scholar—that *judgment*, the most precious of all arts, is not in the curriculum:

The old Lord *Burleigh*, sometime Treasurer of *England*, coming to *Cambridge* with *Queene Elizabeth*, when he was led into the publicke schooles, and had much commended their convenience, beauty, and greatnesse. . .; yea marry, said hee, but I finde one schoole wanting in our Universities, and that is the schoole of *Discretion*.[2]

And many of them would turn to history and biography as the best means of enlarging both their judgment and their grasp of life; agreeing with Sir Thomas North, the translator of Plutarch's Lives (1579) who lived in Cambridge, that

there is no profane study better than Plutarch. All other learning is private, fitter for Universities than cities, fuller of contemplation than experience, more commendable in the students themselves than profitable to others. Whereas stories [*i.e.* histories] are fit for every place, reach to all persons, serve for all times, teach the living, revive the dead, so far excelling all other books as it is better to see learning in noble men's lives than to read it in philosophers' writings.[3]

---

[1] *The Progress of Meum and Tuum*, 15.
[2] Henry Peacham, *The Truth of our Times* (1638), 158–159.
[3] *Plutarchs Lives* (1579), sig. *iij. Spelling modernized.

THE ARMS OF
WILLIAM HATCLIFFE

For Will Hatcliffe, Plutarch's *Lives* held a peculiar intimacy beyond all this: for it was *from Plutarch's Life of Pompey the Great that the heraldic crest of the Hatcliffes had long ago been drawn.* The family bore a (red) *lion holding a sword. Not* a medieval two-handed sword, but a classical short sword or cutlass in one paw. This lion-with-sword was the device of Pompey's own signet, and doubly asserts the ruler: for the majestic lion 'beareth in himself a princely port . . . such is the haughty courage of his high stomach that he accounteth himself without peer', and power is shown by his sword 'that menaceth punishment to the evil, defence and safety to the good'.

Hatcliffe's lion would at once remind every young gentleman of the story of Pompey—his generous friendship to the father of the treacherous Egyptian king Ptolemy, the son who repaid kindness with murder. The tale was common in the Renaissance. You read of it in Legh's *Accedens of Armory* (1562) and elsewhere long before Plutarch had appeared in English:

Plutarke writethe of a Ringe with a precious stone, whiche was taken from Pompey the great, when he was slaine. That Ring saith hee made Cesar weepe. . . . That Ringe had graven in it a Lion bearing a Sworde.[1]

And John Bossewell's *Workes of Armorie*, 1572:

Pompey the great had such a Lyon [bearing a sword] graven in hys signet, *vide in vitis Plutarchi* [97ᵛ]. . . . I dare boldly affirme the bearing of [the lion, 'king of all beastes'] one way to be most of honor & soveraity: as when he is *passant*, gardant [21ᵛ] . . .

—and Hatcliffe's kingly lion was borne *passant*, that is, 'pacing'. In 1511 Francesco Maria della Rovere, Duke of Urbino, had adopted Pompey's lion for his device[2] and coloured it red—again like Hatcliffe's. More than that, shortly before Hatcliffe was admitted at Gray's Inn two other widely-read works brought it

---

[1] (Ed. 1576), 109.
[2] Giovanni Ferro de' Rotarii, *Teatro d'Imprese* (1623), 434; Giacopo Gelli, *Divise . . .* (1928), 355.

again to public notice. Samuel Daniel's 1585 version of Paolo Giovio's book on heroical devices gave Pompey's arms as 'a Lyon with a sword clasped in his claw'; and Ferne's *Blazon of Gentrie* (1586) presents the sword-holding Lion as Pompey's 'insigne, and banner of Armes'.[1]

Will Hatcliffe and Pompeius Magnus. There is much to be added on this curious subject; and when Will Hatcliffe achieves greatness, and rides in triumph as Prince of Purpoole, neither he, we, nor his subjects will forget to recall great Pompey's story.

In the spring of his third or 'sophister' year, 1585, Hatcliffe suffered a grave loss: his aunt Lady Anne Ayscough died at Lincoln, following the death in January of her father, the Earl of Lincoln. The Earl's great offices were now filled by successors— Charles Lord Howard of Effingham becoming the new Lord Admiral, and Robert Dudley Earl of Leicester Lord Steward of the Household. If his aunt and her father could have lived a few years longer, possibly Hatcliffe might have secured a post in the Queen's household.

Since at seventeen he was still young for service in the Low Countries before entering Gray's Inn, if he had enough Greek he doubtless went on for the fourth Cambridge year, which in the curriculum was devoted to philosophy; but like most of the gentlemen, he took no degree. From the years at Cambridge he must have acquired as much learning as befitted a gentleman, greatly widened his circle of friends, perfected himself in dancing and in graces of conversation, and gained enough practice in disputation and declamation to prepare him for the bolting or mooting of a case at Gray's Inn, as well as for making a reasoned reply to his wise councillors, or an eloquent speech from the throne as Prince of Purpoole.

And so, with the motto of Jesus College to speed him better than anyone could foresee, Bishop Alcock's *Prosperum iter facias*—'May your journey be successful'—to London forward by Trumpington he goes, to be admitted at Gray's Inn, as we

---

[1] Qu. R. David, ed. *Love's Labour's Lost* (New Arden), 172.

have seen, on 4 November 1586, aged eighteen years and two months. Here he joined not only his friend the poet Thomas Campion (admitted in the April preceding) but also his first cousin Francis Manby, heir of Sir Francis Manby of Elsham and son of his mother's sister Anne. Manby, admitted two and a half years before, shared Campion's friendship with Cousin Will. Acquaintance among the other gentlemen, senior, contemporary, and junior-to-come, must for Will Hatcliffe have been both wide and increasing.

It was now, as I think, that he met the rising poet-player, Shakespeare. For the gowned collegiate students of the law— like one of their number, 'Mr. John Dunne . . . a great frequenter of Playes'—appreciated 'an excellent player', as John Earle did:

Your inns-of-court men were undone but for him; he is their chief guest and employment, and the sole business that makes them afternoon's men . . . to give him his due, one well-furnisht actor has enough in him for five common gentlemen, and, if he have a good body, for six.[1]

They valued both his example and his teaching; for they agreed with Mr Francis Bacon of Gray's Inn, himself a distinguished deviser of dramatic masks:

It is a thing indeed, if practised professionally, of low repute; but if it be made a part of discipline, it is of excellent use. I mean stageplaying: an art which strengthens the memory, regulates the tone and effect of the voice and pronunciation, teaches a decent carriage of the countenance and gesture, gives not a little assurance, and accustoms young men to bear being looked at.[2]

On the question of the propriety of gentlemen consorting with professional players, they could point to Cicero and Roscius:

Thys *Roscius*, for his excellencie in pronunciation and gesture, the noble *Cicero* called hys Jewell, and so much delited in hym, that he contended with hym, whether *Roscius* coulde set forthe one sentence

---

[1] *Microcosmographie* (1628), Character xxiii.
[2] *De Augmentis Scientiarum* in *The Philosophical Works of Francis Bacon* (tr. and ed. J. Spedding 1905), 560.

in more fashions of gesture and contenance, or he expresse the same sentence in a more diversitie of eloquente wordes.[1]

Among the actors to be carried off to a party at a tavern after the play, Shakespeare, excelling in kingly parts, could not fail to be sought out. Noble and gentle by nature, personally handsome, a poet and a pleasant cheerful wit, he made a most delightful companion. John Aubrey reports Shakespeare as described by those who knew him: 'He was a handsome well shap't man: very good company, and of a very readie and pleasant smooth Witt.' In so small a world as London then presented, it would be curious if two such men as Hatcliffe and Shakespeare should not meet. Still, after first casual acquaintance, the great social disparity, added to the four-and-a-half years' difference in age, made a gap not to be quickly or easily bridged. I conclude that it took nearly a year from the poet's first sight of the beautiful youth for that acquaintance to grow into the warmth of friendship which speaks in the Sonnets.

Hatcliffe's 'punyship' or first year at Gray's Inn must have been an active one, to make his rare qualities and accomplishments so widely known among the elder members as to secure his election over all others as their Prince in his second November. Why Gray's Inn decided to inaugurate a Prince in 1587 we can only guess. No hint has been found of any Christmas Prince there in the years immediately preceding; and certainly the political situation of England before Christmas 1587 was far from favourable for the planning of elaborate, expensive, and light-hearted celebrations.

For like the opening of *Hamlet*, it was an anxious time of watch, post-haste, and romage in the land. Parma was thought to be planning to attack Flushing, and a 'hot alarm' had just been sounded—a rumoured descent of the Spanish Armada. As John Chamberlain writes from London on December 15th:

. . . his Excellency [the Earl of Leicester] returned two days since out of the Low Countries, where he hath left the Lord Willoughby [of

---

[1] Bossewell, *op. cit.*, 91ᵛ.

Eresby, Lincolnshire] lieutenant. . . . The P[rince of Parma] maketh great preparation about Dunkirk. . . . Here is great preparation to sea, for all or most of the Queen's ships are setting forth in all haste, and the Lord Admiral goeth in person, accompanied with the Lord Henry Seymer, the Lord Thomas Howard, the Lord William [Howard], the Lord Sheffeld and others. Sir Fraunces Drake with certain of the Queen's ships and others to the number of forty sail is appointed another way. . . . Our provisions by land go as fast forward as our sea matters, for we have mustering everywhere, and lieutenants and colonels appointed to every shire to be ready upon any sudden invasion. The Earls of Huntington and Cumberland, Sir Henry Lea, Sir Robert Constable, and Captain Banborough are appointed to look to the North, my Lord Chamberlain [Lord Hunsdon] is already at Berwick, Sir Walter Rawly is gone westward; he is sole lieutenant for Cornwall, and joined in commission with the Earl of Bath for Devonshire. . . . Now if you ask me upon what ground we have taken this hot alarm, I can answer you no certainty but upon speech of preparation in Spain and upon the Parma's doings at Dunkirk, and some suspicion of Scotland. . . .[1]

So many noblemen away 'on active service' would explain why Lord Burghley lists only five great lords (including himself) at the Prince of Purpoole's entertainment and comedy one month after this letter.

The inauguration of Prince William [Hatcliffe], Prince of Purpoole, with his heroical Order and the mighty array of his officers and attendants at his inthronization and 'solemn marches' according to the traditional form revealed in the record of Prince Henry [Helmes], will be seen in the sequel.

Meanwhile we may turn back to Shakespeare with the question, What fresh light does our new knowledge throw on the topics, tone, and language of the Sonnets addressed to such a sovereign? One thing is obvious at once: the *kingship* of W. H. was no personal or closet-invention of Shakespeare's to praise or exalt his Friend. It was a public poetical fiction of the select society of

---

[1] From Bodl. MS. Tanner 309, ff. 300 f., with spelling modernized.

Gray's Inn: a fiction maintained in London and at the Court to an extent we can hardly grasp. Once and for all, then, Shakespeare's *my sovereign* is not his private monopoly, but *sovereign* of all the population of 'ancient Purpoole'.

But Shakespeare seized gladly upon a fiction affording such wondrous scope both for poetic eulogy and for the true humble offering of his love; for there is truth in the jingle—

> *The rarest gem that mortal men to Princes can impart,*
> *Renowned* [sovereign], *true love is, proceeding from the heart.*[1]

His jewels of hyperbole are the very language his age employed in the praise of royalty. In view of the extraordinary fiction, such terms do not show his friendship for Will Hatcliffe less sincere, any more than the customary high-flown praise of 'divine' Elizabeth shows insincerity in her subjects' love, which was world-famous.

Thus his praise of Prince Will's beauty, unexampled in English verse addressed to a male friend, is proper for a *king*, and is found in every age: Athenaeus writes:

> At least he [Priam] admires Agamemnon for beauty, uttering praise such as this: 'Yet I have never beheld with my eyes one so beautiful or so majestic; for he is like unto a king.' And many people have set upon the throne their handsomest men as kings . . .[2]

In *The Governor* (II. ii) Sir Thomas Elyot declares,

> Majestie . . . is proprelie a beautie or comelynesse in his countenance, langage and gesture . . .

And of a royal Duke in 1680 we read that

> an incredible number of people crowded to see him, every one extolling him to the Skies, crying one to another, Oh what a brave [fine-looking] man he is! Some admired the Beauty and make of his Person, some

---

[1] Nichols, *Progr. James I*, ii. 652.
[2] *Deipnosophistae* xiii. 566c. (Tr. C. B. Gulick, Loeb-Harvard (1937), VII. 59.)

the Majesty and Port of his Carriage . . . all admired his Affable and Courteous Disposition.[1]

Again, when one knows the Sonnets' frame of reference, and compares contemporary poets' praise of a young prince or half-god *in terms of a woman's beauty*, one cannot sink into the ignorance of imagining anything queer in Shakespeare's lines *A woman's face . . . Hast thou . . . And for a woman wast thou first created.* Sidney in his *Arcadia* describes the lovely Prince Pyrocles:

they saw a young man (at least if he were a man), bearing show of about eighteen years of age . . . full of admirable beauty . . .

And Chapman, Hymen and Perseus:

> Now a god of nuptial love, Hymen once
> Of Athens was a youth so sweet of face
> That many thought him of the female race.
>
> Amongst the fairest women you could find
> Than Perseus, none more fair; 'mongst worthiest men,
> No one more manly. . . .
> Such was the half-divine-born Trojan Terror
> Where both sex' graces met, as in a mirror.[2]

Above all, if anyone should object that such are fables, not real men like Shakespeare's fair Friend, one has only to read Heywood's description of the youthful Frederick, Count Palatine, at his royal marriage in 1613:

> A lovely youth, upon whose face appears
> True signs of manhood; yet he for his years
> And beauty, such a general name hath won,
> They take him all for Venus, or her son.

---

[1] *An Historical Account Of the Most Illustrious Protestant Prince, James Duke of Monmouth*, 1683.
[2] *Hero and Leander*, v. 93–94; *Andromeda Liberata*.

A mixëd grace he in his visage wore,
And but his habit show'd what sex he bore,
The quickest-sighted eye might have mistook,
Having female beauty in a manly look.[1]

They take him all for Venus or her son. That is to say, their love
for Prince Frederick makes him seem either Cupid, God or Master
of Love, or Venus, Goddess or Mistress of Love—each is Passion
or Love. Here Heywood repeats, for his Prince, Shakespeare's
thought in Sonnet 20 about his: Will, his beautiful sovereign or
god, is Love—Cupid or Venus—*the master-mistress of my
passion.*[2] Quite needless to add that any homosexual notion is as
foreign to Heywood's conception as it is to Shakespeare's.

Now let us consider the great initial 'mystery' of the Sonnets.
For perhaps no feature of the whole series has been more puzzling
than its opening: the first seventeen poems urge, persuade, beg,
and warn the Friend to marry and beget a child. *Why?* There is
nothing like it in all poetry. Ordinary common sense dismisses
the Just So Story which informs the credulous reader that 'Shakespeare was hired by a worried mother to write a lot of poems to
make her son marry'. Only complete bafflement could force even
a theorist quite unacquainted with the Elizabethans to suggest
such an absurdity. The truth is that no *explanation* has ever been
offered. As the late C. S. Lewis acutely remarked of this 'in-
cessant demand' to marry, 'It is indeed hard to think of any real
situation in which it would be natural. What man in the whole
world, except a father, or a potential father-in-law, cares whether
any other man gets married?'[3]

It is the inauguration of Prince William of Purpoole which
gives the answer. We can now reply, 'The *subject of a boy-king* or

---

[1] *A Marriage Triumphe . . .* 1613. From the Aungervyle Society reprint
(1884), 8, but with spelling modernized.

[2] In *Love's Labour's Lost* 4.3 Shakespeare again presents Love at once as
master-mistress: (340) 'is not Love a Hercules . . .?' (366) 'Saint Cupid,
then!' (379) 'merry hours Forerun fair Love, strewing her way'.

[3] *English Literature in the Sixteenth Century* (1954), 503.

of an *unmarried ruler* cares, and cares deeply: the birth of an heir will bulwark the commonwealth against civil war or anarchy.' No anxious hope was more universal in Elizabethan minds than that the sovereign would produce a child to secure the succession:

We have just cause to think that our sins have provoked the wrath of God, that in so many years he hath not inclined her heart to marriage, that we might see the desired fruit we have and do so much long for.[1]

Or, as Shirley has it, the ruler being addressed in more Shake-spearean vein,

> If not for your propitious love to us,
> Yet for your own sake, for your glory, hasten
> The cure of these our fears. Time is the moth
> Of nature, devours all beauty.[2]

For more than a generation, Queen Elizabeth's subjects anxiously pestering her to marry were enough to drive frantic a woman whose sound judgment told her that England was safer under her rule, though childless, than if she were subject to a husband.[3] To quiet them, and 'to make the world think she should have children of her own,' as her godson Sir John Haryngton relates, 'she entertained till she was fifty years of age motions of marriage' —accepting from the Earl of Arundel a New Year's gift of a gold hair-pin ornamented with 'a cradle garnished with small dia-monds' when she was forty-seven.

After decades of such experience, could any feature of Eliza-bethan monarchy show more essentially characteristic than a sustained, persistent urging of the sovereign to marry? To marry, not at all to gain a beloved or an able helpmeet; but to marry only *to get an heir*. First in importance, vital to the state, stood the *succession*.

---

[1] Anon., 'At Greenwich 6 Octob. 1579'. B.M. MS. Harl. 6265, f. 104. Spelling modernized.
[2] *The Humorous Courtier* 1.1.
[3] Sir John Neale's *Queen Elizabeth* tells the long, fascinating story.

Accordingly, if upon its creation the Kingdom of Purpoole is to present a reasonable facsimile, be made to look and to sound like the real article, the first thing to reproduce is Exhortation of the Sovereign to Marry and Get an Heir.

'The Kings of England have been pleased usually to consult with their Peers in the Great Council and Commons in Parliament of Marriage, Peace and War.' Yes, but only *after* the high matter had been thoroughly canvassed with their privy councillors. Immediately upon his election, the Prince of Purpoole was assigned a Privy Council to advise him. First in order of business comes the Succession; and texts for its members' loyal and learned arguments are not hard to supply—such as

> *Princes most strength by good succession gather;*
> *With future hopes all present smarts are eas'd.*

or

> *Kings live most safe who of their own have heirs.*[1]

As their sovereign's chosen friends, we may believe that Prince William's councillors did not omit any persuasion which their long-practised art of rhetoric or the example of Erasmus's eloquence to a young gentleman on this very subject could afford.

But no rhetoric is so persuasive as poetry's. And Shakespeare, the new Prince's poet-friend, easily outstrips the official councillors in his opening address of seventeen sonnets. For he is able to infuse argument with the most subtly pleasing praise of his sovereign's *beauty*. With every art he presses his winning point: it is that precious, flower-like, short-lived royal gift of his Prince's which only an heir can preserve:

> 1 *From fairest creatures we desire increase,*
> *That thereby beauty's rose might never die,*
> *But as the riper should by time decease,*
> *His tender heir might bear his memory . . .*

---

[1] Cotgrave, *English Treasury* (1655), 269; Sir William Alexander, *The Alexandraean Tragedy*, line 1210.

2 *When forty winters shall besiege thy brow*
And dig deep trenches in thy beauty's field,
Thy youth's proud livery, so gazed on now,
Will be a tottered weed of small worth held:
Then being asked where all thy beauty lies, . . .
If thou couldst answer, 'This fair child of mine
Shall sum my count and make my old excuse,'
Proving his beauty by succession thine.

6   *. . . thou art much too fair*
To be death's conquest and make worms thine heir.

And more than that, uninhibited by the gravity of the council-
board, he can add the personal plea:

10 *Be as thy presence is, gracious and kind,*
Or to thyself at least kind-hearted prove:
Make thee another self for love of me,
That beauty still may live in thine or thee.

An outsider, no member of Gray's Inn, Shakespeare yet shows
himself perfectly apprised of the Privy Council's duties—both
here and at the later fixture in the programme when the Councillors played leading parts, as follows. At a full Court in Hall,
the Prince presiding in state, his Councillors about him and before
him, the Sovereign made them a speech, requiring their opinions
touching the scope of his government. What royal enterprise,
what plan of life would best conduce to his happiness, glory, or
eternal fame?

The replies of six Councillors to this question as propounded
by his successor Prince Henry of Purpoole have been preserved,
and ascribed by Spedding to the pen of Francis Bacon. The six
advocated respectively War, Philosophy, Building, Absoluteness
of State and Treasure, Virtue and Gracious Government, and
Pastimes and Sports. This looks like a customary form; and
Prince Henry's gracious reply to the extended oratory, thanking
them and choosing Pastimes and Sports, was no doubt also a
stock part of the 'drill'.

How closely such 'consultation' resembled the real thing is

139

evident by a surviving *Aunswer made by command of Prince Henry* [Prince of Wales] *to certaine Propositions of Warr, and Peace.* Also in Sir William Alexander's *Paraenesis* to that same Prince, where he asserts

> In Mars his mysteries to gaine renowne,
> It gives Kings glory, and assures their place.

Shakespeare, too, mentions the glorious enterprise to Prince Will, but only to suggest a better way to perpetuate his memory—to beget a child:

> 16 *But wherefore do not you a mightier way*
> *Make war upon this bloody tyrant, Time?*

War led the list; what then of *Philosophy*, whose royal pursuit Shakespeare reserved for a play later presented before his Prince:

> Let fame, that all hunt after in their lives,
> Live regist'red upon our brazen tombs
> And then grace us, in the disgrace of death,
> When, spite of cormorant devouring Time,
> Th' endeavour of this present breath may buy
> That honour which shall bate his scythe's keen edge
> And make us heirs of all eternity.

Despite the adage 'Philosophers must be Kings and Kings Philosophers', for most Kings it would, however, be 'Hang up Philosophy'; and next to *War*, the third—*Eternizement and Fame by Buildings and Foundations*—would appeal to them: recalling from Herodotus the Pharaohs 'who contended who should excell in these woorkes, some in Labyrinthes, some in building of *Piramides*, and some in monsterous great Temples for their burials.'[1] Certainly it appealed to Francis I of France, who used to say

'Princes and great Lords should . . . signalize their memory by some sumptuous building to show future ages how magnificent and splendid they were.' He had his Fontainebleau and his Chambord built, his

---

[1] Lodowick Lloid, *The Dial of Daies* (1590), 204.

Louvre and other great edifices begun; and would say that even if those who came after him left them to decay, at least the great ruins would be certain evidence of his magnificent splendour.'[1]

Naturally the satirist's view is different:

The Magnificos of this world rear up sumptuous buildings only for show and ostentation . . . depopulate and level with the ground whole Towns . . . only to lay the *Basis* of their Babel-outbraving Palaces.[2]

The honour of giving his Prince such delusive counsel, laying *great bases for eternity, Which proves more short than waste or ruining* has no attraction for Shakespeare. Would it mean anything to him to be such a Privy Councillor? Or, for that matter, to be one of the Barons of the Four Ports of Purpoole, whose proud right (modelled upon that of the Queen's Barons of the Cinque Ports) it was to bear the canopy over the Prince at his inthronization? What are such outward forms and ceremonies compared to the loving friendship he craves?

125

Were 't aught to me I bore the canopy,
With my extern the [thy] outward honouring,
Or laid great bases for eternity,
Which proves more short than waste or ruining?
Have I not seen dwellers on form and favour
Lose all, and more, by paying too much rent,
For compound sweet forgoing simple savour—
Pitiful thrivers, in their gazing spent?
No, let me be obsequious in thy heart,
And take thou my oblation, poor but free,
Which is not mixed with seconds, knows no art
But mutual render, only me for thee.
Hence, thou suborn'd informer! a true soul
When most impeach'd stands least in thy control.

---

[1] Tr. from Antoine de Laval, *Desseins de Professions nobles et publiques* (1605), sig. p3.
[2] John Heath, *This Worlds Folly* (1613), B3ᵛ–B4. Spelling modernized.

Seen in the context of Prince William's reign, the difficult opening lines of this sonnet are now much clearer. But the close remains a mystery. Who was this base informer?[1] Who suborned him? And of what crime did he impeach or accuse Shakespeare to his Prince? Anyone who can throw light here will earn our gratitude.

Will Hatcliffe's reign and his character as sovereign have solved for us the chief puzzle of the first seventeen sonnets, and made sense of the opening of Sonnet 125. And while the point is fresh in mind, I think that the underlying thought of his kingship will help in our reading of Sonnet 94—one of the finest poems, and most difficult, occasioned by the spectacle of the young sovereign's wrong-doing:

94

They that have pow'r to hurt and will do none,
That do not do the thing they most do show,
Who, moving others, are themselves as stone,
Unmovëd, cold, and to temptation slow—
They rightly do inherit heaven's graces
And husband nature's riches from expense;
They are the lords and owners of their faces,
Others but stewards of their excellence.
The summer's flow'r is to the summer sweet,
Though to itself it only live and die;
But if that flow'r with base infection meet,
The basest weed outbraves his dignity:
 For sweetest things turn sourest by their deeds;
 Lilies that fester smell far worse than weeds.

The character which Shakespeare describes in the opening lines, held up as the standard from which the erring Will has shamefully fallen away, sounds strange to modern ears. So strange that the baffled reader such as Lytton Strachey takes refuge in absurdity:

Lytton Strachey, quoting these lines in *Eminent Victorians* (apropos of Cromer in Egypt), decided they were simple condemnation: in

---

[1] Certainly not that universal villain, Time. He cannot be suborned.

them, he thought, Shakespeare described a kind of man 'whom he did not like'.[1]

Returning to sense, I think we shall find that this controlled, universally admired character was familiar. It was that of the *ideal king*.

The first line shows it, reminding us of Massinger's *'T is truly noble, having power to punish, Nay, kinglike, to forbear it*.[2] For the essence of a king is *justice*:

> True justice is the chiefe and onely thing
> That is requir'd and lookt for in a king.[3]

> *Andrugio.* Why, man, I never was a Prince till now.
> 'T is not the barëd pate, the bended knees,
> Gilt tipstaves, Tyrian purple, chairs of state,
> Troops of pied butterflies, that flutter still
> In greatness' summer, that confirm a prince:
> ... No, Lucio, he's a king,
> A true right king, that dares do aught, save wrong;
> Fears nothing mortal but to be unjust,
> ... Who stands unmov'd
> Despite the justling of opinion . . .[4]

And in 1588 the Justice of a King was *as stone, Unmovëd, cold*: shown in the frontispiece to Case's *Sphaera Civitatis* as the fixed Ptolemaic centre of Queen Elizabeth's royal universe— IUSTITIA IMMOBILIS.[5]

---

[1] Patrick Cruttwell, *The Shakespearean Moment* (1955), 31.

[2] *The Bashful Lover* 4.2. Cf. *Measure for Measure* 2.2.107: 'It is excellent To have a giant's strength; but it is tyrannous To use it like a giant.' For many examples of this *posse et nolle, nobile* see Tilley, *Dict. Prov.* H170, and G. C. Moore Smith's ed. of Fraunce's *Victoria* (1906), 71, 119.

[3] Bodenham, *Belvedere* (1600) repr. 1875, 61. On the front-valance of an Elizabethan throne-canopy at Westminster stood the great gold-embroidered word IUDEX (JUDGE). I find this canopy phonetically listed in the Wardrobe Accounts as 'Hughe Dyxe'.

[4] Marston, *Antonio and Mellida* 4.1.

[5] See the illustration in Roy C. Strong, *Portraits of Queen Elizabeth I* (1963), 127.

To be *just* and *unmoved* was to be a king. A true king is not lightly tempted, does not dare do wrong. Shakespeare's Prince, in so daring, degenerates from his right character. 'He is no king, that is affection's slave.' And what mortal men *rightly do inherit heaven's graces* but kings—

> The glorious list
> Of heirs of God, . . .
> Who royalize it there by Grace's high acquist . . .?[1]

They, and only *They are the lords and owners of their faces*, gifted with beauty—'that rare and royal face'.

Underneath this noble attempt to recall Will to a self-control more like a true king's, lies Shakespeare's own painful thought, 'Those have most pow'r to hurt us, that we love.'[2] And why, when employing Pliny's simile[3] from the *roses, lilies, violets* which quickly putrefy, does he choose *lilies*, but for the reason that the white lily means or signifies *purity of heart, good and holy love?*[4]

A later chapter will suggest that Will Hatcliffe, whatever his youthful faults and errors, did not abandon the ideal of true and constant love. But here we must turn back to the fascination of a world-renowned Shakespearean puzzle, and to the story of how the key to its solution proved to be *a knowledge of his name*.

---

[1] Benlowes, *Theophila* (1652), VI. xxxv. 85.

[2] Beaumont and Fletcher, *The Maid's Tragedy* 5.4.129.

[3] 'As in the nature of things, those which most admirably flourish, most swiftly fester or putrefy (*marcescunt*), as roses, lilies, violets, while others last: so in the lives of men, those that are most blooming, are soonest turned into the opposite.' Pliny, *Naturalis historia*, lib. 16. c.15. Tr. from Langius, *Polyanthea* (1607), 453a.

[4] 'Giglio bianco sign[ifica] purità di cuore, amor buono, & santo.' *Il Mostruosissimo Mostro di Giovanni De' Rinaldi* (1584), 90.

TO.THE.ONLIE.BEGETTER.OF.
THESE.INSVING.SONNETS.
M^r.W.H. ALL.HAPPINESSE.
AND.THAT.ETERNITIE.
PROMISED.

BY.

OVR.EVER-LIVING.POET.

WISHETH.

THE.WELL-WISHING.
ADVENTVRER.IN.
SETTING.
FORTH.

T. T.

THE DEDICATION PAGE OF *SHAKES-PEARES SONNETS*, 1609

VI

THE OPENING OF THE ODD

REPRODUCED opposite is perhaps the most famous dedication in all literature. In this curious form Thomas Thorpe inscribes his 1609 publication of *Shake-speares Sonnets Neuer before Imprinted* 'to the onlie begetter of these insuing sonnets Mr. W. H.'

The natural view of its meaning, and the one most generally taken, is that Master W. H. (the dedicatee) and Shakespeare's Friend (who inspired most of his Sonnets) are one and the same. As Sir Edmund Chambers puts it,

> To me it seems more difficult, every time I read the dedication, to believe that, even in Thorpe's affected phrasing, the person to whom he wished eternity was any other than the person to whom the 'ever-living poet' promised eternity.[1]

But some disagree. Those who must have Shakespeare's Friend a Right Honourable peer naturally want to get rid of W. H., who was only a Master. This drives them to follow the eighteenth-century George Chalmers. Chalmers fancied that W. H. was *not* the Friend to whom the poet promises 'eternitie', but some obscure fellow whose fame Thorpe strangely thought to perpetuate in a couple of initials *for having procured him the manuscript*. Even more absurd is it to adopt Massey's notion— that a Jacobean publisher could conceivably address a Right Worshipful knight (*e.g.*, Sir William Hervey) as 'Master'.

Yet few readers who recall Sonnets 38 and 78 have been persuaded that anyone can force the phrase *the onlie begetter of these insuing sonnets* to mean 'the procurer of the copy'—or anything at all but 'the inspirer of these poems'. Whatever else he may have been, Thorpe was literate. He would no more be guilty of

---

[1] *William Shakespeare* (1930), 1.566.

saying 'Beget me a manuscript to publish' than a publisher with elementary-school training would today. Before writing *begetter*, Thorpe had evidently read these two sonnets. In them Shakespeare assures his comely inspirer 'True-love', his *'tenth Muse'*—the begetter or father of the thought, by whom poets' brains conceive and *'bring forth'* ideas—that his poems are *'born of thee'*.

This authoritative testimony has long made the identity of Friend and Begetter plain enough to common sense. Nevertheless, we still occasionally hear it objected that 'no one has ever tangibly connected the Friend of the Sonnets with the Master W. H. of Thorpe's dedication'. And doubtless those who refuse to accept a plain Master for the poet's Friend will go on believing anything rather than the reasonable identification until confronted with conclusive proof that Thorpe knew what he was talking about. Few developments could be more welcome to Shakespeare's readers than discovery of such proof.

No effort should be spared which might lead to that result. Yet if we are not to fail through simple inadvertence, we must learn from the long-experienced to take every possible means of recognition into account. Of the enormous files composing the *Modus Operandi* index at Scotland Yard, the first and foremost is the Nominal Section, 'giving the name and every alias known to have been used by the criminal'.[1]

First of all, then, we should closely examine the *name* of Shakespeare's beautiful Prince, Master William Hatcliffe. And we find at once that his surname, like that of many another Elizabethan, was subject to variation both in pronunciation and spelling. In such names of two syllables we notice it is usually the final one which shows most variants. As familiar examples, we have *Shakespeare* written *Shaxberd* and signed *Shaksper*; *Marlowe* as *Marley, Morley, Marlin*; and *Grenvile* commonly written and always pronounced *Greenfield*. In similar fashion I find Shake-

---

[1] Sir Harold Scott, *Scotland Yard* (1954) Penguin ed., 1957, 138.

146

speare's Hatcliffe described by two of his closest Lincolnshire neighbours as *William Hatley esquire*.[1]

But the name's usual variant, so frequent as to be common, was *Hatliff*. For at Cambridge his father was entered as *Thomas Hatlefe*, his uncle as *George Hatlyffe*;[2] and at Great Grimsby his son and heir was buried as *Mr. Thomas Hatlyff Esquire*.[3] Two cousins prominent in the borough appear in the 1582 subsidy roll of *Grimsby magna* as *Xpofer* [Christopher] *Hatlyffe maior* and *John Hatlyffe*,[4] and his Greenwich cousin and namesake, an officer of King James's Household, was left a legacy as *William Attlife*.[5] In their armorials the contemporary heralds frequently note, trick, or blazon the ancient bearings of Hatcliffe under this same form: *Hatlyff* of *Hatlyffe, Hatelyffe, Hatliff, Hatlif*.[6]

In short, the monotonous repetition of the final syllable as *life, lefe, lif, liff*, and *liffe* shows how the name of Shakespeare's Prince was sounded. Contemporaries almost always gave him his *Hat*. But his *cliff* was commonly only *liff*.[7] Remembering how a '*Morley*'—which had stood for years in print quite unsuspected —led to the discovery that Christopher Marlowe was employed confidentially by the Queen,[8] we should bear in mind this common pronunciation *Hatliff*. It might in the sequel prove similarly useful.

Brief and baffling, the dedication of *Shake-speares Sonnets* stands well in the front rank of major riddles endlessly attacked

---

[1] Episcopal Visitation, Lincoln and Stow Archdeaconries, 1604, f. 119ᵛ. Lincolnshire Archives Committee, The Castle, Lincoln.

[2] John and J. A. Venn, *Matriculations and Degrees, 1544–1659* (1913), 330.

[3] *Registers of St James, Grimsby*, ed. George Stephenson (1889), 132.

[4] P.R.O., E179/138/546.

[5] Will of Matthew Kaye, gent., dated 14 Nov. 1610 (P.C.C. 77 Fenner), qu. H. F. Waters, *Genealogical Gleanings* (1901), 939–940.

[6] B.M. MSS. Harl. 1048 f. 40ᵛ; 1459 f. 275; 1471 f. 50ᵛ; 1475 f. 40.

[7] The same phenomenon is seen in such names as Hinchcliff, Ratcliff, Shertcliff, Topcliff—which often appear as Hinchliff, Ratliff, Shertliff, Topliff.

[8] Hotson, *The Death of Christopher Marlowe*, 1925.

and never solved. In his egregious inscrutability 'Thorpe appears as the Sphinx of literature,' declares Richard Grant White. 'What a Medusa's head!' exclaims W. Carew Hazlitt. 'Thorpe has indeed played Puck among the commentators.' 'It would be rash to guess, and impossible to calculate,' confesses George Saintsbury, 'how many million words of comment these simple nouns and verbs have called forth.' 'An entire library has been written,' observes Hyder E. Rollins, 'on the four opening words, *To the onlie begetter.*' Sir Israel Gollancz concludes that 'T. T. has set the world a conundrum which will probably bring him immortal fame.'

Fame, perhaps. But with it, a generous portion of infamy. For nettled by Thorpe's cool impertinence in baffling them with a couple of initials, some writers show him no mercy. They put him in the pillory as an unscrupulous 'procurer', quite ignorant of the identity of Shakespeare's fair Friend. As for his inscription, they dismiss it as negligible.

But is anything gained by abusing the man who earned our gratitude by preserving a priceless jewel of poetry? And is inability to read his enigma a sufficient excuse for ignoring it, or for attempting to force its words—such as *begetter*—to mean something they obviously don't say?

Now if after all this we venture once more to examine Thorpe's inscription—'so worded,' remarks Mackail, 'as to excite curiosity by a suggestion of some mystery'—we shall certainly stand no chance of success unless we can hit upon some way of looking at it never tried by any one of the authors of those millions of words. As we grope for some possible point of attack, Sherlock Holmes, laying it down that 'Detection is, or ought to be, an exact science,' offers an expert's counsel: '*What is out of the common is usually a guide.*' This might prove to be the golden hint, for herein the skilled scientific investigator strongly seconds the detective: '*Watch out especially,*' he tells us, '*for anything odd.*'[1]

Thorpe and his dedication are certainly odd enough. And at

---

[1] W. I. B. Beveridge, *The Art of Scientific Investigation* (1950), 34.

one time I fancied I might strike a clue by digging into the judicial archives in search of some of his activities. Weary hours of spade-work uncovered nothing but other men of the same name. But at length I was guided to a solitary deposition unquestionably made by the elusive publisher, with his signature, exactly as it appears printed in his earliest publication: *Lucans First Booke translated line for line by Chr. Marlow. 1600—Thom: Thorpe.*

It revealed only two new facts: (*a*) that in September 1611 Thorpe's friend Richard Wallys—a carpenter—thought or pretended to think that the publisher might be good for a loan of five pounds, and (*b*) that Thorpe's friends called him 'Odd':

comming downe to Pawles Wharffe in London where the said Richard Wallys dwelt whilest he lived, and this deponent [Thorpe] & the said Wallys being familiarly acquainted togither, he merrily spake unto this deponent theis, or like words in effect, *vizt*. Odd (For so hee called this deponent, by a by name) wilt thou lend me any money[?] I have fifty poundes to pay . . . to morrow . . . and James . . . can help me but to five & forty poundes.

Again Thorpe produces a puzzle. His very by-name is ambiguous. For in Elizabethan idiom *odd* can be disparagement or ridicule, and on the other hand it can be high esteem, meaning (like *rare*) 'singular or distinguished', thus:

> Go to, go to, y'are odd companions.
> Mistake not *odd*; ye deal unfriendly then:
> This *odd* makes even your commendations,
> For still odd fellows are the wisest men.

Possibly, too, at this date Thorpe might have earned the by-name *Odd* through his recent piratical publication—as *The Odcombian Banquet*—of the many amusing verses contributed by the wits to the *Crudities* of 'odd Tom' Coryate of Odcombe. In short, we cannot be sure what it was that made Thorpe Odd. It must be enough for us that he *was* Odd.

And Odd's printed dedication of *Shake-speares Sonnets*, when

149

we consider it more closely, discovers suitably odd features, some of them very odd, beginning with its arrangement on the page as three triangles of type. No reader, however, of the first volume added in 1780 to the Johnson–Steevens *Shakespeare* would suspect the presence of many of these oddities; for this is how Edmond Malone had it printed, all in capital letters, as though reproducing Thorpe's original:

TO THE ONLY BEGETTER
OF THESE ENSUING SONNETS,
Mr. W. H.
ALL HAPPINESS
AND THAT ETERNITY PROMISED
BY OUR EVER-LIVING POET
WISHETH THE
WELL-WISHING ADVENTURER
IN SETTING FORTH,
T. T.

To compare this with the facsimile at the beginning of this chapter is to see that Malone has 'improved' it out of all resemblance to Thorpe's page. You notice first that he has abolished the three triangles—changed the composition of every line except the final T. T., reducing thirteen lines to ten. Second, he has altered the spelling. Third, he has suppressed all the full-stops or periods between words, and introduced a couple of commas. We cannot reasonably expect better things of the eighteenth century. But in our own day it is not encouraging to find some very recent editions not much more reliable. One of these alters the spelling and suppresses the full-stops. And another alters the lineation by setting PROMISED.BY. on one line, instead of on two.

But it is just this oddness in the original which not only sounds a clear warning to us not to tamper with it, but counsels us to scrutinize the precise form which Thorpe gave it. For its very shape may be emblematical or significant. George Herbert in writing of wings, pillars, and altars was not the first to arrange his lines in visual forms to correspond. When Ben Jonson writes

To my perfect Freind Mr.
Francis Crane.
I erect this Altar
of Freindship.
And leaue it as the eternall
Witnesse of my Loue.

his lines form the altar. On Thorpe's page, not only are the three triangles set all in Roman capitals, but the words are all divided from each other by full-stops. Why this *three*? Can it be some sign of W. H.'s? Why all capitals? And especially, why all these unexampled full-stops? Their painstakingly regular placing gives the whole an unmistakable air of *pattern* or *scheme*. Could these full-stops be meant to be reckoned as items, like the letters? What is more, the sentence is laid out like a monumental inscription, and so curiously arranged that the little word BY. is given a line all to itself, though there is ample room for it beside PROMISED. Again, why? And still we have not done with peculiarities. Thorpe strangely omits his dedicatee's 'estate or degree'. We look in vain for the expected GENT. or ESQVIER. immediately after M^r. W. H. Why is it left out?

To add to all this, as we look at it we are now arrested by an outstanding oddity in the very form of the phrase. For reference to quantities of other dedicatory sentences of the time shows them invariably following the natural grammatical order. Thorpe's therefore strikes the eye at once, for his sentence *inverts the natural order*. Where the others all have 'To the dedicatee (1)the dedicator (2)wisheth (3)blessings', Thorpe upsets this normal and proper 1, 2, 3, into a preposterous 3, 2, 1—'blessings wisheth the dedicator'. Thorpe's is the odd one, the *only* one I have seen which puts the sentence backwards. To compare it with a representative handful of other dedications will expose its conspicuous peculiarity:

151

To our most noble and vertuous quene Katherin,

1 Elizabeth, her humble daughter [*translator*]
2 wisheth
3 perpetual felicitie and everlasting joye.[1]

To the right honorable Ferdinando Stanley, Lord Strange, ennobled with all titles that Honor may afforde, or vertue challenge,

1 Robert Greene [*author*]
2 wisheth
3 encrease of vertuous and Lordly resolutions.[3]

To the Right Honorable his verie good Lord, Sir Christopher Wray, Knight, Lord Cheife Iustice of England . . .

1 Jhon Swan [*translator*]
2 wisheth
3 such condition, as hath promise, both of this life, and of the life to come.[5]

To the right worshipfull the Gouernor, Deputies, Assistants, and generalitie of Marchants aduenturers:

To the Right Worshipful Sir Edward Dimmock, Champion to her Majestie,

1 Samuel Daniel [*translator*]
2 wisheth
3 happie health with increase of worship.[2]

To the Right worshipful, most valiant, and famous, Thomas Candish Esquier:

1 L. Wright [*author*]
2 wisheth
3 all happinesse in this life, and in the world to come, to ioy with Christ in felicitie for euer.[4]

To the right worshipfull and his especiall good friend, M. Nicholas Sanders of Ewell Esquier,

1 T. Newman [*publisher*]
2 wisheth
3 all felicitie.[6]

To the right Vertuous and modest Gentlewoman Mistris M. B. wife to the Right worshipfull D. B. Esquier,

---

[1] 1544. Bodl. MS. Cherry 36.
[3] 1589. *STC* 12224.
[5] 1589. *STC* 6229.

[2] 1585. *STC* 11900.
[4] 1589. *STC* 26025.
[6] 1592. *STC* 12261.

1 I. T. [*author*]
2 wisheth
3 prosperous successe in all their affaires.[1]

1 R. R. [*author*]
2 wisheth
3 the eternizing of her vertues, by the daily practise of her christian life.[2]

To the worthie cherisher and nourisher of all generous studies, S. W. C. Knight,

To the onlie begetter of these insuing sonnets Mr. W. H.

1 R. B. His affectionate Countryman [*author*]

3 all happinesse and that eternitie promised by our ever-living poet

2 wisheth

2 wisheth

3 the increase of all honour, health, and happinesse.[3]

1 the well-wishing adventurer in setting forth T. T. [*publisher*][4]

If, as Sherlock Holmes holds, *singularity is almost always a clue*, here it is. What is the reason for this extraordinary inversion? Plainly, the effect of it is *to call attention to the 'blessings' part of the sentence* by forcing it in directly after M^r. W. H. And on looking again at the facsimile, we now observe that this same spot is further marked in the composition *by a unique blank space or white*, placed where the eye expects the 'estate or degree', immediately following the initials W. H.

Thorpe's inscription has been termed *enigmatic, puzzling, cryptic*, recalling the Elizabethans' characteristic fondness for anagram, rebus, acrostic, concealment, cryptogram, 'wherein my name ciphered were'. In these ensuing sonnets Shakespeare declared, *Your monument shall be my gentle verse*, and Thorpe has set out a monumental inscription TO . . . M^r. W. H. Is there possibly something more than initials, hid and barr'd from common sense here in his text, which we are meant to look for?

The unique blank space set by the compositor just before the peculiar sentence-inversion looks like an index, marking the

---

[1] 1597. *STC* 23621. [2] 1599. *STC* 21137.
[3] 1621. *STC* 3571. [4] 1609. *STC* 22353.

point for attack. Let us therefore start with this third line, beginning M ʳ . W . H ., and for convenience of inspection set it out with the remaining lines of the phrase in tabular form. Observing the curious full-stops or periods marking abbreviations and word-divisions exactly as printed, we get the following:

	1	2	3	4	5	6	7	8	9	10	11	12	13	14	15	16	17	18	19	20	21	22
line 3	M	ʳ	.	W	.	H	.	A	L	L	.	H	A	P	P	I	N	E	S	S	E	.
4	A	N	D	.	T	H	A	T	.	E	T	E	R	N	I	T	I	E	.			
5	P	R	O	M	I	S	E	D	.													
6	B	Y	.																			
7	O	V	R	.	E	V	E	R-L	I	V	I	N	G	.	P	O	E	T	.			

We see that for the first six places, line 3 reads

	1	2	3	4	5	6
3	M	ʳ	.	W	.	H

followed by a period. As a consequence we cannot proceed (as some have done) to read a possible *Hall*; for the full-stop after the initial H puts such a reading out of the question.

But right under that sixth-place H stopped by a period, *the sixth place of the next line*, we notice, *likewise presents* H. Might not this H repeated be an indicator or signal *to continue the stopped message in that next line*? For here we see the H followed by two letters before a full-stop again calls a halt, thus:

	1	2	3	4	5	6	7	8	9	10	11
3	M	ʳ	.	W	.	H	.	A	L	L	.
4						H	A	T	.		

For places 1–8 these additions give us Mʳ.W.HAT. The children would say we are getting warm.

Referring once more to line 3 for an indicator, in the next place, 9, we are given the letter L. Again we follow this column down to the next line which affords letters: line 7. And we not only find—as we already found with H—this L repeated, but again followed by two significant letters. In line 7, places 9, 10, and 11 read LIV.

Putting together, for places 1 through 11 we now have

```
     1  2  3 4  5  6 7  8  9  10 11
3        Mr . W . H .         L
4                    H A T .
7                          L  I  V
```

—or, read consecutively,

3+4+7   Mr . W . H A T L I V .

Here, it seems to me, the much-sought, lightly concealed name of the 'onlie begetter' is at length uncovered. Heralded by the phrase THESE.INSVING.SONNETS., it begins the ensuing line 3, continues in 4, and is completed in 3 plus 4, or 7; figures which together add up to 14—the sum of a sonnet. So neat a flourish no doubt pleased the clever T. T. while deftly including in his text as *Mr. W. Hatliv* the name of 'the onlie begetter of these insuing sonnets', the celebrated William, Prince of Purpoole: Master W. Hatcliffe or *Hatliff*, as we have seen that his name was commonly both pronounced and written.

No doubt, as Cordelia says, Time shall unfold what plighted cunning hides. Yet T. T.'s scheme of folding in his dedicatee's name, while cunning enough, is plainly of the simplest. Beginning with its initial, at full-stop halts the hidden surname—which contains no more than two clear syllables—is carried on from that same place in the next line. Merely a step-down arrangement, with clues given by repeated indicator-letters. Even without these, the message is readily followed *by counting letters and fullstops in lines 3, 4, and 7,* or—even more readily—by inspection, when one sets the lines out in tabular form.

Odd's ingenuity appears chiefly in his adroit choice of words, and in their carefully contrived composition and pointing on the printed page. For example, it is evident that he cannot follow Mr.W.H. with the expected GENT. or ESQVIER. That is why he omits it, marking the spot with a white. Likewise it is clear that he must have THAT.ETERNITIE and not THE.

ETERNITIE, as well as the unusual epithet EVER-LIVING
and not the far more common IMMORTAL.[1]

And his eye-catching inversion 'blessings wisheth the dedicator', aided by a unique blank space, not only directs attention,
but brings his cipher-words THAT. and EVER-LIVING.
up close to the initials M^r.W.H. Further, we now understand
why the little word BY. cannot possibly be set alongside
PROMISED., in the same way that OF. is set alongside
BEGETTER., and IN. alongside ADVENTVRER., at the
ends of lines. For if BY. were not removed to a line all to itself,
it would put letters in places 10 and 11, and thus obstruct those
significant places of the cipher-line below.

Clearly, this grammatically inverted inscription at the fore-
front of our never-dying poet's *pow'rful rime* setting forth *the
living record* of Master W. H.'s memory presents in its three triangles a sufficiently 'questionable shape' to arrest the attention of
an alert reader. Yet however oddly chosen and composed, full-
pointed everywhere, and weighted throughout with capitals, it is
a mark of Thorpe's cleverness that the words of his dedication as
they stand, even in their inverted order, make undeniably good
sense to the uninstructed eye. They give up their secret chiefly,
if not indeed exclusively, to those who—like ourselves, and like
Thorpe's readers in 1609—already know the identity of Master
W. H. the True Love of the Sonnets, his royal arms Three Primroses or Three True-loves, and are curious enough to examine
this Oddity of Three among inscriptions for his lightly veiled
name.

Thorpe has suffered enough and too much from those frivolous
charges, (*a*) that he knew so little English as to think that *begetter*
means 'procurer' or 'obtainer',[2] (*b*) that he was such an oaf as to

---

[1] Shakespeare himself employs *immortal* twenty-nine times, and *ever-
living* only once.

[2] As little indeed as Dekker's Sir Rees ap Vaughan, who like Shakespeare's
Welshman, Parson Evans, makes fritters of English: 'I have some cossens
Garman at Court, shall beget you the reversion of the Master of the Kings
Revels.' *Satiromastix* 4.1.244.

address a Right Worshipful knight as 'Master', and (c) that he was so ignorant of *our ever-living poet* and *these insuing sonnets* of his as not to know Hatcliffe-Hatliff, Shakespeare's friend and sovereign, the high and mighty Prince, William, Prince of Purpoole.

To vindicate Thorpe is however less important to us than to ask him some pertinent questions. Why did he take all this trouble to include the name *Hatliv* in his dedication? Might he have been encouraged to the task by finding a precedent for it in these ensuing sonnets? Did he perhaps feel his resourcefulness challenged by the ingenious and shining example of our ever-living poet?

Clever inclusion of the name of the person addressed appears as a poets' device common in the Renaissance ever since Petrarch in his fifth sonnet played on Laura's worshipped name. Sidney in one sonnet vituperates the husband of Penelope Lady Rich as *that rich fool*: and in two others he writes *rich, naming my Stella's name* and *no misfortune but that rich she is*. Simplicity itself: *rich* is a common adjective. Somewhat more difficult for Spenser in writing his *Prothalamion* was the surname of Elizabeth and Katherine Somerset. But he got it in:

> Yet were they bred of *Somers-heat* they say.

Shakespeare is harder, whether the writer be friend or foe, yet both managed it allusively: Jonson twice, with

> *to heare thy Buskin tread*
> *And shake a Stage . . .*
> *he seemes to shake a Lance,*
> *As brandish't at the eyes of Ignorance . . .*

and Greene with

> in his owne conceit the onely Shake-scene in a countrey.

But as for *Hatcliffe* or *Hatliff*, we ask ourselves How could a writer contrive to work that name in?

Acrostic verse, as everyone knows, was a favourite resource. Ben Jonson's epitaph of *MARGARET RATCLIFFE* is made in seventeen moving lines which spell her name, beginning *Marble, weep, for thou dost cover* . . . And John (later Sir John) Davys[1] achieved no fewer than twenty-six acrostic *Hymnes* of the virgin Queen as *Astræa*, each of them spelling *ELISA BETHA REGINA*. But we find no sonnet of Shakespeare's whose initials read *WILLIAM HATCLIF, WILLIAM HAT-LIFF, WILLIAM HATLEFE*, or any possible form of it. And if he did not resort to acrostic, any method less obvious and mechanical of bringing in so unmanageable a name would seem to present formidable obstacles. Have we any reason to think that he might have made the effort required to surmount them?

Let us see. To begin with, his readers, like Thorpe's later ones, might well expect to find the Prince's familiar name somehow woven into the text. And with Shakespeare himself, in writing *the living record of your memory*, its thought is dominant: *Unless thou take that honour from thy name . . . a better spirit doth use your name . . . Naming thy name blesses an ill report*. But in one prophetic line he goes farther, and reveals his plan for eternizing it:

Your name from hence immortal life shall have.

Here he is unmistakable. For how could he possibly give that name immortality *by these sonnets unless he put that name into them?* It must be there. And it is only because—when the Prince had slipped from memory—posterity *could not see it* that his Friend's name was not immortalized, but lost.

On the strength of the poet's own promise we turn once more to the Sonnets, with *Hatcliffe-Hatliff* now at last as fresh in mind as it was with his readers in the Wonderful Year, 1588. And it acts like magic. We find it leaping to the eye, introduced throughout in the sonnets on the Friend, and even with its syllables reversed,

---

[1] To distinguish him readily from the Welshman John Davies of Hereford the writing-master, it seems best to write the Wiltshire poet-statesman-knight's name *Davys*, as he always signed it himself.

as Shakespeare skilfully rings the changes on [w]*hat leave*, [t]*hat live*, [w]*hat live*, [t]*hat life*, and the like.

In the first group, the poet urges his Prince to marry, that *his tender heir might bear his memory*—might carry on his beauty with his name:

4 12 W*HAT* acceptable Audit can'st thou *LEAVE*
                                  HATLEAVE

6 11 Then w*HAT* could death doe if thou should'st depart,
   12 *LEAV*ing thee *LIV*ing   *HATLIV*

9 2 T*HAT* thou consum'st thy selfe in single *LIFE*
                                  HATLIFE

9 6 T*HAT* thou no forme of thee hast *LEF*t behind
                                  HATLEF

10 14 T*HAT* beauty still may *LIVE* in thine or thee
                                  HATLIVE

11 3 And t*HAT* fresh bloud which yongly thou bestow'st . . .
   5 Herein *LIVE*s wisdome, beauty, and increase
                                  HATLIVE

13 1 O t*HAT* you were your selfe, but love you are
   2 No longer yours, then you your selfe here *LIVE*
                                  HATLIVE

16 9 So should the lines of life t*HAT LIFE* repaire
                                  HATLIFE

17 13 But were some childe of yours alive t*HAT* time,
   14 You should *LIVE* twise in it, and in my rime.
                                  HATLIVE

Throughout the sonnets which follow, his name is interwoven with his praise:

25 4 Unlookt for joy in t*HAT* I honour most;
   5 Great Princes favorites their faire *LEAVE*s spread
                                  HATLEAVE

31 8 But things remov'd t*HAT* hidden in thee lie.
   9 Thou art the grave where buried love doth *LIVE*
                                  HATLIVE

38 11 And he t*HAT* calls on thee, let him bring forth
   12 Eternal numbers to out-*LIVE* long date   *HATLIVE*

159

41 7 And when a woman woes, w*HAT* womans sonne,
8 Will sourely *LEAVE* her   HATLEAVE

54 4 For t*HAT* sweet odor, which doth in it *LIVE* . . .
13 And so of you   HATLIVE

55 13 So til the judgement t*HAT* your selfe arise,
14 You *LIVE* in this   HATLIVE

63 11 T*HAT* he shall never cut from memory
12 My sweet loves beauty, though my lovers *LIFE*
                                         HATLIFE
66 14 Save t*HAT* to dye, I *LEAVE* my love alone
                                         HATLEAVE
67 11 For she *HAT*h no exchecker now but his,
12 And proud of many, *LIVE*s upon his gaines
                                         HATLIVE
79 12 No praise to thee, but w*HAT* in thee doth *LIVE*
                                         HATLIVE
81 13 You still shall *LIVE* (such vertue *HAT*h my Pen)
                                         LIVE HAT
93 5 For there can *LIVE* no *HAT*red in thine eyes
                                         LIVE HAT
94 10 Though to it selfe, it onely *LIVE* and die,
11 But if t*HAT* flowre with base infection meete
                                         LIVE HAT
97 14 T*HAT LEAVE*s looke pale   HATLEAVE

And since he and his Friend are one—*thou art all the better part of me . . . T'is thee (my selfe)*—Shakespeare makes the Friend's name his own:

22 5 For all t*HAT* beauty t*HAT* doth cover thee,
6 Is but the seemely rayment of my heart,
7 Which in thy brest doth *LIVE*   HATLIVE

37 11 T*HAT* I in thy abundance am suffic'd,
12 And by a part of all thy glory *LIVE*   HATLIVE

39 4 And w*HAT* is't but mine owne when I praise thee,
5 Even for this, let us devided *LIVE*   HATLIVE

160

39	9	Oh absence w*HAT* a torment wouldst thou prove,	
	10	Were it not thy soure leisure gave sweet *LEAVE*	
			HATLEAVE
72	2	W*HAT* merit *LIV*'d in me that you should love	
			HATLIV
73	1	T*HAT* time of yeare thou maist in me behold,	
	2	When yellow *LEAVE*s, or none, or few doe hange	
			HATLEAVE
	14	To love t*HAT* well, which thou must *LEAVE* ere long	
			HATLEAVE
74	3	My *LIFE HAT*h in this line some interest	*LIFE HAT*
92	6	When in the least of them my *LIFE HAT*h end	
			LIFE HAT
92	10	Since t*HAT* my *LIFE* on thy revolt doth lie	
			HATLIFE
109	8	So t*HAT* my selfe bring water for my staine,	
	9	Never be*LEEVE* though in my nature raign'd,	
			HATLEEVE
	10	All frailties that besiege all kindes of blood,	
	11	T*HAT* it could so preposterouslie be stain'd,	
	12	To *LEAVE* for nothing all thy summe of good	
			HATLEAVE
111	3	T*HAT* did not better for my *LIFE* provide	
			HATLIFE
112	7	None else to me, nor I to none a*LIVE*,	*LIVE HAT*
	8	T*HAT* my steel'd sence or changes right or wrong	
113	1	Since I *LEF*t you, mine eye is in my minde,	
	2	And t*HAT* which governes me to goe about	
			LEF HAT
145	13	. . . from *HAT*e away she threw,	
	14	And sav'd my *LIFE* saying not you	*HATLIFE*
146	9	Then soule *LIVE* thou upon thy servants losse,	
	10	And let t*HAT* pine	*LIVE HAT*
147	5	My reason the Phisition to my love . . .	
	7	*HAT*h *LEF*t me	*HATLEF*

Shakespeare is as good as his word. Henceforth the name can never be lost. Throughout his Sonnets it remains indeed so thickly sown that we can almost say of W. H. what Leonard Digges said in love and glad remembrance of never-dying Shakespeare—

ev'ry line, each verse
Here shall revive, redeem thee from thy hearse.

One could, of course, find in other poems occasional similar examples appearing by accident. What rules out accident here is the overwhelming mass of occurrences. The sustained skill displayed in weaving it unobtrusively into some forty places, and so smoothly that the poetic texture shows no slightest blemish, marks the genius.

Yes, Hatcliffe's name is there, and Shakespeare put it there. But the highest poet had an aim far nobler than to send the syllables of a Lincolnshire name down the centuries. Worthy of his gentle verse, his underlying purpose was to eternize the essence of his Friend's poetic name: True Love. *The beauty of thy budding name* is the beauty of the budding True-love flower. *Thy sweet belovèd name*, that *fair name* which he has *hallow'd*, is the belovèd name *True Love.*

True Love is the only name and nature which can never die— 'True Love *from hence immortal life shall have.*' True Love shall live for ever in men's mouths:

Your monument shall be my gentle verse,
Which eyes not yet created shall o'erread;
And tongues to be your being shall rehearse
When all the breathers of this world are dead.
You still shall LIVE (*such virtue* HAT*h my pen*)
Where breath most breathes, even in the mouths of men.

To the world's end, in the poet's verse and in the eyes of lovers— True Love:

Not marble nor the gilded monuments
Of princes shall outlive this pow'rful rime . . .
*So, till the judgment t*HAT *yourself arise,*
You LIVE *in this, and dwell in lovers' eyes*

162

VII
TRUE LOVE

No writer on Elizabethan literature today needs to apologize for turning his attention to symbols. All realize that 'Elizabethan imagery is emblematic'.[1] Interest in the subject is fortunately keen. It is shared by students of Elizabethan art, who are continually discovering significance in the drawings and the portraits of the time. And it is only those advanced in the study who know what a tremendous deal still lies before our eyes, unseen. Mr John Pope-Hennessy declares that 'the Elizabethan miniature illustrates the visual imagery of Elizabethan poetry . . . [and it] presents an iconographical problem of the first magnitude'.[2] Experts have learned that every detail in a picture is chosen for a purpose, that *everything bears a meaning*. It amounts to a rich language, of which we today have deciphered a handful of words.

In mentioning Hatcliffe's coat of arms I hinted that his rare four-petalled Primrose or True-love would prove important for the Sonnets. For me, to establish that importance meant a long dive into the Elizabethan depths, with discovery of things as precious to the Shakespearean as

> Wedges of gold, great anchors, heaps of pearl,
> Inestimable stones, unvalued jewels—
> All scatt'red in the bottom of the sea.

To begin the story with the known, no one requires to be told that finding a four-leaved clover or shamrock brings good luck. But why does it? Well, perhaps because in the multitude of trefoils it is rare: Lady Luck helped you find it, and may stay with you. But formerly you could count upon it *to win you love*. Your

---

[1] George Rylands on 'Shakespeare the Poet', *Companion to Shakespeare Studies* (1934), 96.
[2] *The Burlington Magazine* 83 (October 1943), 259–260.

luck would be a 'true love'—a faithful lover, whether friend or spouse. A four-leaved clover-form tiara is still traditionally worn by the bride at weddings of the Hohenzollerns. The four-leaved or four-petalled true-loves get their name from their similarity to the four loops of that ancient and mystical folk-emblem, the true-love knot.

> The girls ... had their omens ... and true-love knots lurked in the bottom of every teacup. (*Vicar of Wakefield*.)

> > And thrice three times tie up this true love's knot,
> > And murmur soft, she will, or she will not.
> > > (Thomas Campion.)

Percy Macquoid describes Elizabethan brides' favours 'made of ribbons, tied in a true-lover's knot (a form of Runic origin) ... emblematical of love, friendship, and the ties of duty. ...'[1] Runic the knot may be, but its mystic FOUR dates at least from Empedocles and Pythagoras. Like ONE, FOUR is the number of perfection, figure of God. 'Adore the sacred quaternion. The quaternion four alone is one and uncompounded.' The Tetragrammaton,[2] four Gospels, four cardinal virtues, four elements, four winds, four 'humours'. The bishop's cross in the twelfth-century ruin of Torcello, Venice, is carved with quatrefoils of deep significance. At Lincoln Cathedral the 'Dean's Eye' rose-window is a 'four'.

Accordingly, a rare four-leaved clover or shamrock, or a four-petalled primrose long-sought was eagerly plucked by gentry as well as by folk, to be worn for a 'true-love'.

> > In a valley of this restless mind
> > I sought in mountain and in mead,
> > Trusting a true love for to find.[3]

---

[1] *Shakespeare's England* (1916), 2.146.

[2] The Quaternion is the holy Tetragrammaton, the same awful name variously pronounced among the sons of men: whether Jeva, Isis, θεος, Zeus, or Deus; or ... Tien, Alla, Idio, Dieu, or Lord.' A. Tucker, *The Light of Nature Pursued* 1768 (1834, I. 463), qu. *O.E.D.*

[3] Anon., *Quia amore langueo*.

Mr John Donne confides, 'I walk to find a true love'—the primrose. Also the regularly four-leaved Herb Paris[1] or One Berry, blooming in April, was commonly called *True-love grass* or *True-love*. The quatrefoil had such magical power to produce love that when Chaucer's Absolon set off to court Alisoun,

> Under his tonge a trewe-love he beer,
> For ther-by wende he to ben gracious.

And the supernatural fairies adorned their powerful king Oberon with it:

> The out side of his doublet was
> Of the four-leav'd truelove grasse.[2]

Before Chaucer, a religious writer—to lure folk to his verse-sermon on the Trinity-plus-the-Virgin—chose a most seductive title: *The Four Leaves of the Truelove*.[3]

Seekers for almost anything you can name among the Elizabethan arts will find their steps drawn, as with a magnet, to the Queen herself: the essential Elizabethan. Our Quatrefoil of Love, the true-love, or the true-love knot is no exception. What prince in history could match her in the supreme royal art—the art of winning the love of her subjects?

> *Who ever found on earth a constant friend*
> *That may compare with this my Virgin Queene?*[4]

Her devotion to these magical emblems began early. At the Bodleian Library we see it in 'The Glasse of the Synnefull Soule' —the New Year's gift she created at the age of eleven for her stepmother Queen Katharine Parr. This she translated from the French, wrote fair, and bound in a sky-blue cloth, which she embroidered with flowers, leaves, and figures in gold and silver

---

[1] 'Herbe Paris hath . . . foure leaves, set . . . like a crosse. . . . This herbe floureth in Aprill, and the seede is ripe in Maie. . . . The fruite and seede . . . are verie good against al poison, especiallie for such as by taking of poison are become peevishe or without understanding: inasmuch that it healeth them.' Dodoens' *Herbal* (tr. Henry Lyte 1586), Ii6ᵛ–7.

[2] Herrick, *Oberon's Feast*.

[3] Pr. *Early English Text Society* (1935) as *The Quatrefoil of Love*.

[4] Thomas Churchyard, *A Discourse . . . 1578*.

thread. On both the covers she enclosed the monogram KP within four-looped true-love knots; and on the spine presented four true-loves—primroses of four silver petals, each growing on the same stem with a golden oak leaf: primrose for True Love, oak for Constancy. These are for Queen Katharine, whose motto is *Amour avec Loyaulte*.

Thus colour, metal, figure, flower, leaf—literally everything, each carries its message to Queen Katharine; and to us, but only if we have learned the language in which that age was eloquent. To realize how poor in comparison our 'Say It With Flowers' is today (how much *can* we say with them?) we have only to read Donne's seventh Elegy:

> I had not taught thee then the Alphabet
> Of flowers, how they devisefully being set
> And bound up, might with speechlesse secrecie
> Deliver arrands mutely, and mutually.

An inkling of the importance of the true-love to Queen Elizabeth can be gained by a glance at lists of her jewels and a look at some portraits of her. Certain of her jewels are described in scattered surviving 'Rolls of New Year's Gifts to the Queen'. Naturally in the effort to please, the givers closely studied her preferences in their orders to the goldsmiths and jewellers.

Since the descriptions are far too long to reproduce in full, the following are snatches only, in modern spelling; the Quatrefoils of Love appearing variously as *trueloves, caters,* and *caters or trueloves.*

In 1580 the Earl of Leicester (whose badge or cognizance was the Ragged Staff) gave the Queen 'a cap . . . with 14 buttons of gold . . . being ragged staves and true-love knots, garnished with rubies and diamonds, and 36 small buttons, being true-love knots and ragged staves'. In 1585 the Earl of Arundel's offering of a 'carcanet (hanging collar) of gold' included '6 true loves of small sparks of diamonds'; the Countess of Oxford's carcanet, 'knots of true-loves or small pearl'; and half of the Countess of Warwick's gift of three dozen gold buttons were 'set with true-loves of small pearl'.

An inventory of 1587 includes '152 buttons with trueloves of pearl'; two bodkins (hair-pins) of gold with pendants—one with 'a Truelove of sparks of rubies and a diamond in the end', the other 'a Truelove of sparks of diamonds'; and 'a Caul (hair-net) with 9 Trueloves of pearl'. The roll for New Year's Day 1592–93 lists a 'cap of pearls' which included '12 Trueloves of diamonds and rubies'; a gold bracelet with 'a Truelove of pearl'; a 'pair of bracelets of gold', four pieces of them 'with Caters of pearl'; and 'two pendants of gold garnished with diamonds in Caters or trueloves'.[1]

As for her portraits, I picked up the following from some of the reproductions—those large enough to show detail—in Roy C. Strong's excellent book *Portraits of Queen Elizabeth I* (1963). Anyone examining the originals could readily extend the list. The references here are to Dr Strong's numbering:

Paintings.

   7. (Pl. IV) True-loves of pearl on belt.
   8. Double carcanet of quatrefoil jewels.
   12. (Pl. V) True-loves of pearl on sleeves.
   24. (Pl. VII) Carcanet, true-loves of pearl.
   26. About fourteen true-loves of pearl on breast of bodice.
   33. Carcanet with true-loves of pearl.
   39. True-loves of pearl in head-dress.
   45. (Pl. X) Quatrefoils on lace cuffs.
   46. True-loves of pearl in head-dress.
   53. True-loves of pearl in embroidered fore-part.
   72. (Pl. XV) Many true-loves of pearl on kirtle.
   75. True-loves of pearl in head-dress and at top of bodice.
   79. True-loves of pearl in head-dress.
   85. (Pl. XI) Four-petalled true-loves on kirtle.
   100. (Pl. XVII) Four-looped true-love on breast-pendant.
   101. (Pl. XIX) Dress covered with quatrefoils, their centres jewels.

---

[1] Nichols, *Progr. Elizabeth* (1788), ii. B.M. MS. Royal App. 68.

Miniatures.

    18. (Pl. XVIII) True-love jewels alternate with arrow-heads on ruff.

Engravings.

    17. True-love knots or quatrefoils between suns on kirtle.

    30. (Pl. XVI) Sleeves and kirtle covered with quatrefoils or true-loves.

Drawings and Illuminations.

    9. Quatrefoils on sleeves.

    10. Quatrefoils on kirtle, and two badges of true-love knot painted below the figure.

Medals.

    1. A true-love at the top on both sides.

    23. (reverse) Rose at base flanked by true-loves.

Sculpture.

    Bust. True-love jewel on breast, and 'fours' on sleeves.

Finally (frontispiece, in colour), the portrait belonging to Lord Tollemache, painted when 'Her circled head Was glorify'd with burnisht Crown of Gold', shows the band set all about with true-loves of pearl, their centres emeralds—*emerald for Virginity.* The typical jewels of the true-love are pearl, white for sincerity or truth. And the resemblance of tears to pearl suggests the natural figure:

    I have . . . tears that might be tied in a True-love Knot, for they're fresh salt indeed.

    And wash him fresh again with true-love tears . . .

            Which bewept to the grave did go
            With true-love show'rs.[1]

---

[1] Webster, *A Cure for a Cuckold* 2.3.19; *Rich. II* 5.1.10; *Haml.* 4.5.39.

Similarly, for the repentant tears of Shakespeare's unkind True-love:

> 34 13 *Ah, but those tears are pearl which thy love sheeds,*
> *And they are rich and ransom all misdeeds.*

The upshot of these catalogues is clear: no more obvious or infallible means of pleasing the Queen could be devised than to play up the True-love. And this is where Will Hatcliffe scored. The College of Arms had found for his ancestors three white True-loves or Primroses, and set them in a field of sky-blue. Just that and nothing more: 'Your coat of arms is richest, when plainest.' When the astute gallants of Gray's Inn, with a great eye to the main chance at Court, were looking about for a Prince whose arms would give them a winningly heroical Order, what could match Will Hatcliffe's True-love? If he had any competitors, whether for *beauty, birth, or wealth, or wit,* this ace alone eclipsed their hopes.

Love was the theme of Elizabeth's Court, with every courtier by definition in love high-fantastical with the Queen whose badge was the True-love Knot.[1] And withal with somebody else as well, as Lyly avers: 'Why, in courts there is nothing more common. So to be in love among courtiers it is no discredit: for that they are all in love.'[2] And the knightly lovers—as Coleridge says Donne does with iron pokers—wreathe swords into true-love knots:

on the inside [of his shield] a naked sword tyed in a true-love knot; the mot [from Ovid], *Militat omnis amans:* Signifieng that in a true love knot his sword was tied to defend and maintaine the features of his mistres [whose picture was on the outside of it].[3]

Is there any reason in the world why the Middle Temple with its Prince d'Amour should be allowed to engross to itself all the

---

[1] It is shown twice below her figure in the frontispiece to Georges de la Mothe's *Hymne* (Bodl. MS. Fr. e. I, f. 7), reproduced in Strong as 'D. & I. 10', p. 104.

[2] *Sapho and Phao* 3.1.33.

[3] Nashe, *Works* (ed. McKerrow) ii. 273.

purveyance of Love to the Court? As for founding a royal and heroical Order of the True-love, the pundits of Purpoole would promptly adduce high precedent. The Kings of Savoy made famous their Order of the True-love Knot, with the FOUR again exhibited in the mystical letters F.E.R.T., linked by true-love knots. The meaning of these letters is uncertain.

The perfection of the quatrefoil True-love Primrose or the True-love Knot showed in its power to create both kinds of true love—the love of married partners, and the love of true friends for each other, like that of the Queen and her subjects. For the two are in essence the same, *the marriage of true minds*: 'Matrimony containeth the Flower of Friendship.' 'Friendship ought to resemble the love between man and wife; that is, of two bodies to be made one will and affection.' 'Friendship is, without comparison, the only true-love knot, that links in conjunction thousands together.'

Spenser calls the rare four-petalled primrose 'the Primrose true'; and Suckling, 'Primroses . . . Of the Mysterious Number' to which lovers shall come 'as to an oracle'. But why, it will be asked, should the perfect FOUR inevitably signify true love? The Renaissance would give the reply: 'The outward and visible number of a couple of true friends or true lovers is of course TWO. But their secret or mysterious number is both ONE and FOUR.' We all know the first: the union or unity of true love— 'Joined in one by God alone'; ''Tis love alone makes two but one'. But the FOUR, which has lapsed from memory today, in Shakespeare's time was as beautiful and essential a thought in the philosophy of true love as the ONE. The concept is traced to the *Dialogues of Love* of Leone Ebreo (Judah Abravanel), whom Burton in his *Anatomy* takes as the leading authority on Love. Miss Helen Gardner has recently demonstrated[1] that this ONE-and-FOUR accounts for Donne's 'difficult' line

And makes both one, each this and that.

---

[1] 'The Argument about "The Ecstasy"' in *Elizabethan and Jacobean Studies presented to Frank Percy Wilson*, 1959.

How it comes about that true lovers are no longer two, but only one or else four, is patiently explained in the *Dialogues*:

Each one being transformed into the other becomes two: at once lover and beloved; and two multiplied by two makes four, so that each of them is twain, and both together are one and four.

The *Dialogues of Love* was a work very widely read in the sixteenth century. Yet did Leone Ebreo's arithmetic of love present a fundamentally novel idea? What of the *allos* (*heteros*) *ego* or *alter ego* of the ancients? '. . . like as *Cato* the Romane said, that the soule of the lover lived & dwelt in the soule of the loved'?[1] If each friend in the union of love is also the other's second self, you have the ONE-and-FOUR without waiting for the Renaissance philosopher to work out the delightful paradox. At all events, both Donne's ready use of it, and Shakespeare's line in *The Phoenix and the Turtle* 'Either was the others mine', show the familiarity of the conception at the time. And show us also how the rare heraldic Primrose is the sign and symbol of True Love. As a Flower it is ONE; as a Quatrefoil it is also FOUR.

The wealth of reference is pouring in under our eyes. Shakespeare's *my sovereign, Will, beauty's Rose, my rose, love, true love* is Prince Will, the Primrose, the True-love. In addressing his distant Quatrefoil of Love, this same ONE-and-FOUR of true loving friends—unmistakable in separation, when 'thou, residing here, go'st yet with me, And I, hence fleeting, here remain with thee'—makes the soul of his theme:

39

O, how thy worth with manners may I sing
When thou art all the better part of me?
What can mine own praise to mine own self bring?
And wHAT is't but mine own when I praise thee?
Even for this let us divided LIVE
And our dear love lose name of single one,
That by this separation I may give
That due to thee which thou deserv'st alone.

---

[1] *Plutarch's Morals* (tr. Holland 1603), 1143.

O absence, wHAT a torment wouldst thou prove,
Were 't not thy sour leisure gave sweet LEAVE
To entertain the time with thoughts of love,
Which time and thoughts so sweetly doth deceive,
And that thou teachest how to make one twain—
By praising him here who doth hence remain!

62   1   *Sin of self-love possesseth all mine eye*
           And all my soul and all my every part; . . .
    13   *'T is thee (myself) that for myself I praise*

74   8   *My spirit is thine, the better part of me.*

But there is more. We learn that the true-love knot and the
sonnet are identified: being called by the same name. The *Oxford
English Dictionary* gives '*Amoret* 3. A love-knot. . . . "Painted
alle with amorettes"; and spangles forged, of shape "like to the
amorettis".' Also '*Amoret* 4. A love sonnet: "wryting amorets"
(Lodge).' And again, '*Amoretto* A love-sonnet. Spenser (title of
Love-sonnets) Amoretti.' To this we may add from Heywood,
'no sooner in love, but . . . he will be in his amorets'. Since both
are *amorets*, no wonder Marston finds them together:

> His windows strow'd with Sonnets, and the glasse
> Drawne full of love-knots.[1]

But far more vividly than in any gloss or literary collocation, that
sweet singer William Browne of Tavistock sets the unity of
amorets before our eyes—a love sonnet in fourteen four-beat
lines, winding on the page in the loops of a double true-love
knot, *still beginning, never ending*—for in its end is its beginning.

> This is love and worth commending,
> Still beginning, never ending,
> Like a wily net ensnaring
> In a round shuts up all squaring.

---

[1] *The Metamorphosis of Pygmalions Image* (1598), 3.140.

In and out, whose every angle
More and more doth still entangle.
Keeps a measure still in moving,
And is never light but loving.
Twining arms, exchanging kisses,
Each partaking other's blisses.
Laughing, weeping still together,
Bliss in one is mirth in either.
Never breaking, ever bending,
This is love and worth commending.[1]

In view of this identity, what form of verse could rightly extol the True-love knot but the Sonnet? The amoret sounding the praise of the amoret. And if so, which type of sonnet would befit Shakespeare's Prince of the True-love—the Italian or Petrarchan in two parts of eight and six, or the English with three fours and a couplet? Is there any question? Hatcliffe's coat of arms shows *three fours*, three Quatrefoils of Love.

In the three quatrains of each of 125 sonnets, Shakespeare mirrors their perfection without change—*Still such, and ever so*—although this fidelity, this truth gives him problems in the final couplet, noticed by every critic. For since the *three fours* of the 'invention' complete the picture, the couplet can only be an addition: an 'inscription' or title, a comment, a summation. To look again at the four petals of the True-love Primrose as Shakespeare so often looked, is to understand why he kept 'the lines end-stopped in a proportion quite unknown in his blank verse. The greater number of the sonnets are end-stopped in every line.'[2] Each petal is a shape, and should have a sense to itself. To see how the poet has coupled thoughts and shapes lovingly together in producing his poetic shadow of perfection, one has only to impose the lines of a sonnet on the True-loves of Will Hatcliffe's shield. (See accompanying illustration.)

---

[1] *Britannia's Pastorals* (1613), Bk. 1, Song 3, p. 61.
[2] Enid Hamer, *Metres of English Poetry* (1930), 196–197.

Let not my love be call'd idolatry
   Nor my belovëd as an idol show,
Since all alike my songs and praises be
   To one, of one, still such, and ever so.

Kind is my love to-day, to-morrow kind,
   Still constant in a wondrous excellence;
Therefore my verse, to constancy confin'd,
   One thing expressing, leaves out difference.

'Fair, kind, and true,' is all my argument,
   'Fair, kind, and true,' varying to other words;
And in this change is my invention spent,
   Three themes in one, which wondrous scope affords.

Fair, kind, and true have often liv'd alone,
Which three till now never kept seat in one.

One note might be added to the reading of *leaves out difference.*
I have never seen this *difference* explained as anything but 'variety'
or 'variation'. That is of course its surface-meaning here, but
clearly present is its other Shakespearean sense of 'disagreement'
or 'quarrel'. His verse expresses only the *constancy*, omitting any
'falling-out of faithful friends'. Browne has something similar in
his love-knot, that 'In a round shuts up all *squaring*'—which
means both 'right angles' and 'quarrelling'.

Like other sovereigns identified with their cognizance or badge
(as Richard III, 'this most bloody boar'), Prince Will became
'True-love' or 'Love'. The arresting discovery of this name of
his alters at once our view of Shakespeare's uses of these nouns.
Obviously we must consider them all afresh, in order to distinguish where possible 'my [emotion of] true love or love' from
'my [beloved Prince] True-love or Love'. For example:

61   11   *Mine own true love* [for you] *that doth my rest defeat*

72   9   *Lest your true love* [for me] *may seem false in this*

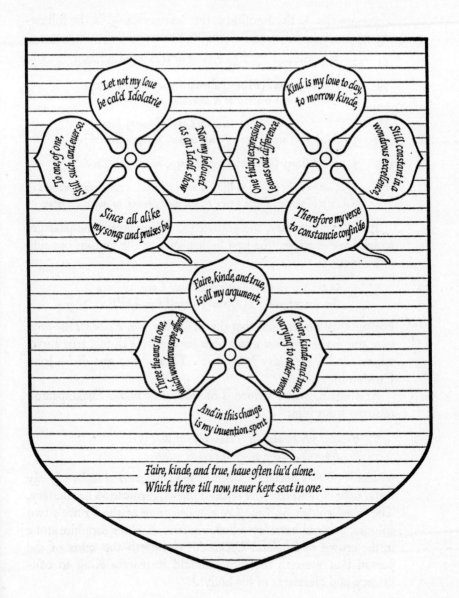

These are clearly the emotions. But just as clearly, in the following we have the beloved Prince:

51   12   *But* [Prince] *Love for love shall thus excuse my jade*

79   5   *I grant, sweet* [Prince] *Love, thy lovely argument*
     6   *Deserves the travail of a worthier pen*

93   2   . . . *so Love's* [your] *face*
     3   *May still seem Love* [you] *to me, though alter'd new*

105 5   *Kind is my* [Prince] *Love to-day, to-morrow kind*

107 3   *Can yet the lease* [of life] *of my* [Prince] *True-love control* . . .
     10 *My* [Prince] *Love looks fresh, and Death to me subscribes*

Just as importantly, the knowledge illuminates some passages which have exercised the best brains, such as the famous opening of Sonnet 13:

> *O tHAT you were yourself! but, Love, you are*
> *No longer yours than you yourself here* LIVE:

For now we understand that this is *O that you, Prince True-love, were true love—the love which lives for ever!* ('Tell me, true Love, where shall I seek thy being? . . . Thou canst not die'—John Dowland.)

And again, when Prince True-love has taken Shakespeare's mistress from him:

40   7   *But yet be blam'd if thou thyself deceivest*
     8   *By wilful taste of what thyself refusest*

—which now is perfectly clear: *if thou deceivest true love by thy wilful taste of what true love refuses*: that is, fornication or adultery. The 'true' colour of True Love is *blue*, one of the Prince's two colours, in royal heraldry called *sapphire*. And the sapphire stone in the crown of England 'because it chastiseth the reins of the person that weareth the same, should instruct a King to continency and cleanness of his body'.[1]

---

[1] John Ferne, *The Blazon of Gentrie* (1586), 143. Spelling modernized. And cf. John Swan, *Speculum Mundi* (1635), 293.

In Sonnet 38 we have it once more: *thyself* describing the Prince not as Will Hatcliffe but as his poetic or heroical self, True Love. Here Shakespeare makes the immortal True Love his Muse. That Muse is not Will Hatcliffe, but his Idea—Love, that *ever-fixèd mark*, that *star*—far more powerful than all the Nine, which alone can inspire *eternal numbers*:

> 38 7 *For who's so dumb that cannot write to thee*
> *When thou thyself dost give invention light?*
> *Be thou the tenth Muse, ten times more in worth*
> *Than those old nine which rimers invocate;*
> *And he tHAT calls on thee, let him bring forth*
> *Eternal numbers to outLIVE long date.*

In view of his public glory, we should not be surprised to find the Prince celebrated in verse outside the Sonnets. We recall from Sonnet 78 Shakespeare's annoyance with 'alien' imitators of his praise of Prince True-love who, he says, have *got my use And under thee* [with thee as their inspiration] *their poesy disperse.* No trace has ever been found of any such poesy. But the fresh clue of the Prince's name now leads us to the peculiar title of a lost book. This work was entered in the Stationers' Register on 13 January 1587/8—just three days before the Prince royally entertained Lord Burghley and four other great lords at the comedy in Gray's Inn Hall. Its title reads, *Phidamore his fygure of fancye.*[1]

Phidamore is evidently *True-love* (Fidamore) and belongs to a familiar class of names: Philamour, counsellor in the Court of Love; Veramour, 'a loving and loyal Page'; Portamour, bailiff to Cupid.[2] And Fancy is of course Love. 'Tell me, where is fancy bred'; 'all in love? no other food than fancy?'; 'All fancy-sick she

---

[1] Arber (*S.R.* 2.224*b*) mistakenly prints PHIDAMONE; but J. P. Collier (*Notes and Queries* 2.12.22) had correctly read *Phidamore*, which I verified by the original in the Registry, Stationers' Hall, through the kindness of Mr Stanley Osborne.

[2] Massinger, *Parliament of Love*; Fletcher, *Honest Man's Fortune*; Poole, *English Parnassus* (1657), 376.

is'.[1] Put together, it is 'True-love his Figure of Love'. Figure?
At the height of the Prince's reign, what figure could *True-love's
Figure of Love* exhibit but his Quatrefoils of Love? And if this
versifier naturally employed Shakespeare's invariable method of
three fours to show the Figure in sonnets, and (what was worse)
set about vulgarizing it in print, he would rank at least as one of
those many *alien pens* who have *got my use And under thee their
poesy disperse*.[2]

In Phidamore *Love* is seen again *as a name*. Thoroughly to
digest the implications of this fact is to realize that we must re-
examine our view of the 'lover-like' quality of the sonnet-
language. Shakespeare's calling his friend *a God in love* makes
plain Hatcliffe's personification of Love, a concept frequent in
contemporary use: *Dear Love, sweet Lord, goodness-surmounting
God . . . Love, if a God thou art . . . Sweet Love, I will no more
abuse thee . . . Say, Love, if ever thou didst find . . . sweet Love doth
now invite . . . Thou deity, swift-wingèd Love . . . Sweet Love, if
thou wilt gain a monarch's glory . . .* It may be Shakespeare's
repeated and unrecognized use of 'sweet Love' as a title or name
which helps to give the 'extreme' impression—moving the late
C. S. Lewis to say 'I have found no real parallel to such language
between friends in sixteenth century literature.'[3]

At all events, we must not lose sight of the commonness of
sweet and *dear* in ordinary Shakespearean speech. 'Sweet Bottom',
'sweet countrymen', 'sweet masters', 'sweet gentlemen', 'sweet
lords', as well as 'sweet prince', 'sweet sovereign', and 'sweet
majesty'. Antonio was 'how dear a lover' of Bassanio—that is,
how dear a friend. Brutus calls the Roman citizens his 'lovers'.
While it cannot be asserted that whenever in the Sonnets we find

---

[1] *Merch. of V.* 3.2.63; Lyly, *Gallathea* 3.1.89; *Mids. N. D.* 3.2.96.

[2] I should mention the wretched verse-eclogue *Amor Constans* (with its
accompanying sixteen sonnets) by 'Ch. M.' (Bodl. MS. Eng. misc. d. 239)
only to say that it seems definitely too late to refer to Hatcliffe and his reign.
Cf. Roy C. Strong, 'Elizabeth as Oriana', *Studies in the Renaissance* VI
(1959), 256.

[3] *English Literature in the Sixteenth Century* (1954), 503.

sweet love and *dear love* it is always *sweet* [Prince] *Love* and *dear* [Prince] *Love*, it is clear that revelation of the *name* sounds a caution against importing our modern connotations into the words wherever they appear.

We might easily be as wide of the mark here as some have been in reading Meres's epithets: 'the mellifluous & honey-tongued Shakespeare . . . his sugred Sonnets'. For this 'sugred' implies nothing of what we mean by 'sweet verse' or 'love-poetry'. It simply means *eloquent, choice or perfect in expression*.[1] A year after Meres, John Weever (*Epigrams*) in similarly praising Shakespeare speaks of the 'sugred tongues' of his Tarquin and his Richard, and confesses his own inadequacy:

> I cannot shew then in a sugred vein
> Wit, judgment, learning, or invention—

meaning, 'with choice eloquence'. A quarter-century before, Raphe Lever had condemned 'Ciceronian & sugertongued fellowes which labour more for fineness of speech, then for knowledge of good matter'.[2] And as for Mark Antony, whose persuasive eloquence was quite irresistible, Thomas Lodge's Cinna begs him, 'Anthony, seal up those sugar'd lips'.[3] For similar eloquence, we have 'the sugred and renowned Orators *Demosthenes* and *Hortensius*',[4] and 'Homers sugared Muse'.[5] When we are tempted to think of 'sugred Sonnets' as implying verses lusciously sweet, we should take a dose of the sugared *Iliad*, or of the sugared *Odyssey*. In reprinting some of the Sonnets in 1640, John Benson reproduces Meres's praise by calling them 'perfect eloquence'. 'Mellifluous and honey-tongued' means precisely the same as 'sugred'. It is used to describe Nestor, Plato, Pindar, Claudius Ælianus the Roman rhetorician, and St

---

[1] Lorenz Morsbach in 1912 pointed out that this was its meaning from Chaucer to Milton. Qu. Rollins, *The Sonnets* (Varior. Shak.), 2.54.

[2] *The Arte of Reason* (1573).

[3] *The Wounds of Civil War.*

[4] Swetnam, *The Arraignment of . . . Women* (1628), 22.

[5] Greene, *Alphonsus*, Scene 7.

Chrysostom, as well as 'Honie-tongd *Tullie*, Mermaid of our eares'.

In my report of Will Hatcliffe's native county I recalled that Lyly in his *Gallathea*, given at the Court at Greenwich on New Year's Day 1587/8 during our Prince's reign, laid a scene in Lincolnshire. That this may have been done in compliment to Prince Will of the True-love (as well as to the Lincolnshire lords and courtiers) as a guest of the Queen's seems more likely when we find the dramatist also introducing a unique and elaborate discussion of the True-love Knot:

Telusa. Come, Cupid, to your task. First you must undo all these Lovers' knots, because you tied them.

Cupid. If they be true love knots, 't is unpossible to unknit them; if false, I never tied them.

Eurota. Make no excuses, but to it!

Cupid. Love knots are tied with eyes, and cannot be undone with hands; made fast with thoughts, and cannot be unloosed with fingers. Had Diana no task to set Cupid but to things impossible? [*They threaten him.*] I will to it.

Ramia. Why, how now? you tie the knots faster.

Cupid. I cannot choose; it goeth against my mind to make them loose.

Eurota. Let me see. . . . Now 't is unpossible to be undone!

Cupid. It is the true love knot of a woman's heart, therefore cannot be undone.

Ramia. That [one] falls in sunder of itself.

Cupid. It was made of a man's thought, which will never hang together.

Larissa. You have undone that well.

Cupid. Ay, because it was never tied well.

Telusa. To the rest, for she will give you no rest. These two knots are finely untied.

Cupid. It was because I never tied them: the one was knit by Pluto, not Cupid: by money, not love; the other by force, not faith: by appointment, not affection.

Ramia. Why do you lay that knot aside?

Cupid. For death.

Telusa. Why?

Cupid. Because the knot was knit by faith, and must only be unknit of
　　death.
Eurota. Why laugh you [at this next one]?
Cupid. Because it is the fairest and the falsest, done with greatest art
　　and least truth, with best colours and worst conceits.
Telusa. Who tied it?
Cupid. A man's tongue.
. . . .
Cupid. The time may come, Diana, and the time shall come, that thou
　　that settest Cupid to undo knots, shalt entreat Cupid to tie
　　knots . . .[1]

Cupid or Love has here reviewed the True-love Knot in its
several aspects: love, friendship, marriage. True Love in all three
is one and the same. But what a world divides the courtly chop-
logic of Lyly from that supreme sonnet which also takes its
origin in the True-love Knot, the ONE-and-FOUR of loving
friendship. Here high thought's invention mounts the skies for
compare of love's divine constancy in scorn of Time:

116

> *Let me not to the marriage of true minds*
> *Admit impediments. Love is not love*
> *Which alters when it alteration finds*
> *Or bends with the remover to remove.*
> *O, no! it is an ever-fixèd mark*
> *That looks on tempests and is never shaken;*
> *It is the star to every wand'ring bark,*
> *Whose worth's unknown, although his highth be taken.*
> *Love's not Time's fool, though rosy lips and cheeks*
> *Within his bending sickle's compass come.*
> *Love alters not with his brief hours and weeks,*
> *But bears it out even to the edge of doom.*
> 　*If this be error, and upon me proved,*
> 　*I never writ, nor no man ever loved.*

The only True-love *and* youthful Sovereign at the time of
Shakespeare's writing—the Prince of Purpoole—in ordinary life

---

[1] *Gallathea* 4.2.21 ff., in modern spelling.

was a law-student at Gray's Inn. This prosaic fact accounts naturally for the presence of the law-terms and legalisms appearing in a dozen or so of the sonnets addressed to him. There is little point in detailing their familiar features again, with however one interesting exception. And that is the masterly poem beginning *When to the sessions of sweet silent thought.* Our discovery shows us for the first time the frame and richness of its reference.

As King, the monarch of Purpoole inevitably has his Courts. Most material to his state stands Revenue, dealt with at the sessions and audits of his Court of Exchequer. Among its judges are numbered his Lord Treasurer, his Chancellor of the Exchequer, and his Lord Chief Baron of the Exchequer, with subsidiary Barons, Remembrancers, and Tellers understood.

Exchequer. As a court of law its primary business was to call the King's debtors to account. . . . Summons . . . to Sheriffs . . . with the *charge* against the Sheriff showing the . . . debts, arrears, &c. for which he was to answer.[1]

Remembrancers . . . are officers of the *Exchequer* . . . to put the . . . Justices of that Court in *Remembrance* of such Things as are to be called upon and dealt in for the King's Behoof and Benefit. . . . The *King's Remembrancer* . . . writes Process against the Collectors of . . . publicke Payments for their Accounts[2] . . .

For his sonnet, Shakespeare borrows the terms of the audit of moneys by True-love's Court of Exchequer—its summonses, its sessions, its remembrance of things, its debtors, non-appearances, losses, cancellations, old debts, accounts, tellers, payments—to picture his own heart's painful accounting: the real audit of true love.

30

When to the sessions of sweet silent thought
I summon up remembrance of things past,
I sigh the lack of many a thing I sought
And with old woes new wail my dear time's waste.

---

[1] M. S. Giuseppi, *Guide to . . . Public Record Office*, 1.75, 115.
[2] Giles Jacob, *Law Dictionary* (8th ed. 1762), s.v. *Remembrancers.*

Then can I drown an eye (unus'd to flow)
For precious friends hid in death's dateless night,
And weep afresh love's long since cancell'd woe,
And moan th'expense of many a vanish'd sight.
Then can I grieve at grievances foregone,
And heavily from woe to woe tell o'er
The sad account of fore-bemoanèd moan,
Which I new pay as if not paid before.
But if the while I think on thee, dear friend,
All losses are restor'd and sorrows end.

With the fortunate True-loves or Primroses which gave Will Hatcliffe's coat of arms its all-conquering charm in the eyes of the Gray's Inn gallants we have gained some acquaintance. But we have said nothing of a feature equally important—his *colours*, which as retainers and servants they would all wear as their Prince's livery. Were these as winning as the lucky Quatrefoils of Love?

Argent and Azure—primroses pure white in a field of sky-blue. These are the colours of triumphant kings of England, beginning with William the Conqueror.[1] An old heraldic manuscript[2] gives the heavenly pair as the personal colours of Edward III, Henry IV, Henry V, and Henry VI. They are also the colours of Edward III's peerless foundation, the Most Noble Order of the Garter:

blew, and white,
Like sapphire, pearl, and rich embroidery
Buckled below fair knighthood's bending knee.

More, they are the colours of the Stanleys, Earls of Derby, the richest subjects of the Queen, and members of Gray's Inn—their noble arms shining in glass in the Hall windows. Better still, they are the colours of the Grayans' dear ally and loving friend, the the Inner Temple: *Azure, a Pegasus or wingèd horse salient Argent.*

---

[1] John Bossewell, *Workes of Armorie* (1572), 31ᵛ, reports William's coat at the Conquest as 'barrie of vi peces d'Argent and Azure'—the same as Lord Gray's and Gray's Inn's.
[2] B.M. MS. Harley 2076, f. 44.

But best of all, they are the ancient colours of Gray's Inn itself; from Lord Grey or Gray, Earl of Kent, whose London inn or mansion-house the honourable society obtained in the time of Edward III, and whose arms 'are still kept as the proper and peculiar ensigne of the said Inne, viz. *Barry of six, Argent and Azure*'.[1]

One cannot doubt that if Hatcliffe found fortune in his Primroses, he was equally lucky in his colours—*silver in sapphire, seemly on sight*. For Honour has no nobler ensigns than the hues Sir Walter Ralegh calls 'snow-driven white and purest azure'.[2] Their respective meanings, according to Henry Peacham, are 'Milk white—Innocency or Purity of Conscience, Truth, Integrity' and 'Blue—Faith, Constancy, or Truth in Affection'.[3] And when worn together, Coronato Accolti tells us what they show: 'If the colour white is accompanied with azure, it signifies a person loyal, constant, just, and humble.'[4] Rinaldi expresses the conceptions in verse: *White shows the candid soul: azure, the mind's high thought*.[5]

Again in *Gallathea* (5.3) we find the two—how true a twain—as the wedding-colours for the true lovers' knot, answering the question 'Is your loves unspotted, begun with truth, continued with constancy, and not to be altered with death?' Similarly, Chapman describes the priest at the marriage of Hymen and Eucharis:

> And from his shoulders to the ground did trail,
> On either side, ribands of white and blue. . . .

---

[1] Randle Holme, *Academy of Armory* II (*ca.* 1688, pr. 1905), 376; who adds, 'but now of late this honorable society have assumed for their proper coate Armour or ensigne of Honor S. a Griffin rampant O.'

[2] 'The Ocean to Cynthia.'

[3] *The Compleat Gentleman* (1661), 156–157.

[4] *Del significato de' colori* (1568), 38ᵛ, 39.

[5] 'L'alto pensiero altrui il *Torchin* dimostra. . . . Si fa d'alma sincera il *Bianco* scorta' Rinaldi, *op. cit.* (1584), A3, with much illustration given on pp. 26–32. The nineteenth century adds, 'Purity is the feminine, Truth the Masculine, of Honour.' J. C. and A. W. Hare, *Guesses at Truth* (Ser. 1), 1827.

Then took he the disparent silks, and tied
The lovers by the waists, and side to side,
In token that thereafter they must bind
In one self sacred knot each other's mind.[1]

Sincerity and True Fidelity remain virtues today, and these colours symbolize them for us still. But what of *Beauty*? Was that a virtue? Yes: one of the five virtues signified by Silver (White) in arms was *Beauty*.[2] And describing the colour *white*, Shakespeare wrote, 'beauty's crest becomes the heavens'.[3] Throughout his Sonnets, as Alden said, he 'was exceedingly fond of coupling the notion of *truth* with that of *beauty*'. We now realize that his True-love is identified with Beauty not only in his 'outward fair' but also in the Beauty symbolized by his *argent*: *That beauty still may live in thine and thee . . . that beauty which you hold in lease . . . beauty's pattern to succeeding men.* And Truth is added by his *azure*:

54   1   *O how much more doth beauty beauteous seem*
      2   *By that sweet ornament which truth doth give . . .*
    13   *And so of you, beauteous and lovely youth,*
    14   *When that shall vade, my verse distils your truth.*

14 14   *Thy end is truth's and beauty's doom and date.*

60 10   *[Time] delves the parallels in beauty's brow,*
    11   *Feeds on the rarities of nature's truth.*

101

O truant Muse, what shall be thy amends
For thy neglect of truth in beauty dy'd?
Both truth and beauty on my love depends;
So dost thou too, and therein dignified.
Make answer, Muse: wilt thou not haply say,
'Truth needs no colour, with his colour fix'd;
Beauty no pencil, beauty's truth to lay;
But best is best, if never intermix'd'?

---

[1] *Hero and Leander* v. 350–358.
[2] Richard Robinson, *The Auncient Order . . . of Prince Arthure* (1582), A2ᵛ.
[3] *Love's Labour's Lost* 4.3.256.

The two colours bring to mind two ideal virtues of Honour. But they also recall the fairest sight in Nature:

the white and azure sky
In Light and Glory raisëd high[1]

—and this presents perfect Day. When we come upon the heraldic epithet appropriated to Hatcliffe's armorial colours, we catch the reference in Shakespeare's famous comparison:

When the Field and Charge is White and Blew, that is most Lovely: because when Aurora's Morning Curtains are dipt within that change-able Die, that day is most pleasant, lovely, and admired by the be-holders.[2]

18
Shall I compare thee to a summer's day?
Thou art more lovely and more temperate.

It recurs again and again—*loveliness, the lovely gaze* (sight), *thy lovely argument* (theme), *lovely youth, lovely boy.*

The alert reader, while agreeing that white is *fair* and blue is *true*, will have a question from Sonnet 105. Here we have *m Love* described as *fair* and *true*, but first of all as *kind; Kind is my Love today.* If Shakespeare's thought is fixed on Hatcliffe's colours, what of *kind*—whose colour is certainly red?

In his blazon of True-love, Shakespeare has not forgotten the red of his crest—Pompey's lordly lion, *gules.* It stands above the *fair* and the *true* of the escutcheon. The poet begins with *Kind*, for Love is the mighty lord, and what are beauty and truth without him?

105   5   *Kind is my Love to-day, to-morrow kind,*
      6   *Still constant in a wondrous excellence . . .*
      9   *'Fair, kind, and true,' is all my argument,*
    10   *'Fair, kind, and true,' varying to other words;*
    11   *And in this change is my invention spent,*
    12   *Three themes in one, which wondrous scope affords.*

---

[1] Lord Herbert of Cherbury, 'A Description.'

[2] Randle Holme, *The Academy of Armory* (1688), 14*a*. For each of the armorial combinations of colours Holme lists the superlative epithet proper to it, as *Most Ancient, Most Glittering, Most Rich*, &c. The seventh, for White and Blue, is *Most Lovely*.

Our realization that argent or white represents *beauty*, and that Hatcliffe's Primrose (First or Chief Rose) is white, makes it clear that 'beauty's Rose' means the Prince:

1 1 *From fairest creatures we desire increase,*
  2 *That thereby beauty's* Rose *might never die* . . .

And if that were not enough to identify him, we have it again in

9 *Thou that art now the world's fresh ornament*
10 *And only herald to the gaudy spring* . . .

This, as Gerard Legh told us, is the Primrose, which 'of all other flowers bringeth good tidings unto man, that the spring of the year is at hand'; or, as the song has it,

> Prim-rose first borne child of Ver,
> Merry Spring-time's harbinger.[1]

And Drayton,

> The Primrose placing first, because that in the Spring
> It is the first appeares.[2]

In the prime flower of his youth, Prince True-love is not only first, but the chosen primate, the paragon, 'the pride and primrose of all the rest', the 'Primrose of Honour'. And that Shakespeare means no ordinary flower, but the rare four-petalled one which Spenser calls 'the Primrose true', is plain from Sonnet 67: *his Rose is true.*

By a part of all his Prince's glory, Shakespeare lived. And if with the ear of mind we are to hear the trumpets' 'flourish when true subjects bow To a new-crown'd monarch', we must try to conjure up some part of that part. First, then, to put us in the mood, here is a magpie-collection (with a couple of names altered) from the poets of the time.

He beareth so prince-like a port in his person as any man living, and his excellent virtues beget a world of love. . . . We'll do thee homage, and be rul'd by thee, Love thee as our commander and our

---

[1] *Two Noble Kinsmen* 1.1.7–8.   [2] *Poly-olb.* xv. 150.

187

king. . . . Where's this prince? He's studying some speech, I'll lay my life, Against his coronation, to thank all His loving subjects, that as low as earth Thus offer him their duties. . . .

The trumpets show Prince William is at hand. . . . That's the prince: the rest are bare. . . . Room for the Prince! As well beseems so brave a prince as he, They bring him with great reverence and worship Unto his regal seat. . . . Sound, trumpets! William shall be here proclaim'd.

Gentlemen, I am your Prince. (All.) A prince! a prince! a prince! . . . I thank you, my good people, for your loves. My life is but the gift of heav'n, to waste it For your dear sakes. My people are my children, Whom I am bound in nature and religion To cherish and protect. . . . In progress will I now go through my realm. Sound loudest music: let's pass out in state.

Order and degree Duly observ'd is Majesty's defence. Generous Pensioners their axes bear For state and ornament. Then follow forth The noble ranks, and senators of worth . . . and march amidst his royal equipage.

The people swarm to gaze him in the face. Make room for the Prince! Fellows, bear back! 'T is he, indeed . . . Crown'd with the loves and honours of the people, With all the gallant youth of Gray's, Who could deny him love?

But this is no more than 'atmosphere'; and the only firm means at hand is to take passages of the *Gesta Grayorum*[1]—the traditional ceremonies of Hatcliffe's successor of seven years later, Henry Helmes—and project them back *mutatis mutandis* to Prince William's inauguration before the Armada.

The great number of gallant Gentlemen that *Grays-Inn* afforded at ordinary Revels [dancing on Saturdays] between *All-hollontide* and *Christmas*, exceeding therein the rest of the Houses of Court, gave

---

[1] Since no chronicle survives of the reigns of Hatcliffe (1587/8), Perient (1614/15), or Vivian (1635/6), we can be grateful for the luck which preserved the story of Helmes (1594/5). The manuscript is unknown, but fortunately someone printed from it in 1688—nearly a hundred years after it was written. While modernizing spellings, I have kept the Restoration's capitalizations, which lend a touch of grandeur.

occasion ... to wish an Head answerable to so noble a Body, and a Leader to so gallant a Company. .... After many Consultations, ... about the 12th of *December*, with the Consent and Assistance of the Readers and Ancients, it was determined that there should be elected a Prince of *Purpoole*, to govern our State for the time; which was intended to be for the Credit of Gray's Inn.

Helmes was elected, a Privy Council appointed, and together they created his Court—whose size and impressiveness can only be appreciated by the list (the incumbents' names here omitted) which follows. We note that after the under-officers come the great lords, climaxed by Lord Chamberlain, Lord High Steward, Lord Chancellor, and Archbishop. Then the Mace and the Sword, followed by the Shields of the Inner Temple and Gray's Inn; then the King at Arms or chief herald (here called 'Helmet' and no doubt in the earlier reign 'True-love'); then the great Shield of the Prince's Arms—a fanciful and highly ingenious elaboration of his real coat—immediately before the Prince of Purpoole himself; the rear brought up by courtiers and a guard led by the Master of the Horse. All told, well over one hundred and fifty in number, and with 'Townsmen, Family, and Followers' probably two hundred at the least.

The Order of the Prince of Purpoole's *Proceedings, with his Officers and Attendants at his honourable Inthronization; which was likewise observed in all his solemn Marches on Grand Days, and like Occasions; which Place every Officer did duly attend, during the Reign of His Highness's Government.*

A Marshal.   A Marshal.

Trumpets.   Trumpets.

Pursuivant at Arms.

Townsmen in the Prince's   Yeomen of the Guard,

Livery, with Halberds.   three Couples.

Captain of the Guard.

Baron of the Grand Port.

Baron of the Base Port.

Gentlemen for Entertainment, three Couples.

Baron of the Petty Port.

Baron of the New Port.
Gentlemen for Entertainment, three Couples.
Lieutenant of the Pensioners.
Gentlemen Pensioners, twelve Couples.
Chief Ranger, and Master of the Game.
Master of the Revels.
Master of the Revellers.
Captain of the Pensioners.
Sewer.
Carver.
Another Sewer.
Cup-bearer.
Groom-porter.
Sheriff.
Clerk of the Council.
Clerk of the Parliament.
Clerk of the Crown.
Orator.
Recorder.
Solicitor.
Serjeant.
Speaker of the Parliament.
Commissary.
Attorney.
Serjeant.
Master of the Requests.
Chancellor of the Exchequer.
Master of the Wards and Idiots.
Reader.
Lord Chief Baron of the Exchequer.
Master of the Rolls.
Lord Chief Baron of the Common Pleas.
Lord Chief Justice of the Prince's Bench.
Master of the Ordnance.
Lieutenant of the Tower.
Master of the Jewel-house.
Treasurer of the Household.
Knight Marshal.
Master of the Wardrobe.

Comptroller of the Household.
Bishop of St. *Giles*'s in the Fields.
Steward of the Household.
Lord Warden of the Four Ports.
Secretary of State.
Lord Admiral.
Lord Treasurer.
Lord Great Chamberlain.
Lord High Constable.
Lord Marshal.
Lord Privy Seal.
Lord Chamberlain of the Household.
Lord High Steward.
Lord Chancellor.
Archbishop of St. *Andrew*'s in Holborn.
Serjeant at Arms, with the Mace.
Gentleman Usher.
The Shield of *Pegasus*, for the *Inner Temple*.
Serjeant at Arms, with the Sword.
Gentleman Usher.
The Shield of the *Griffin*, for *Gray's Inn*.
The King at Arms.
The great Shield of the Prince's Arms.
The Prince of *Purpoole*.
A Page of Honour.
Gentlemen of the Privy Chamber, six Couples.
A Page of Honour.
Vice-Chamberlain.
Master of the Horse.
Yeomen of the Guard, three Couples.
Townsmen in Liveries.
The Family, and Followers.

Busy times in the land of Purpoole. The time cries haste.
When we reflect that only eight days were allowed between the
election of Prince Henry and his 'inthronization', to which all
these aforenamed officers marched, fully accoutred in rich and
proper dress, we may imagine the activity of an army of tailors,
as well as much rushing-about and borrowing. Not to mention

preparation of speeches, of the Shields, and of the Hall as a Presence. I have always believed the Elizabethans far more quick and efficient than we are, and now I know it.

Upon the 20th day of *December*, being St. *Thomas*'s Eve, the Prince, with all his Train in Order, as above set down, marched from his Lodging, to the great Hall; and there took his place in his Throne, under a rich Cloth of State: his Councillors and great Lords were placed about him, and before him; below the Half-pace, at a Table, sat his learned Counsel and Lawyers; the rest of the Officers and Attendants took their proper Places, as belonged to their Condition.

Then the Trumpets were commanded to sound thrice; which being done, the King at Arms, in his rich Surcoat of Arms [*in Hatcliffe's case the herald's coat would be True-loves*], stood forth before the Prince, and proclaimed his Style as followeth:

> *By the sacred Laws of Arms, and authorized Ceremonies of the same (maugre the Conceit of any Malcontent) I do pronounce my Sovereign Liege Lord, Sir* Henry, *rightfully to be the high and mighty Prince of* Purpoole, *Arch-Duke of* Stapulia *and* Bernardia, *Duke of the High and Nether* Holborn, *Marquis of St.* Giles's *and* Tottenham, *Count Palatine of* Bloomsbury *and* Clerkenwell, *Great Lord of the Cantons of* Islington, &c. *Knight of the most Heroical Order of the* Helmet, *and Sovereign of the same.* [*For* Henry *and* Helmet, *substitute* William *and* True-love.]

After that the King of Arms had thus proclaimed his Style, the Trumpets sounded again; and then entered the Prince's Champion, all in complete Armour, on Horseback, and so came riding round about the Fire; and in the midst of the Hall stayed, and made his Challenge in these Words following:

> *If there be any Man, of high Degree, or low, that will say that my Sovereign is not rightly Prince of* Purpoole, *as by his King at Arms right-now hath been proclaimed, I am ready here to maintain, that he lieth as a false Traitor; and I do challenge, in Combat, to fight with him, either now, or at any time or place appointed: And in token hereof, I gage my Gauntlet, as the Prince's true Knight, and his Champion.*

When the Champion had thus made his Challenge, he departed; then the Trumpets were commanded to sound, and the King at Arms blazoned the Prince his Highness's Arms, as followeth:

The most mighty Prince of Purpoole, *&c. beareth his Shield of the highest* Jupiter. *In Point, a Sacred Imperial Diadem, safely guarded by the Helmet of the great Goddess* Pallas, *from the Violence of Darts, Bullets, and Bolts of* Saturn, Momus, *and the* Idiot; *all environed with the Ribband of Loyalty, having a Pendant of the most heroical Order of Knighthood of the Helmet; the Word hereunto,* Sic virtus honorem. *For his Highness's Crest, the glorious Planet* Sol, *coursing through the twelve Signs of the* Zodiac, *on a Celestial Globe, moved upon the two Poles, Arctic and Antarctic; with this Motto,* Dum peragraverit orbem. *All set upon a Chapeau:* Mars *turned up,* Luna *mantelled,* Sapphire *doubled* Pearl [*i.e.* Azure *and* Argent, *the colours of Gray's Inn and of the Inner Temple*] *supported by two anciently renowned and glorious* Griffins, *which have been always in League with the honourable* Pegasus [*of the Inner Temple*].

The Conceit hereof was to show, that the Prince, whose private Arms were three Helmets, should defend his Honour by Virtue, from Reprehensions of Malcontents, Carpers, and Fools. The Ribband of Blue, with an Helmet Pendant, in intimation of St. *George.* In his Crest, his Government for the twelve Days of *Christmas* was resembled to the Sun's passing the twelve Signs, though the Prince's Course had some odd degrees beyond that time: But he was wholly supported by the Griffins; for *Grays-Inn*-Gentlemen, and not the Treasure of the House, was charged. The Word, *Sic virtus honorem,* that his Virtue should defend his Honour, whilst he had run his whole Course of Dominion, without any either Eclipse or Retrogradation.

The figure comparing the Sun's progress to the Prince's reign emphasizes our memory of Shakespeare's use of *my sun* and *the sun* for his sovereign Prince William. We also recall that his Order of the True-love, following the Purpoole tradition, had to be Most *Heroical.*

Here is an excellent opportunity for an important digression: *recognition of early critical tributes to Shakespeare as the poet of the Sonnets.* First, we shall see these conceptions, *sun* and *Heroical,* revealing the final evidence that the prince of English poets, Edmund Spenser, was the earliest of all to hail the *gentility* of Shakespeare's *gentle verse*—to pay high tribute both to his character and to his art.[1]

Spenser's tributes were two. First, in his *Teares of the Muses*, written 1589. At the height of the scurrilous Martin Marprelate controversy—in which both Lyly and Nashe were employed— Spenser recognizes the *gentle*[2] *Spirit*, Shakespeare, maker of the Sonnets' noble eloquence, as above prostituting his pen to this vulgar brawl:

> *But that same gentle Spirit, from whose pen*
> *Large streames of honnie and sweete Nectar flowe,*
> *Scorning the boldnes of such base-borne men,*
> *Which dare their follies forth so rashlie throwe;*
> *Doth rather choose to sit in idle Cell,*
> *Than so himselfe to mockerie to sell.*[3]

We have already learned (apropos Meres's 'his sugred Sonnets') that *honnie and sweete Nectar* does not mean 'luscious, sweet verse', but 'choice eloquence'. And *gentle* means 'of high, noble character'. True gentility has no relation to social rank. Some of the scurrilous may write themselves 'gentlemen', but to Spenser they are *base-borne*. For he agrees with Chaucer, *that good poet* who said *The gentle mind by gentle deeds is known.*[4]

---

[1] In *Shakespeare's Motley* (1952), 25–32, my surmise of this was correct; but in the state of my knowledge when I wrote, I missed the clinching connotations of *Aëtion, high thought,* and *Heroically.*

[2] Now *Stratford* upon *Avon,* we would choose
  Thy gentle and ingenuous *Shakespeare* Muse . . .
  Sir Aston Cockain, *Small Poems* (1658), 111.

[3] *Shakespeare's Motley,* 26–28. Rowe's testimony will be recalled: 'the incomparable Mr *Edmond Spencer* . . . speaks of him in his *Tears of the Muses.* . . . Mr *Dryden* was always of Opinion that these Verses were meant of *Shakespeare.*' The instinct of latter-day Shakespearean criticism has not proved as sound as Glorious John's.

[4] *F.Q.* 6.3.1.

194

> ... that man whose actions
> Purchase a real merit to himself,
> And rank him in the file of Praise and Honour,
> Creates his own advancement.[1]

At a time when the humble station in the world to which Fortune has condemned him seems peculiarly galling to Shakespeare—his rival Marlowe has recently, as we shall see, become his social better—Spenser, best judge of spiritual worth, proclaims the Stratford poet's true gentility, unmistakable in the high thought of his Sonnets.

The second dates from about 1591, the writing of *Colin Clout's Come Home Againe.*[2] Here in *gentler shepheard* Spenser again hails the generous Shakespeare as a poet second to none in nobility of utterance:

> *And there though last not least is* Aetion,
> *A gentler shepheard may no where be found:*
> *Whose* Muse *full of high thoughts invention*
> *Doth like himselfe Heroically sound.*

Before we knew the circumstances of the Sonnets, we could not catch the peculiar force of the name *Aëtion* for Shakespeare. Chambers correctly gave it as the Greek for 'eaglet', and saw no personal applicability in it. But Pliny (lib. X c. 3) lists six kinds of eagles; and *Aëtion* describes none but the young of the *Haliæetus*: the one truly noble kind of eagle *which can gaze at the sun.* In poetry, the sun is the King, or the heaven-graced majesty of Beauty. Shakespeare knew the Aëtion:

> Nay, if thou be that princely eagle's bird,
> Show thy descent by gazing 'gainst the sun [the throne].
> > *3 Hen. VI* 2.1.91–92.

> What peremptory eagle-sighted eye
> Dares look upon the heaven of her brow
> That is not blinded by her majesty?

> A lover's eye will gaze an eagle blind
> > *L. L. Lost* 4.3.226–228, 335.

---

[1] Fletcher, *Fair Maid of the Inn* 3.2.
[2] Chambers, *William Shakespeare* (1930), 2.187.

As Spenser did:

> And like the native brood of Eagle's kind
> On that bright Sun of glory fix thine eyes
>
> *Hymn of Heavenly Beauty*, 138–139.

And Lodge in his *Rosalynde*:

... prooving himselfe like the *Eagle* a true borne bird, since as the one is knowen by beholding the Sunne, so was he by regarding excellent beautie. . . .[1]

By their *gentle* or noble verse, the Sonnets of Shakespeare reveal him as Aëtion, the true-born noble eaglet, proved by his fixing his eyes upon the excellent beauty of his Sun, Prince True-love. And to leave no room for mistaking, Spenser adds

> *Whose* Muse *full of high thoughts invention*
> *Doth like himselfe Heroically sound.*

What is an 'heroically' sounding Muse? The modern reader's eye can miss here almost by as much as it misses in *pyramids* and *sugred*. For in Shakespeare's time *heroical* was far richer in meaning than it is now.

> *Preceptes Heroical.*

... worship God. Honour thy King. Obey the lawes. Be merciful. Desire honour and glorye for vertue. . . . Perfourme what so ever thou promisest.

> J. Bossewell, *Workes of Armorie*, 1572.

In short, be a *gentle* man, a hero.

> No, none can barre a Prince from being kind,
> The honour'd badge of an Heroicke heart.
>
> Sir W. Alexander, *Tragedy of Crœsus* 4.2.

---

[1] And compare

> ... my Eaglets would aspire,
> Straight mounting up to thy celestial eyes ...   Drayton, Amour 3.

> As none but Eagles gaze against the sun,
> So none but virtuous eyes discerne nobility.
>
> Bodenham, *Belvedere* (1600), F2ᵛ.

> Do not eclipse the splendour of that sun
> My eagle's eye must gaze at ...   Shirley, *Humorous Courtier* 4.1.

196

Similarly, Spenser of Belphoebe, who is Perfect Love and Chastity:

> Nathlesse she was so curteous and kind,
> Tempred with grace, and goodly modesty,
> That seeměd those two vertues strove to find
> The higher place in her Heroick mind.
>
> *F.Q.* 3.5.55.
>
> This well became a mynd heroicall
> Inly to greive at others' overthrowe:
> Sencelesse they are, & more then Stoicall,
> Whose harts are sear'd from feeling neighbours' woe.
>
> John Ross, *The authors teares*, 1592.[1]

It is not mainly because of the great single combats which the *Faerie Queene* recounts, but because it sets forth *the noble or kingly virtues* that Spenser's Muse is *heroic* or *heroical*. Davys sings of '*Colins* fayre heroike stile', and Richard Zouche reports '*Spencer*, having . . . delivered Morall and Heroicall matter for use and action.'[2]

Some of the finest heroical matter is presented by the paragons of true-loving friendship—David and Jonathan, Orestes and Pylades, Damon and Pythias—whom Spenser describes as '*lovers linkěd in true harts consent*, who *on chast vertue grounded their desire*

> *which in their spirits kindling zealous fire,*
> *Brave thoughts, and noble deedes did evermore inspire.*[3]

In the same way, planning to write on Prince Jonathan, 'linkěd in love' with David, Sir William Alexander begins,

> Muse sound true valour, all perfections parts,
> The force of friendship, and th' effects of faith,
> To kindle courage in those generous hearts
> Which strive for vertue to triúmph o're death.

This tale of loving friends was to be 'An heroicke Poeme'. As Professor Northrop Frye well says, 'In Shakespeare's Sonnets,

---

[1] Bodl. MS. Douce 277, f. 15.　　[2] *The Dove* (1613), E6ᵛ.
[3] *F. Q.* 4.10.26.

the beautiful youth group tells a "high" story of devotion'[1]—
and we look again at Spenser's Aëtion, the True Eaglet, the Sun
Gazer

> *Whose* Muse *full of high thoughts invention*
> *Doth like himselfe Heroically sound.*

The high thought is True Love. The Most Heroical Order of
Shakespeare's Prince is True-love. And the *only* name among all
the poets which sounds heroically is Shake-spear.

None but virtuous minds discern nobility, and one noble mind
recognizes another on sight. To the humbly born future King,
the Prince of English Poets' accolade was promptly and royally
accorded—in 1589 and 1591.

And now our recent recognition of the colours White and
Blue of Prince True-love in the Beauty and Truth of the Friend
discloses another early tribute to the Shakespeare of the Sonnets.

If one had to put the Sonnets into one word, that word would
be *Truth*: devotion, fidelity. For the poet is *true*,

21	9	*O, let me, true in love, but truly write*
40	4	*All* [*my true love*] *was thine*
61	11	*Mine own true love*
82	11	*Thou, truly fair, wert truly sympathiz'd*
		In true plain words by thy true-telling friend
113	14	*My most true mind*
123	14	*I will be true*
125	13	*a true soul*

their love is *true*,

116	1	*Let me not to the marriage of true minds*

and the Friend is *true*:

14	14	*Thy end is truth's and beauty's doom and date*
54	14	*my verse distils your truth*
72	9	*your true love*
105	9	*'Fair, kind, and true,' is all my argument*

---

[1] 'How True a Twain' in *The Riddle of Shakespeare's Sonnets* (1962), 38.

198

And we have already seen Shakespeare's Muse recalled to her true self, in hymning *azure-blue Truth*:

101   1   *O truant Muse, what shall be thy amends*
        2   *For thy neglect of truth in beauty dy'd . . .*
        6   *'Truth needs no colour, with his colour fix'd . . .'*

Spenser calls Shakespeare's Muse *full of high thought's invention*; and we have learned that it is *Azure* which *shows the mind's high thought*.[1]

If any poet's Muse is Azure or True Blue, it is Shakespeare's. With this firmly in mind, we open Gabriel Harvey's *Foure Letters* (1592) to his Sonnet X. Here he praises contemporary poets, as they look to him A.D. 1592:

Yet let Affection interpret selfe:
Arcadia *brave, and dowty* Faery Queene   [Sidney [Spenser
Cannot be stain'd by Gibelin, *or* Guelph,   [Daniel, *Civil Wars*
Or goodliest Legend, *that Witts eye hath seene.*
                        [Drayton, *Legend of Matilda*
The dainty Hand of exquisitest Art,
And nimble Head of pregnantest receit,
Never more finely plaid their curious part,
Then in those lively Christals of conceit.
Other faire Wittes I cordially embrace:
And that sweete Muse of azur Dy, admire: [Shakespeare, *Sonnets*
And must in every Sonnet interlace
The earthly Soveraine of heavenly fire.   [Queen Elizabeth
  A fitter place remaineth to implore,
  Of deepest Artists the profoundest lore.   [? Theology

Harvey follows his friend Spenser in admiration of Shakespeare's Muse, the Muse of *high thought* and True Love:

    And that sweete Muse of azur Dy, admire.

When to the foregoing we add John Davys's

      O could I sweet Companion, sing like you,
      Which of a shadow, under a shadow sing

---

[1] 'L'alto pensiero altrui il *Torchin* dimostra.' Rinaldi, *op. cit.*

we can enumerate four early tributes to the Shakespeare of the Sonnets. Two by Spenser, written 1589 and 1591, a third by Gabriel Harvey 1592, and a fourth by John Davys before June 1594. And though the Sonnets were unprinted, only 'spread abroad in written copies', all these tributes were published. It is plain that we cannot accuse the Elizabethans of representing Shakespeare (in modern academic style) as a mentally backward sonneteer writing in the middle 1590s, or later. Nor can we accuse them of tardiness in saluting the Stratford yeoman's high character and his achievement in poetry.

Before our digression, we were seeing the Prince's reign likened to the progress of the sun: a thought which recalls Shakespeare's figure for his radiant sovereign—*my sun, sun of the world.*

33 1 *Full many a glorious morning have I seen*
Flatter the mountain tops with sovereign eye,
Kissing with golden face the meadows green,
Gilding pale streams with heavenly alchemy . . .

25 5 *Great princes' favourites their fair leaves spread*
But as the marigold at the sun's eye . . .

18 5 *Sometime too hot the eye of heaven shines,*
And often is his gold complexion dimm'd.

Nothing is more familiar than the *golden* sun; and we also know that Gold—the heraldic metal *Or*—stands for *dominion* or *kingship.*[1] No question but that Shakespeare's sovereign is *the sun* by day; but what of the night? On looking further, we find that by night he becomes a *radiant, shining jewel*:

27 9 *Save that my soul's imaginary sight*
Presents thy shadow to my sightless view,
Which, like a jewel hung in ghastly night,
Makes black night beauteous . . .

What gem would that be? Obviously a 'gold' one, as the next sonnet implies:

28 12 *When sparkling stars twire not, thou gild'st the even.*

---

[1] 'E di dominio il *Giallo* inditio porta' Rinaldi, *loc. cit.*

However vague our ideas may be, both Shakespeare and his readers have a clear picture of this 'gold' gem, and we find it at once in Legh's familiar *Armory* (1562, p. 4*b*):

That precious stone, which ye Herhaughts [Heralds] do use in blason, for and in ye name of this mettall [*Or*, gold] and Planett [the sun] that is called a Topace.

Shakespeare's Prince, his jewel that makes black night beauteous, is the Topaz, known as 'the Sun of Gems'. When we turn to another popular work, Sir John Ferne's *The Blazon of Gentrie*, published in the year before Hatcliffe's election as Prince, we learn what the gold of the Topaz signifies. And the quantity of its given meanings applicable to Prince True-love is astonishing:

Topaz The cullor is yellow, & signifieth in		Prince True-love (William Hatcliffe)
Planets	*The Sunne*	*my sun sun of the world* (33.9, 14)
Vertues	*Faith & Constancy*	Argent & Azure, Hatcliffe colours *truth in beauty dy'd* (101.2)
Celestial signes	*The Lion*	The Lion, Hatcliffe crest
Ages of man	*Yong age of ado- lescentia* [given as from 14 to 20]	19 years, Hatcliffe's age
Flowres	*The Marygold*	*the marigold at the sun's eye* (25.6)
Elements	*Ayre*	*Shall I compare thee to a summer's day* (18.1)
Seasons of the yere	*Springtime*	*herald to the gaudy spring* (1.10) *Speak of the spring* (53.9) *the treasure of his spring* (63.8)
Numbers	*1.2.3.*	3 Quatrefoils, Hatcliffe arms 3 Quatrains, Shakespearean sonnet '*Fair, kind, and true*' (105.9)
Mettailes	*Gold*	*gold complexion* (18.6) *golden face* (33.3) *gilding the object* (20.6) *gilding pale streams* (33.4) *thou gild'st the even* (28.12)

Further, another passage in this same book of 1586 solves one of the chief sonnet-puzzles, contained in the famous description of the Friend's beauty contrasted with that of women:

> 20 5 *An eye more bright than theirs, less false in rolling,*
> *Gilding the object whereupon it gazeth;*
> *A man in hue all hues in his controlling,*
> *Which steals men's eyes and women's souls amazeth.*

To begin with, it has not been noticed that two terms here plainly connote the King: *Gilding* (as the *sun's* eye), and *controlling* (royal power).

> Yet looks he like a King: behold his Eye
> ... lightens forth
> Controlling Majesty.   (*Rich. II* 3.3.68.)

Now what of *A man in hue all hues in his controlling?* *Hue*—like the Latin *color*—is recognized to mean 'beauty' as well as 'colour'.[1] *A man in hue* means 'Of manly beauty'. But the ultimate bafflement lies in *all hues*; and none of the many guesses at its meaning carries conviction.

Shakespeare himself repeats of his Prince the first sense of *hue* —'beauty':

> 63 6 ... *all those beauties whereof now he's King*

The second, 'colour', is now revealed by the sun or king of gems, the Topaz:

> '... the Topazion, conteyning in it (as dyvers do write) the cullors of all stones, whereby Kynges are warned, to exercise all Vertues.[2]

Among the 'divers', the eleventh-century St Bruno of Asti writes, 'The Topaz ... is said to have the colours of all stones in it-self ... chiefly of gold and blue, for the virtues of wisdom and

---

[1] '*Color civitatis*, Cic. The beauty or stateliness of a City' (Littleton); 'Beauty is a colour' (Bodenham, *Politeuphuia*, 1597, 27ᵛ); 'Beautie is a blessed hue' (*Choice, Chance, and Change*, 1606, 12ᵛ).
[2] Ferne, 142.

chastity';[1] Sts Isidore and Gregory describe it 'shining with every colour'—*omni colore resplendens*; Carducci says 'It shines, all-hues—*omnicolor radiat*—a picture of those perfect ones wondrously shining with all the virtues'; Hugh of St Victor concurs.[2]

Now at length we understand *A man in hue all hues in his controlling*. It means 'Of manly beauty, and King (Sun-gem, Topaz) of all beauties, hues, or virtues.' And this fresh perception of the master-poet's picture of his Prince True-love's beauties and virtues brings us prepared and equipped to understand the master-painter's portrayal of the same—as we shall find in the pages which follow.

---

[1] 'Topazius . . . fertur autem quod omnium lapidum in se colores habeat, duos tamen, id est auri et coeli principaliter possidet per quem eos figurari putamus qui non solum sapientiâ et castitate verum etiam caeteris omnibus virtutibus rutilare videntur.' *Praefat. in lib. Apoc.* c. 21. Qu. Mme Félicie d'Ayzac in *Annales Archéologiques* v (1846), 216–233.

[2] 'TOPATIO . . . conchiuse Sant' Isidoro lib. 16. c. 7. che sia OMNI COLORE RESPLENDENS . . . ò pure col Carducci, OMNICOLOR RADIAT; idea di quei perfetti, che di tutti le virtù mirabilmente illustrati compaiono. San Gregorio 18. Moral. cap. 27. *Quia Graeca lingua pan omne dicitur, pro eo quod omni colore resplendet, topazium, quasi topandium vocatur* . . . Ugon Vittorino lib. 3. de Bestijs &c c. 58. *Topatius, qui omnium lapidum colores in se obtinet significat sanctos omnium virtutibus refertos.*' Filippo Picinelli, *Mondo Simbolico* (1689), 573a.

VIII

THE PORTRAIT OF MR. W. H.

As a heading for these pages I reproduce the title of Oscar Wilde's famous fantasy, universally enjoyed and admired. I recall fantasy as a foil to the recovered diamond of fact. For here we have emerged from the enormous and shifting world of dream. No longer are we looking at 'monsters and things indigest', but at an historical figure. London's poetical Prince True-love, A.D. 1587–88. Her youthful shadow-king of the Christmas Saturnalia. Bringing back the golden age of Friendship loving and true.

> A kingdom for a stage, princes to act,
> And monarchs to behold the swelling scene.

The beautiful stripling prince to act this ideal rôle in the amphitheatre of Elizabeth's England for his monarch to behold is Master William Hatcliffe. And the second monarch to behold it —*whose pen The scepter was, which rul'd the souls of men*—is still a young man not yet come to his kingdom. But he will be proclaimed by Fame,

> Which crown'd him *Poet* first, then *Poets* King:[1]

—William Shakespeare, the generous in mind and mood. Although in the scale of the world cruel Fortune pressed him down to *plebeian*, his spirit was royal. And in eternal lines he crowned Prince True-love his Friend—

> King of his thoughts, man's greatest empery.

We are now aware that the badge of Prince William's heroical Order and the public theme of his reign was the True Love of a True Friend. And that Shakespeare—his poet—in his Sonnets not only renowned the Prince who symbolized it, but himself exemplified the virtue in his own true love.

---

[1] Hugh Holland 'Upon ... Master William Shakespeare' in the First Folio of Shakespeare, 1623.

But as we noticed in Chapter II, Shakespeare was not alone in picturing the True-love Prince. The greatest painter had joined the greatest poet; and Shakespeare could feast his eyes upon the treasured portrait, the work of *this time's pencil*—the master-limner of the age, Nicholas Hilliard. Our own age has learned to appreciate the stature of this Elizabethan genius. Mr Raymond Mortimer writes:

Hilliard, I consider, has been equalled by none of his compatriots, except possibly Gainsborough, in the power of making a likeness into a thing of beauty. . . . I do not know of any portraits more delicately poetic.[1]

We have learned, moreover, not to look at Elizabethan art in the belief that a picture is an artist's self-expression, its elements and details chosen to further that expression. In those days, as we know, painters were still considered 'workmen'; the customer in ordering a picture gave directions for the details to be included:

> Sir painter, are thy colours ready set?
> My mistress cannot be with thee today . . .
> Come draw her picture by my fantasy. . . .

Instructions are given, ending with

> Before her feet, upon a marble stone
> Inflamëd with the sunbeams of her eye,
> Depaint my heart that burneth passionately;
> And if thy pencil can set down such moan,
> Thy picture self will feeling semblance make
> Of ruth and pity for my torments' sake.[2]

As in the jewels for Queen Elizabeth, each detail in the order to the artisan was selected for a purpose, designed to carry a meaning. Two examples of this in Hilliard's portrait-miniatures will

---

[1] Review of Dr Erna Auerbach's *Nicholas Hilliard* in *The Sunday Times* (London), 28 May 1961.
[2] *The Phoenix Nest* (1593), 99–100 (spelling modernized). The custom produced a well-known literary form, the 'Directions to a Painter'.

show both the principle, and the extent to which knowledge of their eloquent language has been lost.

The first is the familiar *Unknown Man against a background of flames*.[1] This shows the *lover*, 'burning in flames beyond all measure', as Mr Winter writes, pointing also to the significance of his 'holding a locket, doubtless containing a portrait of his mistress, towards his heart'. Yes, and there is more. He is *en déshabillé*, his fine linen shirt wide open, baring his breast. The meaning, his suffering withdraws him from society, he lives alone with his love's thought, and the white of his shirt and the nakedness of his breast both show his Sincerity or Truth. The locket is fixed to a chain round his neck: he is chained to the Idea of his mistress. On the little finger of the hand nearest his heart he wears a ring. This speaks it again, for as the fourth finger is the 'wedding finger', so *the little finger is the finger of lovers*.[2] If we could distinguish the material and form of the ring, it would tell more of the same story—as would also the ornamentation of the locket and the figures of the lace on his shirt. Finally, he is wearing a pendant ear-drop *in the form of a true-love*, the ONE-and-FOUR; whose jewels, if we could make them out, would not fail to carry the message as plainly as does the playing-card on which the portrait is mounted—the *ace of hearts*: 'my heart is single and it is thine'. Faced with this kind of thing, we come to realize that *far-fetched* can be an epithet of ignorance. Painting, in short, aspired to communicate as clearly and richly as language—to be 'dumb poetry'.

The other is a miniature portrait of that great sea-dog George Clifford, Earl of Cumberland, *il più gran corsaro del mondo*.[3] To his right is pictured a cloud emitting lightning and rain, and the legend reads *Fulmen aquasque fero*, 'I bear lightning and waters'. Everyone has noticed the allusion to the Earl's sea-service. But this personal thought or 'conceit' is not the primary message.

---

[1] Carl Winter, *Elizabethan Miniatures* (1955), pp. 25–26 and Pl. VI.
[2] John Minsheu, *The Guide into Tongues* (1627), 11096i.
[3] Graham Reynolds, *Nicholas Hilliard 1547–1947* (1947), No. 55.

The miniature must have been painted as a *wedding-gift to a bride*: for what it says is 'I bring fire and water to bless your marriage.'

What is the reason that new wedded wives are bidden to touch fire and water?

> Before them [the bride and groom] he presented
> Both fire and water . . .

The *fire and water* were the symbol of the union . . . the bride was sprinkled with the water.[1]

Finally, and more amusingly, if we look at the oil-painting (*not by Hilliard*) of the Earl of Southampton prisoner in the Tower of London, and find him accompanied by a cat, how do we read it? What is the cat doing there? His biographer sees a touching domestic scene:

> One likes to believe that it was [his wife's] happy thought to take his favourite cat with her to help to comfort, and to help calm the excitement of meeting again after such a long and anxious separation.[2]

Acquaintance with the Elizabethans should however tell us that it is a matter of indifference whether a harmless necessary cat was with the Earl in the Tower or not; or indeed whether the Earl cared for cats, or ever owned a cat. The important thing is that *in the picture* a cat is shown with the Earl in the Tower:

> Cat. To this animal it is natural and inborn to be extremely desirous of liberty, and most impatient of imprisonment.[3]
> Liberty. . . . At her feet is a cat, an animal that never lets its freedom be taken from it.[4]

---

[1] *Plutarchs Morals* (tr. Holland, 1603), 850; Chapman, *Hero and Leander* v. 359–360; P. J. Percival, ed. *Faerie Queene* Bk. I (1893), 332, on *F.Q.* 1.12.37. And see La Primaudaye, *French Academy* (1577), c. 46; *Jonson* (ed. Simpson), vii. 211, 215; x. 467–468.

[2] Mrs C. C. Stopes, *Southampton* (1922), 246. And later writers can see no more in the cat than Mrs Stopes could.

[3] J. Camerarius, *Symbolorum . . . Quadrupedibus Cent. Secunda* (1595), LXXVIII. p. 80. Cf. Pierius Valerianus, *Hieroglyphica*, de Fele.

[4] J. J. M. Timmers, *Symboliek en Iconographie der Christelijke Kunst* (1947), 802.

To the Victorians, the picture may say *Dear Pussy*. What it was painted to say is *Give me back my freedom*.

Most of us know Liberty's cap and her pole. But every Elizabethan knew her cat as well: knew why it is that a Cat may look at a King; why Hamlet says 'the cat will mew'; why in the scales of government the Serpent (Prudence) balances the Cat; and why (after the tribunes have roused the populace against Coriolanus with 'He was your enemy, ever spake against your liberties', 'You are at point to lose your liberties') Volumnia calls these 'liberty'-demagogues *cats*: ''Twas you incensed the rabble. Cats!'

Background of this kind will come to our aid in looking again at Hilliard's masterpiece (see Frontispiece), the *Unknown Youth leaning against a tree amongst roses, circa* 1588.

First consideration: this is not an artist's fancy, but a portrait; and no ordinary portrait either, for the presence at the top of a 'word' or motto shows it as an *impresa* or 'heroical device'. Just what an *impresa* consisted of is precisely explained by Ben Jonson's teacher, William Camden:

> An Impress (as the Italians call it) is a device in picture with his motto, or word, borne by noble and learned personages, to notify some particular conceit of their own, as Emblems (that we may omit other differences) do propound some general instruction to all. . . .
>
> There is required in a Impress (that we may reduce them to a few heads) a correspondency of the picture, which is as the body, and the motto, which as the soul giveth it life. That is, the body must be of fair representation, and the word in some different language, witty [*i.e.* full of meaning], short, and answerable thereunto; neither too obscure, nor too plain, and most commended when it is an hemistich, or parcel of a verse.[1]

What we have here in Hilliard's miniature, then, is an 'heroical device'. We are to find correspondency of the picture with the motto which gives it life and notifies some particular conceit of

---

[1] *Remains* . . . (ed. 1674), 366–367. Spelling modernized.

the sitter's,[1] who chose it, and is more than likely to have chosen the costume and its colours, the essential pose, and the accessories too—although the limner may certainly have contributed suggestions.

Second, what is this youth, this noble or learned personage? Obviously not (like the man frying in flames) an amorous lover. There are no signs whatever of a lady-love. Nor is he a sufferer from love-melancholy. Unlike Prince Hamlet, he is dressed to perfection. He has no *sombrero* pulled down over his eyes, nor does he 'lay his wreathèd arms athwart His loving bosom to keep down his heart'. Yet 'a lover' is all we have imagined, or perhaps 'a dreaming youth'. Rather, it now appears that so far from mooning, he is thinking, purposeful, resolved. It is we who have been wool-gathering. For what he is, and what he would at once be recognized to be, is The Picture of True-loving Friendship.

The gesture which shows it is *his hand upon his heart*. Greene gives a list of Virtues, represented by female figures; and after 'kind Hospitality . . . with her Cornucopia in her fist' and 'Courtesy whose face was full of smiles' comes

Friendship with her hand upon her heart.[2]

But Allot's *Wits Theater of the Little World* (1599, p. 66) gives full detail:

The Romaines . . . Shadowed [Friendship] in the shape of a young man whose heade was bared . . . putting his finger to his harte.

We look back at the painting, and 'lo, here the figure'—young man, head bared, hand to heart. In love with the classics, the Elizabethans drew their ideas of Friendship from Cicero. And as for the picture of *Amicitia* or Friendship, Erna Mandowsky

---

[1] As Cumberland's *Fulmen aquasque fero* notifies his endurance of perils at sea.
[2] *A Maidens Dreame* (1591), line 240. Spelling modernized.

traces it back to Fulgentius, and down through Holcot, Lilius Gyraldus, Alciati, and Ripa, to Falconet.[1]

Knowing what we know, can we still label this masterpiece of about 1588 *An Unknown Youth?* For about 1588 Shakespeare testifies that Hilliard painted his Friend, Prince True-love—*my Love's picture.* The public theme of the beautiful nineteen-year-old Will Hatcliffe's London reign was True-loving Friendship, and he was its Type and Exemplar.[2] If there were no more evidence, here already would be enough to identify for me this *young man whose head was bared . . . putting his finger to his heart* as William Hatcliffe: The Portrait of Mr W. H.

Yes. But it is more than a portrait, a 'body of fair representation' which says 'Friendship'. It is an *impresa,* and bears an answerable motto in some different language, neither too obscure nor too plain, and most commended when it is an hemistich (half-verse), or parcel of a verse. Here the different language is Latin; the motto is most commended, because it is a half-verse from the favourite poet 'rich Lucan': *Dat poenas laudata fides.* Is it also answerable, and neither too obscure nor too plain? We shall see presently.

First, however, beyond the beauty of his *outward fair,* we should examine this Picture of Friendship painted by *this time's pencil.* What of the colours of his costume? With exception of the golden-brown hatching of his white doublet to match his

---

[1] *Untersuchungen zur Iconologie des Cesare Ripa* (1934), 27–29.

[2] No wonder that so lovely and welcome a theme inspired contemporary works—as Thomas Churchyard's *A Sparke of Frendship and warme Goodwill, That Sheweth The Effect of True Affection* (1588), Walter Dorke's *A Tipe or Figure of Friendship* (1589), and 'In prayse of friendship' in L. Wright's *A Display of dutie* (1589)—or that its fashionable currency shows in Mundy's *Banquet of Daintie Conceits* (1588): 'To . . . his especial good freend. . . . In respecte of the manifolde . . . deedes of freendship . . . your wonted freendlie iudgment . . . your worships poore Freende. . . . To the gentle and freendlie Reader. . . . Thine to vse in freendship, A. Munday.'—as well as in Greene's *Perimedes the Blacksmith* (1588): '. . . to his freend the Author . . . freend Robin . . . my very good freend . . . if not, *Actum est de Amicitia* . . . mine especiall good freend . . . his freendship whom I haue euer found as faithfull as familiar and so familiar as can come within the compasse of amitie.'

210

hair—the dark auburn or 'brown madder' *buds of marjoram* of Sonnet 99—they are only two, the personal colours of Queen Elizabeth: Black (short cloak) and pure White (ruff, cuffs, legs, and feet). On the picture of sincere white Friendship in the symbols-book are painted the words MORS ET VITA, Death and Life: meaning that 'a perfect friend . . . is for ever inseparable: for however great the change of fortune, whether for better or for worse, he is glad to live and die for the sake of a true love'.[1] White, as everyone knows, is the colour of Truth or Faith; and Black is Constancy, for *black will take no other hue*: 'Galen . . . attributeth . . . to the blacke, constancie.' 'Black . . . signifies Constancie.'[2] White and Black, then, for True Friendship Eternal. For 'the love of men to women is a thing common and of course: the friendship of man to man infinite and immortal.'[3]

The strong tree on which he leans is naturally again Steadfastness, Constancy. The constant, immovable Oak is frequent in the collections of 'heroical devices' and symbols.[4]

> As hardened oke that fear'th no sworde so kene
> So fast am I to you, and aye have bene . . .
> But ever one, yea both in calme and blast,
> Your faithfull frend, and will be to my last.[5]

'The greatest treasure in adversitie, is the truth of a friend immoveable.'[6]

And why is he standing among the large sharp thorns of the white brier-rose or dog-rose? To say that *he will be with his friend in adversity or trouble*: he is not one 'at need that leaves a man

---

[1] Cesare Ripa, *Iconologie* (ed. J. Baudoin, 1698), 10.
[2] Harrison, *Descr. of Britaine* (1577), I. xx.; Sylvanus Morgan, *The Sphere of Gentry* (1667), 3.
[3] Lyly, *Endimion* 3.4.114–116.
[4] 'Semper Immota'—Ruscelli, *Le Imprese illustri* (1584), 281; 'Semper Eadem '—Ferro de' Rotarii, *Teatro d'imprese* (1623), ii. 592; 'Ventis Immoto Superbit'—Camerarius, *Symbolorum . . . Centuria Unus* (1590), 19; F. Picinelli, *Mondo Simbolico* (1689), 443, 444, 460, gives several more.
[5] Tottel, *Songes and Sonnettes* (Arber repr.), 199.
[6] Bodenham, *Politeuphuia* (1597), 10.

sticking in the briers', or that 'hath left his friend in the briers'.[1]
Here, as in Shakespeare's Helicanus, who stood by Pericles in
his misfortune,

may you well descry

> A figure of truth, of faith, of loyalty.

Hatcliffe's friend Campion sings, '*Earth hath no Princelier
flowers Than Roses White*'. Many today would choose the brier-
or dog-rose as the loveliest rose of all. And in heraldry the
'White Rose was the type of Love and Faith'.[2]

53 13   *In all external grace you have some part,*
         But you like none, none you, for constant heart.

54   1   *O how much more doth beauty beauteous seem*
         By that sweet ornament which truth doth give:
         The rose looks fair, but fairer we it deem
         For that sweet odor which doth in it live . . .
         And so of you, beauteous and lovely youth,
         When that shall vade, my verse distils your truth.

The message of this *painted counterfeit* is unmistakable. And
just as in the case of the Lover frying in flames, every last feature
repeats it with the language of symbolism and connotation.
Hilliard's Youth presents *True-loving Friendship, for ever faithful,
and constant in adversity*. To my mind, this Friend can be no
other than Shakespeare's Friend, that constant heart, *fair, kind,
and true*.

For the word or motto to give his picture life, the sitter has
chosen the half-verse *Dat poenas laudata fides* from a famous
'speech out of Lucan'. How is it appropriate?

It recalls a classical and most extreme test of True Friendship.
Put directly, it is this: When your father's great benefactor and
faithful friend comes to you in defeat, hunted with overwhelming
power by his deadly enemy, what do you do? Loyally to
succour and support him will certainly get you the revenge of his

---

[1] Tilley, *Dict. Proverbs*, B673.
[2] W. C. Wade, *The Symbolism of Heraldry* (1898), 133.

conqueror. The fidelity which one of your advisers recommends is all very fine; but as a coward and a traitor you prefer to follow the worldly-wise counsel of the other. He tells you not to put your neck in the noose for friendship, but to join cruel Fortune in crushing your friend: turn on him, murder him, and claim reward. The grim story is the Fall of great Pompey; and you are young Ptolemy, King of Egypt:

Pompey. Trusting upon King Ptolemy's promis'd faith,
　　　　　And hoping succour, I am come to shore.[1]

The half-verse in Latin is from the speech (*De Bello Civili* viii. 485–486) of the eunuch Pothinus, who 'with base breath Durst thus presume to counsel Pompey's death'—

　　　　　'*Dat poenas laudata fides*, dum sustinet,' inquit,
　　　　　'Quos fortuna premit.'

which may be rendered

He said, '*We all praise fidelity; but the true friend pays the penalty* when he supports those whom Fortune crushes.'[2]

---

[1] *The Tragedy of Caesar and Pompey* 2.4.
[2] I subjoin four versions from the seventeenth century:
　　　　　　　　　　a praysed faith
Is her own scourge, when it sustaines their states
whom fortune hath deprest;
　　　　　　　　　Ben Jonson, pr. W. D. Briggs, *Anglia* 39.247.
Obserued faith so much commended,
Hath with repentance often ended,
When men will striue to eleuate
That Fortune meanes to ruinate.
　　　　　　　　　Sir Arthur Gorges, Lucan's *Phars.* (1614), 337.
And faith, though prais'd, is punish'd, that supports
Such as good fate forsakes.
　　　　　　　　　Fletcher, *The False One* 1.1.303–304.
Faith suffers, Ptolomey, when it would aide
Whom fortune hates.　　　Thomas May, Lucan's *Phars.* (1627), P2.

Marston brings Lucan's *laudata fides* familiarly in with the heart-less talk of common fair-weather 'friends' who are no friends at all:

> But he is dead; or—worse—distress'd; or—more
> Than dead or much distressëd (oh, sad!)—*poor.*
> Who ever held such friends? No, let him go.
> Such faith is prais'd, then laugh'd at.[1]

The distressed Lear's loyal Kent is told he's a fool 'for taking one's part that's out of favour'. But Kent is glad to suffer for his friend. And his reply would be the faithful Shakespeare's own: '*So true a fool is Love*'.

Neither too obscure nor too plain, the motto gives life to the Picture of True Friendship standing in the thorny briers. It says, 'The True Friend pays the penalty': *suffers* by supporting his friend whom Fortune crushes:

29   1   *When, in disgrace with Fortune and men's eyes,*
        I all alone beweep my outcast state . . .

111 1   *O, for my sake do you with Fortune chide,*
        The guilty goddess of my harmful deeds,
        That did not better for my life provide
        Than public means which public manners breeds.

37   3   *So I, made lame by Fortune's dearest spite,*
        Take all my comfort of thy worth and truth.

This picture by Hilliard, or another example of it, could be the very one on which the Prince's unfortunate friend feasted his eyes.

Yet the most interesting question is still to ask. And its answer should contain a crowning piece of evidence for identi-fying Hilliard's Youth as a portrait of William Hatcliffe.

Since this is an 'heroical device', the motto must 'notify some particular conceit' of Hatcliffe's beyond the general instruction of 'True-loving Friendship' as an emblem. This 'conceit' should be a personal allusion 'to be understood by some but not by all': a kind of signature, like the *Fulmen aquasque fero* of the sea-warrior

---

[1] *Sophonisba* 3.1.

Cumberland. The question therefore puts itself, Is there something in *Dat poenas laudata fides* which identifies William, Prince of Purpoole?

Answer, Yes: *Pompey the Great*, called by St Augustine 'the most famous prince of the Roman people'. Pompey is Lucan's hero, and Pompey's signet (the Lion bearing a sword), as we have already seen, is the proud crest of Hatcliffe. Out of all hemistichs of Friendship in Latin, Italian, French, or Spanish poetry, he chooses the one which recalls Pompey, and Pompey recalls the Hatcliffe crest. One wonders what Hatcliffe's personal motto was, to compare with Sidney's *Vix ea nostra voco* from Ovid and Essex's *Virtutis comes invidia* from Cicero. I have not been able to find it. But I should not be surprised if it turned out to be *Dat poenas laudata fides* from Lucan.

This choice of Lucan puts the sitter in noble contemporary company. Ottavio Farnese, Duke of Parma (d. 1586), took for his *impresa* Lucan's *Nubes excedit*, the cloud-overtopping Olympus. And the proud canting device of the House of Umbrosi was Lucan's *Stat magni nominis umbra*—'The shadow of a great name stands.'[1] If (as I believe) Hilliard's Youth was William Hatcliffe, this motto of his was not the only appearance of Pompey in Shakespeare's circle. For Sir Dudley Digges—stepson of the poet's intimate friend Squire Thomas Russell—borrowed from Lucan, as a title for his book (1611) urging American discovery, Pompey's farewell on sailing to Egypt and to his death: *Fata mihi totum mea sunt agitanda per orbem*, 'I must follow up my destiny throughout all the world.'[2]

Pompey stirs another question. How did the first armigerous Hatcliffe get Pompey's Lion? In devising crests, the common effort was to secure a 'correspondency' with the heraldic charge of the escutcheon. Thus, when the shield of Shakespeare bore a spear, the crest granted with it was a noble falcon supporting (or shaking) a spear.

---

[1] Giacopo Gelli, *Divise, Motti e Imprese* (1928), 367, 92.
[2] Hotson, *I, William Shakespeare* (1937), 229.

Hatcliffe bore three True-loves. What is there in the thought of Love or True Love to suggest Pompey the Great, and give reason for adopting his Lion? We turn to page 678 of North's Plutarch, and read

The Love of the Romanes unto Pompey.

The Romanes seeme to have loved Pompey from his childhoode ... never any other ROMANE (but Pompey) had the peoples earnest goodwilles so soone, nor that in prosperitie and adversity continued lenger constant, then unto *Pompey*.

More, we find the popular handbook *Belvedere* (1600, p. 153) drawing the following from Plutarch's *Morals*:

> *Augustus* wished Scipioes valiancie,
> And *Pompeys* love ...

As early as 1511 in his *Pompeius Fugiens* the widely read teacher Vives had presented Pompey saying

All ... embraced me with love, and marvellously favoured me. What father ever loved his son ... as all the people, all the knights, all the senators loved me?

And not in books alone, but in London's public poetry the love of Pompey is paralleled only by the supreme love of Elizabeth. In Peele's *Descensus Astræae*, the 1591 Lord Mayor's Pageant, we have

> Our faire Eliza, or Zabeta faire,
> Sweet Cynthias darling, beauteous Cyprias peere
> As deere to England and true English heartes,
> As Pompey to the Citizens of Rome.

When Prince True-love the shadow-king rode through the thronging Londoners in imitation and sincerest flattery of his all-loved Queen, his crest, Pompey's Lion, also implied 'I am the people's Love'. For, as Shakespeare wrote, Will was *lov'd of more and less*—of high and low.

Along with Love, the quatrefoil Primrose or the 'lucky four-leav'd grass' also signified Good Fortune. And never was there a Roman captain so fortunate as Pompey, glorious so long. 'That Pompey whom the gods loved without rival in this world.' 'Fifty-eight years in Fortune's sweet soft lap.'

Great Rome's paragon of Love and Luck. Here is ample reason for crowning a shield of lucky true-loves with Pompey's Lion. With all this in mind, we can now make a more-than-probable guess at Will Hatcliffe's favourite reading in boyhood. It was the Life of Pompey the Great:

> But *Pompey* his sonne was for many occasions beloved. As, for temperance of life, aptnesse to armes, eloquence of tongue, faithfulnes of word, and courtesie in conversation: so that there was never man that requested any thing with lesse ill will then he, nor that more willingly did pleasure any man when he was requested. For he gave without disdaine, and tooke with great honor.

The favour of Pompey.

> Furthermore, being but a childe, he had a certain grace in his looke that wan mens good willes before he spake: for his countenaunce was sweete, mixed with gravetie, & being come to mans state, a grave & princely majestie . . . the cast and soft moving of his eyes had a certaine resemblaunce (as they sayd) of the statues and images of king *Alexander*.

Evidently in some respects Will Hatcliffe could model himself even upon such a paragon as Pompey; his Purpoole election proves him able to 'prince it much Beyond the trick of others'. Shakespeare describes his comely Will as *music to hear*, gracious, kind, constant, sweet; and

> 17 5 *If I could write the beauty of your eyes*
> *And in fresh numbers number all your graces,*
> *The age to come would say, 'This poet lies . . .'*

Beautiful, both in character and countenance. For handsome is that handsome does; and Plutarch would underline the importance of character and behaviour—'If loved for fair and gentle conditions, he hath more honour thereby than if he won love by beauty

217

only.' This axiom Will Hatcliffe would see verified at Queen Elizabeth's Court, where the high mark for all chivalrous emulation was a man quite undistinguished by good looks: Sidney, the 'gentle Sir Philip'.

As for Friendly Love, in Plutarch he would further read that Pompey, reproved by Cato for neglecting his insistent advice either to control Caesar or look to be controlled by him, replied 'Your counsel indeed was wiser, but mine more *courteous and friendly*'. We may also compare Pompey's character in Chapman's *Tragedy of Caesar and Pompey*:

> Pompey.   ... but love me
>   And wish me conquest for your country's sake.
> Statilius.   Our lives shall seal our loves, sir ...
> Pompey.   Y'are my friends. ...
> 1st Consul. See yet, my lord, more friends.
> 2nd Consul.   Five Kings, your servants.
>
>   *Enter five* Kings.

Great Pompey's story was thoroughly familiar not only to the boy who proudly bore his lion for his crest, but to all. An anonymous writer mentions it in 1580[1] as popular material for the playwrights: 'And if they write of histories that are knowen, as the life of Pompeie; the martial affaires of Caesar ... they give them a new face.' And two years later, Gosson in his *Plays Confuted*: 'So was the history of Caesar and Pompey, and the Playe of the Fabii at the Theatre, both amplified there.'

A year and a half before Will Hatcliffe went up to Cambridge, and while he was a boy of twelve still (as I think) with his aunt Lady Anne Ayscough at Court, Pompey 'the people's love' came to Whitehall. On the year's greatest feast of Twelfth Night 1580/1, 'The Children of Pawles' presented before their beloved Queen 'A storie of Pompey'.

How early the dream of greatness was born in the boy's mind

---

[1] *A Third Blast of Retraite* ... 145.

we can only conjecture. As an ambition it was not too fantastical
—'A gentleman may make a king, and a clerk may prove a pope.'

> *Rufinus.* He was a man, you know, of no great birth.
> *Leontius.* A gentleman; that's all.
> *Marius.* A king's no more.[1]

Recalling those 'two suns of our Roman heaven, Pompey and
Caesar', he did not have to be told that

> Two suns are not adorëd in one sky,
> Nor many Kings admired on one throne.

But everyone knew that a monarch of the Inns of Court could
mount the sky up near the 'sun of the world . . . great Gloriana',
and shine in the clouds as a glistering Parhelion—a representation, a resemblance, a shadow of that radiant orb supreme. Such
a mock sun tasted all the sweets of majesty and none of the sour.
As Davies of Hereford put it,

> Then who had better reigns, judge all of sense,
> Either a king indeed, or in pretence?

And beyond that, is there not more solid satisfaction in being
chosen king by one's peers in an open competition, than in gaining
a throne by the accident of having a king for a father? Great
Pompey's soldier-father was no king. He was even bitterly hated
by his men. Yet after 'the wonderfull deedes that *Pompey* did in
his Childhoode' his son's later conquests were rewarded by the
Lex Manilia, which as Plutarch said made him 'monarch and
absolute prince of all the Roman empire'.

On his admission to the society of Gray's Inn in 1586, Will
Hatcliffe found his good genius Pompey actively remembered
there, and by a countryman of his from Lincolnshire. William
Fulbecke, son of the Mayor of Lincoln, and a Fellow of Corpus
Christi College Oxford, had been admitted a couple of years
before; and at Gray's Inn was completing his *Historicall Collection
of the continuall factions, tumultes, and Massacres of the Romans*

---

[1] *The Faithful Friends* 1.1.

and Italians. Writing of Pompey's mighty conquests, Fulbecke relates that 'for a triple reward of these his victories, he had the blazon of three triumphs: the first was of Affricke, the second of Europa, and the third of Asia.' And he recounts his betrayal by Ptolemy, which is recalled by the motto *Dat poenas laudata fides*:

Pompey having procured the restitution of his father to the throne of Egypt, and with many other singular benefites having deserved his favour, thought that the young Prince wold have entertained him according to his honour and desert; but who doth busie his memorie in recounting benefites? and who will think himselfe beholden to one that is distressed? and when doth not fortune chaunge friendship? Ptolome, unthankfull Ptolome. . . . Pompey, whose excellent qualities might encline a massagite to mercie. . . . But how false was this world to Pompey, who had not now earth enough for his sepulture, to whom before the earth was too little for his conquest: but rare is the bird whose feathers do not moult, and happie is that man whose glorie doth not eclipse.

However long it may have been—through the years of boyhood spent probably at Court or near it, and his career as a Jesus man at Cambridge—that Will Hatcliffe held Pompey before his mind's eye with the thought of possible glory to come, he was certainly human. And when at the beginning of his second year at Gray's Inn that glory came, and he was 'happy enough to pity Caesar', it could not have been easy to realize:

> He that in glory of his fortune sat,
> Admiring what he thought could never be,
> Did feel his blood within salute his state
> And lift up his rejoicing soul, to see
> So many hands and hearts congratulate
> Th' advancement of his long-desir'd degree;
> When, prodigal of thanks, in passing by
> He resalutes them all, with cheerful eye.[1]

---

[1] Daniel, *Civil Wars* II. 64.1–8.

Before the greatest fortune had crowned him, Shakespeare had known him—almost an Argalus for 'princely parts':

> A noble, generous, and well-manner'd youth;
> Bears beauty's ensigns in his gracious looks,
> Has that supreme divinity in his eyes
> As sparkles flames able to fire all hearts;
> And the superlative virtue of his mind
> Transcends his outward figure.[1]

In Shakespeare Prince True-love had made a friend who could truly say 'I love thee for thyself, not for thy State'. And if he could discern the mental stature of this player-poet, Wisdom would whisper the Prince in the ear

> Now he o'er all will spread your praises forth—
> A famous witness of your glorious reign.
> The record of one wise man is more worth
> Than what a world of others would maintain.[2]

Time was however to show that Will Hatcliffe was not quite up to it. He took too much pleasure in hearing his own praise. His judgment followed Fashion in preferring the verse of that admired University wit Marlowe to Shakespeare's. And on one occasion he was capable of inflicting an incurable wound on his faithful friend by unkindness:

34

> *Why didst thou promise such a beauteous day*
> *And make me travel forth without my cloak,*
> *To let base clouds o'ertake me in my way,*
> *Hiding thy brav'ry in their rotten smoke?*
> *'Tis not enough that through the cloud thou break*
> *To dry the rain on my storm-beaten face,*
> *For no man well of such a salve can speak*
> *That heals the wound, and cures not the disgrace:*

---

[1] Glapthorne, *Argalus and Parthenia* 2.1. As we shall see, Henry Glapthorne was Will Hatcliffe's nephew, aged twenty-one when his uncle died.
[2] Sir W. Alexander, *The Tragedy of Crœsus* 2.1.275–278.

> *Nor can thy shame give physic to my grief;*
> *Though thou repent, yet I have still the loss.*
> *Th' offender's sorrow lends but weak relief*
> *To him that bears the strong offence's cross.*
>   *Ah, but those tears are pearl which thy love sheeds,*
>   *And they are rich and ransom all ill deeds.*

Forgiveness cannot obliterate unkindness. 'Look what abuse is offer'd to a friend, The shame and fault finds no excuse or end.' Later, in confessing a 'transgression' of his own, Shakespeare can write

120

> *That you were once unkind befriends me now,*
> *And for that sorrow which I then did feel*
> *Needs must I under my transgression bow,*
> *Unless my nerves were brass or hammer'd steel.*
> *For if you were by my unkindness shaken,*
> *As I by yours, y' have pass'd a hell of time,*
> *And I, a tyrant, have no leisure taken*
> *To weigh how once I suffer'd in your crime.*
> *O that our night of woe might have rememb'red*   [reminded
> *My deepest sense how hard true sorrow hits,*
> *And soon to you, as you to me then, tend'red*
> *The humble salve which wounded bosom fits!*
>   *But that your trespass now becomes a fee;*
>   *Mine ransoms yours, and yours must ransom me.*

This, however, is something of a digression, for I have much to say in the behalf of that Pompey. Let us go back to the early days of Prince William's reign, and view him as Shakespeare did when

> the mounted Sun
> Breaks through the clouds, and throws his golden rays
> About the world: so his increasing days
> Succeed in glory.[1]

---

[1] J. Poole, *The English Parnassus* (1657), 313.

By his crest, and (as I believe) his chosen motto for his portrait as True Love Constant in Adversity, and his public appearance in triumph as 'the people's love,' we have seen that Will Hatcliffe's thought was *Pompey*. We should naturally expect to find Shakespeare recalling his Prince's Pompey in the Sonnets. We cannot fail, I think, to see two instances of it, as follows.

First, Plutarch in his *Morals* emphasizes one of the most famous passages in Pompey's life by giving it twice—once in his 'Instructions for them that manage affaires of State' and again in his 'Apophthegmes of Kings, Princes, and Captaines':

And when *Pompey* the great would have entred the citie of *Rome* in triumph, before he had shewed himselfe unto the Senate, and was withstood by *Sylla*, who meant to impeach him, he stucke not to say unto him: More men there be sir, who worship the Sun rising, than the Sun setting; which when *Sylla* heard, he gave place and yealded unto him without one word replying to the contrary.

... when he minded to enter triumphant into *Rome*, *Sylla* would have hindered him, alledging for his reason: That he was not as yet admitted and sworne a Senatour: whereat *Pompeius* turning to those that were present: It seemeth (quoth he) that *Sylla* is ignorant how there be more men that worship the sun rising than setting: which words when *Sylla* heard, he cried out with a loud voice: Let him triumph a Gods name, for I see well he wil have it ...

And in his *Life of Pompey* he gives it a third time:

All this blanked not Pompey, who told him frankely againe, how men did honor the rising, not the setting of the sunne.

This memorable story identified the 'rising sun' proverb with Pompey, as we see it recalled in the tale of his fall by the ingratitude and treachery of Ptolemy

> to whom he did commit his life;
> (But O, who doth remember good turns past?)
> The Rising Sun, not Setting, doth men please.[1]

---

[1] *The Tragedy of Caesar and Pompey* (1607), 2.4.

And at Prince William's inauguration Shakespeare reminds him of the triumphing Pompey's words, 'More men . . . worship the Sun rising, than the Sun setting':

7

> Lo, in the Orient when the gracious light
> Lifts up his burning head, each under eye
> Doth homage to his new-appearing sight,
> Serving with looks his sacred majesty;
> And having climb'd the steep-up heavenly hill,
> Resembling strong youth in his middle age,
> Yet mortal looks adore his beauty still,
> Attending on his golden pilgrimage;
> But when from highmost pitch, with weary car,
> Like feeble age he reeleth from the day,
> The eyes (fore duteous) now converted are
> From his low tract and look another way.
> So thou, thyself outgoing in thy noon,
> Unlook'd on diest unless thou get a son.

Shakespeare's other obvious Pompey-reference is to Cicero's superlative praise, in support of the Lex Manilia which made Pompey 'absolute prince of all the Roman empire': 'in Pompey alone are all sums (*i.e.* perfections).'[1]

Admiring Prince True-love's hoard of perfections—the *all sums* of Pompey—his *sum of sums*, Shakespeare asks

> 4 7 Profitless usurer, why dost thou use
>   So great a sum of sums, yet canst not live?

And now with Hatcliffe-Pompey in mind, let us go back to the very time and place where we first discovered him as Prince.

---

[1] . . . *concedunt in uno Cn. Pompeio summa esse omnia. (De Imp. Pomp.* 17, 51.) In eulogy of the Landgrave of Hesse in 1596 as 'a most perfect Prince', Edward Monings wrote 'a man may say of him without flatterie, as Tullie did of Pompey, *unus in quo summa sunt omnia.*'

The time is Tuesday night, 16 January 1587/8; and the place the Hall of Gray's Inn. Here the Boy-Prince of Purpoole in state is feasting England's greatest lords at the high table. And after the table has been taken up, he entertains them with a comedy (followed by a Mask of six dancers) acted 'in the round' by the ingenious youths in front of the magnates, between the dais and the central fire.

Before we consider the audience, and the persons of the play, we find fascination in looking at the original document carrying the cast of this comedy. It is one of Lord Burghley's papers,[1] endorsed in his own hand. If the Lord Treasurer had not been careful enough to have preserved this programme of an amateur dramatic performance, we might never have learned the identity of Shakespeare's Friend. With this ephemeral-seeming scrap, Queen Elizabeth's greatest minister gives us the key which unlocks the poems of her greatest poet—four centuries after his birth. Possibly some day it may be taken out of its obscurity in the volume and placed on exhibition.

At the performance, then, Burghley—the most distinguished as well as one of the most ancient members of Gray's Inn—was evidently given this paper of the cast of the comedy, headed by his countryman *Hatclyff* as *Dominus de purpoole*. And in his well-known angular hand he endorsed it with the following memorandum:

xvi. Janv. 1587
The Names of yᵉ Jētillmē
of Grays In yᵗ playd ther
a Com̄edy
before yᵉ L. burghly L. Tr.
Er. of lec. L. stuard
Er. of warr
Erl. of ormōd
L. Grey of wiltō
&c

---

[1] B.M. MS. Lansdowne 55, art. 4, ff. 11, 12ᵛ.

This may be expanded in modern spelling—

16 January 1587/8
The Names of the Gentlemen of Gray's Inn that played there
a Comedy before
[William Cecil] the Lord Burghley, Lord Treasurer
[Robert Dudley] Earl of Leicester, Lord Steward
[Ambrose Dudley] Earl of Warwick, [Master of the Ordnance]
[Thomas Butler] Earl of Ormonde, [Lord Treasurer of Ireland]
[Arthur] Lord Grey of Wilton,
and others

As we have seen, further great lords would no doubt have been present, to be noted by Lord Burghley, had not the Spanish alarm sent them to sea and to the borders of England on active military service. But among Prince True-love's guests appeared his friend Shakespeare's own landlord, Ambrose Dudley, Earl of Warwick, Lord of the Manor of Stratford-upon-Avon.

And here is the cast Lord Burghley was given:

Dominus de purpoole	Hatclyff
The prologue:	:Ellis:
Hidaspis yᵉ sonn:	:Campion:
Manilius madd:	:Anderton:
Pvso:	:Farnley:
Lucius:	:Ashley:
Mummius old man	:Toppham:
Byrria parasite:	:Staverton:
Flamantia curtizan	:Sandfort:
Sʳ Delicato:	:Sʳ Peter Shackerly:
Catelyne:	:Rhodes:
Clodius:	:Stanfort:
Salust:	:Crwe:
Cato: ⎱ Censors	:Hutton:
Crassus: ⎰	:Williamson:
Scilla Dictator:	:Montfort:
Cinna: 1: consull	:Davenport:
2: consull	:Starkey:
Tribunus plebis:	:Smyth:

Melancholy:	: Campion:
Epilogue:	: Ellis

Masquers:

Rhodes:	Ross:
Luttrell:	Peniston:
Champnes:	Daye:

One has but to glance at this cast of characters to be astonished. For what can the first half have to do with the second—the stock old man, parasite, and courtesan of a Roman comedy with Cato the Censor and Sylla the Dictator? Percival Vivian remarks of it

Mr. Daniel . . . suggests that the cast involves a confusion of two plays, one on the model of the ordinary Terentine comedy, the other an historical drama, similar to Lodge's *Wounds of Civil War*, based upon Roman history. It will be noted, however, that the historical characters introduced are not all contemporary, and I am inclined to think that the play may really be one, and that it may have contained a review or procession of great Romans.[1]

Possibly; but in any such review Pompey would be included. And I question the procession. The great Romans could hardly be reduced to 'walking gentlemen'. And if they spoke, what did they speak about?

I put forward the suggestion that since Hatcliffe leads the list as Dominus de Purpoole and Pompey is not among the *dramatis personae*, their main topic may have been Young Pompey, the 'people's love'. Note the presence of Pompey's friend Cato and his enemy Crassus, and of Sylla, who greeted him as *Imperator*. The two Cinnas are there as well—which suggests a date about 87 B.C., when Pompey was nineteen: the age of Purpoole's young Prince. Someone with an expert knowledge of Roman history should look into this possibility more narrowly.

Two interesting points may be noted. Hatcliffe's friend the poet Thomas Campion doubles as 'Hidaspis ye sonn' and as 'Melancholy'; and between the two halves of the cast a modern

---

[1] *Campion's Works* (1909), xxxi.

character is shoved in—'Sr Delicato' (*i.e.* 'luxurious'), played by 'Sr Peter Shackerly'. This Shakerley, already a member of the Inn for more than ten years (his 'Sir' is ironical, since he was never knighted), had made himself a by-word in London for ridiculous strutting and vainglory.[1] Apparently he had only to 'come on' as something like himself to raise a laugh—and so was too valuable a property to be omitted.

So much for the Prince's own play in his palace. Of his London triumph, as he rode in state with his Pompey crest to dine with my Lord Mayor Sir George Bond, no record has as yet been found. A note of it may however still turn up, and might prove to be of great interest.

With *The Misfortunes of Arthur*, the play prepared by Purpoole as a climax to Prince True-love's reign, and performed at Greenwich before the Queen on Shrove Tuesday, 20 February 1587/8,[2] we are more fortunate. Not only have we the published play, written by the barrister Thomas Hughes, a Welshman from Cheshire, but also evidence that some of the speeches he wrote were cancelled and supplanted in performance by some written by others. In publishing, Hughes subjoins 'such speaches as were penned by others in lue of some of these hereafter following'. Thus we find William Fulbecke, for one (author of the Roman history we quoted apropos Pompey), giving the Senecan 'Revenge'-ghost Gorlois a more learned prologue and epilogue to speak than this sort of thing by Hughes:

> Ye Furies black
> And ugly shapes that howl in holes beneath;
> Thou Orcus dark and deep Avernus nook
> With duskish glens out-gnawn in gulfs below,
> Receive your ghastly charge, Duke Gorlois' ghost!
> Make room! I gladly, thus revenged, return.

---

[1] See Nashe (ed. McKerrow), 4.155.

[2] The published play gives the date as the 'twenty-eighth', certainly an error for 'twentieth'. To imagine that Queen Elizabeth would countenance a play followed by dancing in her house during the first week in Lent is absurd.

228

And the ingeniously symbolic dumb shows before the acts were
devised by such leaders as Christopher Yelverton (Treasurer,
1585), Francis Bacon (Bencher), John Lancaster, and Francis
Flower. The production was prepared under the direction of
Lancaster, Flower, and John Penruddock.

What moved their legal minds to study so ghastly a theme as
the working-out of 'Duke Gorlois' curse' to solace the Queen
with, we can only guess. Another curiosity is their choosing the
dismal death of Arthur at the hands of his treacherous nephew as
their climax. For their Prince's recent guest at Purpoole, the
ageing Earl of Leicester, less than three years earlier had been
repeatedly likened to Arthur (Champion of Christendom) in
pageantry shown before him in Leyden and The Hague.

We shall find more entertainment in reading the following notice
of the performance written by a dramatic critic. It has lain hitherto
unrecognized among the Sloane Manuscripts. Here the chief misfortune of Arthur is seen to be his treatment by this 'British Bard',
whose 'second Arthur' is rated as not worth publishing:

> O second Arthur, bred in brittishe brayne,
>   Well hath myne host him self a Prophet prov'd:
> For sure when first he sang thou camst again,
>   Cassandra-lyke, his threatnings few men mov'd;
>   Th' effect expounds—that Oracle so dark
>   Forshewed this Brittish Bards surpassing wark.
>
> Strang was thy birth in dede & Giant-lyke;
>   Much payns thy mother bidd, with paciens myld.   [endured
> One noosed the, an other made thy cheke—   [nosëd thee
>   And yet no doubt thow art but one mans child.
>   But who so wash'd thy face in printers inke,
>   Speek on the rest; I know well what I think.
>
> Resigne thy buskins, Sophocles the great—
>   Tread mortar now with thy disarmed shanks—
> For this mans brayne hath had a happier sweat,
>   Whereof the world doth conn him ample thanks.
>   Blush, Seneca, to see thy feathers loose
>   Pluck't from a Swann & sticked on a goose.

And yᵂ, suete gentlemen of Grayan name,
    Well was a solace to her highnes meant;
And all that passed from yᵂ deserv's good fame—
    Your mendments good, your acting excellent.
        But when your Spyks of Poesie be ripe,   [*ears of grain*
        Dance harvest home after a better pipe.[1]

In sum, the fatal blemish on the well-acted show, concludes
this reviewer, was the unhappy choice of author—that *goose*
(*Hughes*). Even the patchwork amendments by better pens rally-
ing round could not save it. We can agree that the sweet gentlemen of Grayan name should have shown more judgment. In
Shakespeare the player they could have found that better pipe.
But no. They must have Gentlemen and University Rhetoric;
and they deserved nothing better than the dreary 'Tragicall
notes' they got.

Even the memory of the Senecan gloom enwrapping Greenwich Palace must have been banished by the delightful Shrovetide revelling which followed, introduced by a Mask led by the
magnificent and all-graceful Prince, Will Hatcliffe. The Queen
had helped him and his *corps de ballet* to appear in splendour by
providing them some 'cloth of gold and other stuffe out of the
store' of her Office of Revels.[2]

Naturally in such a subject as the death-grapple of Mordred
and Arthur to satisfy the ghost of Gorlois howling for revenge,
there could be no trace of Pompey the Great. But when we find
Shakespeare tuning his better pipe to please his Prince's sweet
gentlemen of Grayan name, it is another story.

By many signs we all recognize *Love's Labour's Lost* as a
comedy composed not for the public theatre, but (like *Twelfth
Night*) for a courtly or select audience. And as with *Twelfth
Night*, everyone feels the presence of hits or jokes here, very

---

[1] B.M. MS. Sloane 4125, f. 395.
[2] Revels Charges, Greenwich Palace, Christmas-Shrovetide 1587–88:
'shewes ... the gent of Grayes Inne, on whome was ymployed dyvers
remnantes of cloth of gold & other stuffe out of the store'. B.M. MS. Lansdowne 59, f. 39.

diverting to its particular audience—and perhaps to us too, if we knew what that audience was. Some years ago I made a guess at it—the Christmas court of Richard Prince d'Amour or Love at the Middle Temple, as follows:

... we mark the topicality for a Court of a Prince of Love and his fellow gentlemen-scholars in the philosophy of the law, of a scene laid in the court of a prince whose book-mates and fellow-scholars have sworn to keep the statutes of their fellowship: to study and to see no women. Legal jests are thickly sown: 'intituled, nominated, or called,' 'taken with the manner,' and 'in manner and form following.'[1]

And from West's *Symboleography* I added the *Quis? . . . Quando? . . . Ubi? . . . Quid?* etc. of an indictment for felony, so deliciously hit off in Armado's letter—'The time When? About the sixth hour . . .' and so on, indicting the rational hind Costard of crime with the female Jaquenetta.

As a guess—except for date—this was respectably warm. *Love's Labour's Lost* was certainly written for the entertainment of an Inn of Court ruled by a Prince named Love. But our new knowledge reveals that all this evidence must be transferred to the rival Gray's Inn—ancient Purpoole, under Prince True-love, where it properly belongs, and where it fits like a glove to a hand.

For the date of performance, all the signs point to Christmas 1588/9. The recent visit of the 'invincible Armado' from tawny Spain, which left many travellers behind awaiting ransom, offers the best opportunity for relishing the lies of a refined traveller surnamed Armado. More importantly, the play's sonnets, and its wealth of echoes from the author's own Sonnets, together with the passage on the irresistible *black eyes*, mark it as inseparable from the period of these poems, 1588–89. And when we add Fleay's firm evidence from the play's style, and Baldwin's argument from its structure, both pointing to a very early date, the consenting testimonies carry conviction.

---

[1] *Shakespeare's Sonnets Dated* (1949), 54–55.

The title *Love's Labour's Lost*[1] plays on the Prince (Will Hatcliffe), True-love. Again, we recall that at Gray's Inn among the plans of life advocated for the Prince's glory or eternal fame, the second was Philosophy. At the play's very opening, this is the course which Shakespeare has the monarch choose for himself and his companions:

> *King.* Let fame, that all hunt after in their lives,
> Live regist'red upon our brazen tombs
> And then grace us, in the disgrace of death,
> When, spite of cormorant devouring Time,
> Th' endeavour of this present breath may buy
> That honour which shall bate his scythe's keen edge
> And make us heirs of all eternity.

This primary and peculiar feature at once identifies this play of Love Unrequited with the Kingdom of Purpoole under its Prince True-love. Further, the 'strange pastime' of its Mask of Muscovites or Russians not only connects it with the expedition in aid of the Tsar of Muscovy undertaken by the succeeding Prince, Helmet, but may well have inspired the episode.

This is much; but there must be more topicalities which we have not seen. In scrutinizing the lineaments of *Love's Labour's Lost*, we again apply Sherlock Holmes's rule, 'Singularity is almost always a clue.'

Singularity is certainly presented here, but not by solvable textual puzzles such as 'the charge-house', 'Chirra', ' "Veal," quoth the Dutchman', and 'I will whip about your infamy *vnum cita*', which still baffle the editor. When, however, we come to the show of the Nine Worthies prepared by Holofernes for entertainment in 'the posterior of the day', a genuine singularity confronts us.

We should remind ourselves first of all who the Nine Worthies were. This celebrated novenary was symmetrically made up of trios of heroes: three Biblical—Joshua, David, Judas Maccabeus;

---

[1] Shakespeare's title means *Love Unrequited*; as we find in a manuscript collection of Posies for Rings, 1596 (B.M. MS. Harl. 6910, f. 162ʳ): 'Love unlov'd, labor ill lost.' At the play's ending, Jack hath not Jill; the peccant lovers are all inexorably sentenced to 'twelve months' hard'.

three Classical—Hector, Alexander, Julius Caesar; and three Christian-romantic—Arthur, Charlemagne, and either Godfrey of Bulloigne or Guy of Warwick. Out of these Nine, the Worthies presented in the show are only three: Judas Maccabeus (Holofernes), Hector (Armado), and Alexander (Nathaniel).

Now without any explanation two additional characters are foisted in and blandly presented as if they were Worthies: *Hercules as a child* (Boy or *Mozo*, Moth), and *Pompey the Great* (Costard). Here is our singularity. As early as 1807 Francis Douce (*Illustrations of Shakespeare*) pointed out that no one had explained why Shakespeare dragged Hercules and Pompey in. A century and a half of study has been devoted to Shakespeare since Douce wrote, and still no one has explained why.

To the casual eye they seem singularly inappropriate. Hercules the demigod has less than no business in this select club of human heroes, yet here he is, and diminished to a child. And as for Pompey the Great, why should he, a non-Worthy, be hilariously played up as a target for jesting, while his conqueror, the genuine Worthy Caesar, is not even mentioned?

I am persuaded that the answer lies in the Saturnalian Christmas freedom of ridiculing the master—fully seen in *Twelfth Night*, with Master Controller Knollys presented for mirth as Malvolio or Mal-voglio.[1]

At Purpoole's Christmas, the master or Prince is Will Hatcliffe or True-love, identified as we have seen with Pompey the Great by his family crest, his Friendship and Love with 'Pompey's love', and his early triumphing, like Pompey, 'before, by age, he might'.[2] At the Roman Pompey's triumph the common soldiers

---

[1] See *The First Night of 'Twelfth Night'* (1954), 97–114.
[2] 'But though his freedome to upbraid, and chide
Him who Triúmph'd, were lawfull, it was ty'd
With this, that it might never reference have
Unto the Senate, who this triumph gave;
Men might at Pompey jeast, but they might not
At that authoritie, by which he got
Leave to Triúmph, before, by age, he might.'
Donne, *Obsequies to the Lord Harrington.*

233

had full licence to jest at the triumpher—just as Purpoole has at Christmas: a sort of *Sic transit gloria mundi*, to keep her Prince well reminded that he is mortal.

It is delightfully done. Shakespeare not only brings in a burlesqued Pompey as a Worthy—to point up the discomfortable fact that he is *not* one—but also gives the rôle to the brawny and only-too-commonly-human clown, Costard.

> *Costard.* I Pompey am.
> *Pompey surnam'd the Big—*
> *Dumain.* The *Great*.
> *Costard.* It is *Great*, sir.
> *Pompey surnam'd the Great;*
> *That oft in field*
> *With targe and shield*
> *Did make my foes to sweat.*

And when the great conqueror is aroused to denounce Hector-Armado, infamonizing him among the potentates, it is

> *Dumain.* Most rare Pompey!
> *Boyet.* Renowned Pompey!
> *Berowne.* Greater than Great! Great, great, great Pompey! Pompey the Huge!

So much for Pompey the Big, Pompey the Huge. Today he is still delicious, but at Purpoole under Prince True-love he was topical.

Now for the other non-Worthy. Why is Hercules lugged in? And especially, why is he diminished to a child? The answer again is, to make game of (Prince) Love.

> *Armado.* Comfort me, boy. What great men have been in love?
> *Moth.* Hercules, master.
> *Armado.* Most sweet Hercules!
> . . . is not Love a Hercules,
> Still climbing trees . . .?

234

Berowne has already pointed out what pitiful diminutives *Love* makes of the great—

> To see a king transformed to a gnat!
> To see great Hercules whipping a gig . . .

Accordingly, to show what a ridiculous job *Love* has made of that tremendous demigod,

> Great Hercules is presented by this imp.

But it may be asked Why especially *Hercules*, and not (say) the strong-jointed Samson, befooled by a love of a sea-water green complexion? The answer again is *True-love*. For the true-love knot was known as 'Hercules his knot'.[1] And when the imp came on—'His enter and exit shall be strangling a snake'—(Love makes Hercules strangle Prudence), I have little doubt that Hercules wreathed that convenient reptile into his own true-love knot, and held it up for all the Court of True-love to see.

In *Love's Labour's Lost*, then, we recapture the carefree, genial jollity of the Kingdom of Purpoole 'when the gown and cap is off, and the Lord of liberty reigns'.[2] The young Saturnalian Lord True-love brought back the early Golden Age, when

> youth call'd beauty forth to dance,
> And every grace was by . . .
> 'Twas always spring . . .
> The better acted world did move
> Upon the fixëd poles of truth and love; . . .
> Love the circumference was, and love the centre.[3]

And the Roman Saturnalia resembled the Greek Kronia; for as Dr Percy Simpson points out,[4] Kronos or Time 'was identified with Saturn, the mythical king of Italy', referring to Jonson's *Hymenæi* 696: 'Kronos—Saturne: who indeed with the Ancients,

---

[1] Browne, *Pseud. Ep.* V. xxi. 265, qu. *O.E.D.*
[2] Ben Jonson, dedicating *Every Man Out* . . . to the Inns of Court.
[3] Poole, *English Parnassus* (1657), 325–329.
[4] *Jonson*, 10.654.

was no other then *Time*.' In the dialogue of *Time Vindicated*, a
Twelfth Night merriment, Jonson describes the Lord of Misrule,
Saturn-Kronos-Time:

Fame. I come from *Saturne* . . . he' is *Time* it selfe, and his name
    KRONOS. . . .
Nose. A Fencer, and do's travell with a sith . . .
Eies.   Hath often been called from it [*i.e.* scything]
    To be their Lord of Misrule.
Nose. O, we shall have his *Saternalia*.
Eies. His dayes of feast, and libertie agen.

And we may add from Linche's translation of Cartari,[1] 'Other
would have him [Saturn] signifie Tyme, as that with his sythe he
should measure and proportionise the length of Time.'

Shakespeare's Boy-King of the Saturnalia is therefore not only
True-love, but also Kronos-Saturn or Time. And in the warning
of his hail-and-farewell Sonnet 126 this is the very figure in which
the poet sees his Lord of Liberty—as a Boy and as Time:

126

O thou, my lovely Boy, who in thy pow'r
Dost hold Time's fickle glass, his sickle hour . . .

Time's *fickle glass* is the hour-glass of man's allotted span—
variable, unpredictable;[2] and his *sickle hour* is that inevitable hour
when the Reaper cuts with 'the edge of doom'.

The form of this farewell 126 is distinct. Not the usual fourteen, but twelve lines in couplets, making the Three Fours which
represent the Three Fours of Hatcliffe's arms.

In this Envoy to the Prince, a final and summarizing identification of Shakespeare's Friend as the Boy-King of Misrule, Will
Hatcliffe is however recognized as Time only during the Saturnalia, when he realizes the Golden Age and controls Mutability.

---

[1] *The Fountaine of ancient Fiction* (1599), Dij.
[2] 'not within the hour-glasse of one mans life.' Bacon, *Advancement of
Learning*, qu. *O.E.D.*

And that is but an ideal thought, a poetic fiction, a waking dream.
The dream will evanesce. Youthful beauty, however idealized,
is natural: it must be surrendered.

O thou, my lovely Boy, who in thy pow'r
Dost hold Time's fickle glass, his sickle hour;
Who hast by waning grown, and therein show'st
Thy lovers withering as thy sweet self grow'st;

If Nature, sovereign mistress over wrack,
As thou goest onwards, still will pluck thee back,
She keeps thee to this purpose, that her skill
May time disgrace, and wretched minutes kill.

Yet fear her, O thou minion of her pleasure!
She may detain, but not still keep, her treasure;
Her audit, though delay'd, answer'd must be,
And her quietus is to render thee.

Reluctant Nature had to resign the poet's princely, graceful,
and comely Friend. Will's beauty faded. He died an old man,
having lived eleven years more than Shakespeare's fifty-two.
But I believe that as the True-loving Friend Constant in Adversity, Nicholas Hilliard the master-limner has preserved him before
our eyes in the delicate poetry of painting, ever young, fair, and
true: as Shakespeare drew him in his ever-living lines.

XI

BLACK EYES

SHE was a rare raven-haired beauty, with irresistible black eyes. And she played on the virginals entrancingly. She had acquired both a husband and a wide reputation as a harlot. 'She ties herself in marriage to one, that she may more freely stray out to many.' Although young Shakespeare well knew she deserved the abhorrence in which decent people held her, when she turned her charm upon him he found himself hopelessly bewitched. Only in the intervals of his mad passion could he see clearly enough to hate her—and himself. In these sonnets the young player-poet hands us his fever-chart; and every line seems to say 'I versify the truth; not poetize.'

Her seducing young Will Hatcliffe—thereby for a time alienating the true-loving friends—was but one of her foul deeds. 'A whore thinks herself excellent witty when she can practise disloyalty cunningly, and overreach her friends.' After reading Sonnets 40–42 and 127–152, we can all agree with J. M. Murry: 'She seems to have been a woman of the courtesan type, whose attraction for Shakespeare and whose hold on him was purely sensual.' As for the title 'Dark Lady'—unless we go to the gutter for the phrase 'a perfect lady'—it is too naïf to call this harlot, her prostituted body *the wide world's common place* or *the bay where all men ride*, a lady—an Elizabethan noblewoman. Even if born a gentlewoman, she had long forfeited all claim to respect.

How many weeks or months the wretched infatuation lasted is unknown. But we do know now that it was the aberration of unruly 'heyday in the blood'—of a youthful sinner, and *not* the crime of tamer middle age which a false Shakespeare chronology has made it. Its period can now be fixed, with the rest of the Sonnets, in 1588 or 1589, when Shakespeare was still but twenty-four or -five.

Everyone asks, Who was she? Although in the very nature of

238

the case this woman's identity is insignificant, for Shakespeare's honesty tells us all that anyone needs to know about her, human curiosity remains intense. What we *say* is, If we knew her name it might reveal something more about Shakespeare. But looked at objectively, what is it but this *holding back* from us of the name which makes us so passionate to know it? I should say that the prime value of a discovery of the name would lie in its discouraging effect on the airing of loose theories about Mary Fitton, Penelope Lady Rich, Mrs Davenant, and heaven knows whom besides—not to mention the silly identification of the noble unmarried Lady Rosaline of *Love's Labour's Lost* with this married drab. And to put a damper on that sort of gossip is worth some trouble.

Who is it holds her identity back? Certainly not Shakespeare. The whole tone of these sonnets shows that from his readers he is concealing it no more than he conceals the identity of his young Sovereign. Everybody knows that his Friend is Will Hatcliffe, just as everybody knows who the woman is—and thinks him a fool for becoming her '*slave and vassal wretch*'. Again it is that villain Time who is solely to blame for the 'mystery' surrounding this other associate of the poet's. The old rascal has given criticism a second spectre. George Sampson's 'embarrassing phantom' has a female companion—Mrs Jameson's 'veiled and nameless phantom'. We must understand Time to have supplied the veil—an article she had no use for—and removed her notorious name, which she needed for business purposes. And criticism would preserve her a Phantom Everlasting. Dowden concludes, 'We shall never discover the name of that woman.' Beeching declares of her, 'the sonnets supply no possible clue by which the particular person can be identified'. And Kittredge, 'She must remain a mystery.' Mackail tells us that to identify her is an impossibility, and that 'all the labour that has been spent upon it is pure waste'. His second remark is perhaps not far from the truth.

Before Shakespeare was properly consulted, we heard the same sad presages about the identity of his fair Friend. Yet all through the Sonnets the poet had described him as a King, and repeatedly identified him as Will. It was only a matter of taking Shakespeare at his word and looking about in Elizabethan London at the date of the Sonnets to be enabled to tap Will Hatcliffe on the shoulder. And having learned Will's surname, we now see his constant friend rehearsing its syllables throughout his poems, including those on the Woman:

41   7   *And when a woman woos, wHAT woman's son*
           Will sourly LEAVE her till she have prevail'd? HATLEAVE

145   13   *... from HATe away she threw,*
           And sav'd my LIFE saying not you   HATLIFE

147   5   *My reason, the physician to my love ...*
       7   HAT*h* LEF*t* me   HATLEF

On discovering Will's royal badge or agnomination *True-love*, we find that sweet belovëd name also everywhere. The allusions come crowding, thick and threefold.

This then we have found to be Shakespeare's way with his Love—the right fair White, of *comfort* or hope. His *modus operandi* should be the same with her colour'd ill—the Black, of *despair*. We are to scrutinize the epithets, figures, or topics he repeats, in the certainty that they contain clear allusions—which we have failed to recognize—to the Woman's name.

To begin with, although her hair is black, her eyes are black, and her *brows are raven black*, Shakespeare curiously enough can swear that she is *bright*:

147   13   *For I have sworn thee fair, and thought thee bright,*
       14   *Who art as black as hell, as dark as night.*

150   3   *To make me give the lie to my true sight*
       4   *And swear that brightness doth not grace the day*
           [*sc.* But graces thee who art as dark as night.]

Now, perhaps my ears are over-suspicious in detecting 'particularity' in *bright*. But in dealing with Shakespeare I have learned at least to test what they pick up before discarding it. A 'black' woman may yet be 'bright' *because of her name.* Turning up Camden's *Remains* for 'Christian Names of Women', we find '*Lucia,* Lat. Lightsome, Bright.' Could the woman's name be Lucia, Lucy, Luce? It is worth looking into.

'Bright' and 'brightness' certainly carried *Lucy* to the Elizabethan reader: 'That same other Damzell, Lucy bright'; '*For Lucy's sake, that lady bright . . . As ever man beheld with eye' : 'To Sir Thomas Lucy.* Bright spark of wit and courage';[1] (To Lucy, Countess of Bedford) 'LUCY, you brightness of our sphere'; 'LUCY the bright'.[2]

Shakespeare adds the apparent paradox: this 'bright' woman is in fact *as dark as night.* Which night was Lucy's? Consult the Calendar, Old Style. We find Lucy *on the darkest night of the whole year*: December 13, the winter solstice—'Lucy bright, the shortest day and longest night'. And John Donne writes 'A Nocturnall upon S. Lucies Day'—*Tis the yeares midnight. Lucy* as the name of the Bright-Dark Woman is clearly more than a possibility, as we look further into Shakespeare's topics.

The next one needs no searching for. It so hunts and haunts the reader that there is no escaping it: *eyes, seeing, sight, blind, blindness, eyes corrupt* (diseased) with *plague.*

127	10	*Her eyes so suited*
132	1	*Thine eyes I love*
	9	*those two mourning eyes*
133	5	*thy cruel eye*
139	3	*Wound me not with thine eye*
	6	*forbear to glance thine eye aside*
140	14	*Bear thine eyes straight*
141	1	*I do not love thee with mine eyes*
142	10	*Whom thine eyes woo*
149	12	*Commanded by the motion of thine eyes*
150	3	*To make me give the lie to my true sight*
152	13	*more perjur'd eye*

[1] Spenser, *F.Q.* 5.4.9; Beaumont, *Knight . . . Pestle* 2.8; J. Davies of Hereford, *Scourge of Folly*, Epigr. 103.

[2] Jonson, *Epigr.* 94; *The Forest,* 12.66.

153	9	*my mistress' eye*
136	2	*Swear to thy blind soul*
149	14	*Those that can see, thou lov'st, and I am blind*
152	11	*And, to enlighten thee, gave eyes to blindness,*
	12	*Or made them swear against the thing they see*

153 9 *my mistress' eye*
14 *my mistress' eyes*
136 2 *Swear to thy blind soul*
149 14 *Those that can see, thou lov'st, and I am blind*
152 11 *And, to enlighten thee, gave eyes to blindness,*
12 *Or made them swear against the thing they see*

148

O me, what eyes hath Love put in my head,
Which have no correspondence with true sight!
Or, if they have, where is my judgment fled
That censures falsely what they see aright?
If that be fair whereon my false eyes dote,
What means the world to say it is not so?
If it be not, then love doth well denote
Love's eye is not so true as all men's no.   [eye—'ay' versus *no*
How can it? O, how can Love's eye be true,
That is so vex'd with watching and with tears?
No marvel then though I mistake my view:
The sun itself sees not till heaven clears.
  O cunning Love! with tears thou keep'st me blind,
  Lest eyes well-seeing thy foul faults should find.

137

Thou blind fool, Love, what dost thou to mine eyes
That they behold, and see not what they see?
They know what beauty is, see where it lies,
Yet what the best is take the worst to be.
If eyes, corrupt by over-partial looks,
Be anchor'd in the bay where all men ride,
Why of eyes' falsehood hast thou forgëd hooks,
Whereto the judgment of my heart is tied?
Why should my heart think that a several plot
Which my heart knows the wide world's common place?
Or mine eyes seeing this, say this is not,
To put fair truth upon so foul a face?
  In things right true my heart and eyes have erred,
  And to this false plague are they now transferred.[1]

---

[1] The closing line is glossed by C. K. Pooler, 'are given over to a disease which renders them incapable of distinguishing'.

Has all this—*eyes, seeing, bear thine eyes, blind, eyes corrupt* or diseased—something especially to do with *Lucy*? It would seem so, when we find an ode in Italian to Lucy, Countess of Bedford, entitled *The Eyes*,[1] and Londoners of 1566 reading that 'to heale their eies, these of our time have Saint *Lucie*'.[2]

But let the books of reference tell the story of the noble virgin of Syracuse, martyred A.D. 303:

Lucia, St. Lucy . . . she plucked out her eyes when they threatened to become a snare to her lover . . . they were afterwards restored to her more beautiful than before. She is regarded as the special patroness of those who suffer from diseases of the eyes.[3]

St. Lucy (December 13) . . . is invoked by persons afflicted with diseases of the eyes, because, rather than accept the hand in marriage of a lover who desired her for the sake of her beautiful eyes, she plucked them out and sent them to him. . . . Nevertheless . . . her sight was restored to her the next day. . . . In Christian Art she is generally represented as bearing a dish or platter with two eyes on it.[4]

St. Lucy. Many paintings represent her bearing her eyes in her hand or on a salver. Some artists have even represented her blind.[5]

Bear thine eyes straight . . . Swear to thy blind soul . . . to en-lighten thee, gave eyes to blindness . . . eyes, corrupt . . . Lucy bearing her eyes; *Lucy* blind, enlightened by being given eyes even more beautiful; *Lucy* invoked by men plagued with diseased eyes—beyond question this cluster is the connotation of these sonnets. Joined with *Lucy bright*, in my mind it leaves no room

---

[1] Francesco Peretto, *Gli Occhi. Oda. All'illust. Contessa Lucia Bedford.* Londra 1616.

[2] C. A. Curio, *Pasquine in a traunce*, tr. W. P[histon] (1566), 48.

[3] Paget Toynbee, *Dictionary of . . . Dante* (1898), 343.

[4] Leopold Wagner, *Manners, Customs, and Observances* (1894), 192.

[5] C. Cahier, *Caractéristiques des saints dans l'art populaire* (1867), 1.105. And cf. F. C. Husenbeth, *Emblems of Saints* (1882), 133: (Paintings)

St. Lucy	Eyes in a dish.	Colonna Palace, Rome, Titian.
St. Lucy	Eyes in a dish.	Campidoglio, Rome, N. Cansoni.
St. Lucy	Eyes on a book.	Rood Screen, Eye, Suffolk.
St. Lucy	Presenting her eyes on a dish to the B.V.M.	Turin Gallery, G. A. Razzi.

for doubt that the name Shakespeare is playing upon here, the name of the Bright-Dark Woman, is Lucy or Luce.

We have thus arrived at a beautiful harlot, *black as hell*, notorious in 1588 or 1589, named Lucy or Luce. This at once takes our minds five or six years onward to the *Gesta Grayorum*—the chronicle of Henry Prince of Purpoole's reign 1594/5, and to the unsavoury list of the Prince's feodaries, in which we read of three bawds who hold 'Signiories, Lordships, &c.':

Marotto Maquarillo de Holborn holdeth the manors of *High* and *Nether Holborn* by cornage in *capite* . . .
Lucy Negro, Abbess *de Clerkenwell*, holdeth the nunnery of *Clerkenwell* . . . by night-service in *Cauda*, and to find a choir of nuns . . .
Ruffiano de St. Giles's holdeth the town of *St. Giles's* by cornage in *Cauda* . . .

By this time, then, some five or six years after the Sonnets, Black Lucy or Luce has set up as the 'madam' of a house in Clerkenwell.

'Such beginning, such an end:' This Ile not applaud,
For Luce did like a whore begin, but ended like a bawd.[1]

To Professor G. B. Harrison[2] belongs the credit of first suspecting the truth: 'This "*Lucy Negro* (Abbess *de Clerkenwell*)" I would very tentatively identify as the Dark Lady'—and also the discredit of believing Shakespeare's fair enslaver a blackamoor. Under so dark a misapprehension his 'very tentatively' is commendable, and he followed his negress no farther. Black Luce was of course no more an Ethiop than the Black Prince[3] and

---

[1] Davies of Hereford, *Scourge of Folly* (1611), 'Upon English Proverbes', No. 281.
[2] *Shakespeare under Elizabeth* (1933), 310.
[3] *Edw. III* (apostrophizing his son, the Black Prince):

Thy mother is but blacke, and thou, like her,
Dost put it in my minde how foule she is.   *Edw. III* 2.2.109–110.

'the blacke man is ment to be Sir Walter Rawley.' Examination of one Flood, 15 Mar. 1586/7.   Chetham Soc. XXV (1851).

Note signed by Anderson, L.C.J.: 'Henry Roll off Stevenson the best off yᵗ nayme in the Countie off Devon a little black gent.'

244

Black Tom Wentworth (Lord Strafford) were, or a professional successor of Black Luce's own across the Thames: 'Neer to black *Madges* in the *Paris Garden*.'[1]

In folk-physiology, the 'black' were held to be 'proud'—which is to say *lustful*—a light condition in a beauty dark.

'At a *Pale* man draw thy knife; From a *Blacke* man keepe thy wife.... *The* pale *peevish*, *The* blacke *lusty*.'[2]

'A mayden blacke is always proud.'[3]

The proverb was verified in Black Luce. Shakespeare testifies that she wooed his Friend *with her foul pride*, and the satirical epitaph describes her 'leacherous as any Sparrow'.[4]

Her name was Morgan. She was universally known by it, and not by her husband's name, Parker. Although his baptismal name and the date of the marriage are still to find, the date must have been before 1588. I have been at some pains to collect facts and reports about Luce Morgan, in search especially of her earlier life, before she grew common and infamous. My reward is the discovery of a series of documents indicating that some years before she charmed Shakespeare, she had first charmed Queen Elizabeth.

Study of the very extensive unpublished records of the Queen's Household will bring one sooner or later upon most of the Elizabethans of note. Among these, the Accounts of the Great Wardrobe throw fascinating light upon a few young ladies and

---

John Manningham describes the Puritan preacher Henoch Clapham: 'one Clappam, a blacke fellowe, with a sower looke . . .'

In Dryden's *Troilus and Cressida* 1.2 we have:

Enter Helenus.

Cressi. Who's that black man Uncle?

Of the woman Mrs Pepys thought the handsomest in England, Mr Pepys writes, 'indeed she is a pretty black woman, her name Mrs. Horsely.' And of Mrs Tite's daughters, 'the younger, a pretty black girl . . .'

[1] E. Gayton, *Wil Bagnal's Ghost* (1655), 20.
[2] W. B[?asse] & E. P., *A Helpe to Discourse* (1621), 182.
[3] Bodl. MS. Don. d. 58, f. 14.
[4] *'On Luce Morgan a Common-Whore.' Wit and Drollery* (1656), 19.

gentlewomen of her Court who from time to time enjoyed the Queen's particular favour. This royal favour was shown by occasional gifts of dresses—very rich ones for noble young ladies, and less expensive ones for young gentlewomen, most of whom served the Queen intimately as Ladies or Gentlewomen of the Bedchamber or the Privy Chamber.[1] Others were Maids of Honour, and still others, daughters of officers of her Household.

Now we learn that one of the Queen's familiar Gentlewomen was Luce Morgan. In the two years between March 1579 and March 1581 we find her as one of the very few distinguished by a gift from Queen Elizabeth; and she was thus favoured three separate times:

Warrants to the Great Wardrobe, 1568–1589.

(For the half-year March–September 1579:)

Item for Eleven yards of silk grograin given by our Commandment to Luce Morgan to make her a Gown of our great wardrobe.

(For the half-year September 1579–March 1580:)

Item for three yards [and a] quarter of velvet by us given to guard a gown for Luce Morgan (at 28 shillings a yard, 4 pounds 11 shillings).

(For the half-year September 1580–March 1581:)

Item for six yards of russet Satin and two yards of black velvet by us given to Luce Morgan.[2]

The discerning eye will note how choicely russet satin trimmed with black velvet suited her black eyes and hair.

The last trace I have found of her at Court, nearly a year after this, is contained in Sir Thomas Heneage's office book,[3] recording

---

[1] See B.M. MS. Lansd. 59, f. 43; Chambers, *Eliz. Stage*, 1.44.
[2] B.M. MS. Egerton 2806, ff. 148, 152ᵛ, 167ᵛ. And P.R.O., L.C. 5/35/178, 204, 245; L.C. 9/71/9. Spelling modernized.
[3] Dated 12 Febr. 1581/2. B.M. MS. Harl. 1644, f. 78ᵛ.

Gentlewomen

Mrs Blanch Appereys [Parry's] servant	6s 8d
Mrs Haynes servant	6s 8d
Mrs Morgans servant	6s 8d
The Queens Majestys dwarfs servant	6s 8d

The heading means that the four persons whose servants here received as a reward a gold noble each or its equivalent were Gentlewomen of the Bedchamber or the Privy Chamber; and along with Mistress Blanche Parry, Mistress Haynes, and (Mistress Thomasina de Paris) the Queen's dwarf, is included Mistress Morgan.[1]

Here, then, for a period of some three years, during the time of Anjou's courtship, Luce Morgan enjoys intimate association with Queen Elizabeth, constant attendance upon her, and for the major part of it, the great Queen's particular favour.

Two of the qualities which gained her that favour Shakespeare puts beyond question. Beauty, first, is the best recommendation, and Queen Elizabeth was very fond of handsome young women, later making Mary Fitton her favourite until the girl foolishly ruined herself. Next, of all accomplishments the Queen best loved music and dancing. Among her men-servants no one enjoyed greater intimacy and influence than the musician Ferdinando Heyborne *alias* Richardson, a Groom of the Privy Chamber, who played to her on the virginals. Her constant call for music brought him so close to the Queen that those who wanted something of her were advised to 'see Master Ferdinando'.

But there was inevitably much time during which even Master Ferdinando was not admitted—when the Queen depended for solace and distraction upon the talents of her women. Here

---

[1] Luce Morgan, the Queen's unmarried gentlewoman, is not to be confused with a later 'Mrs. Morgan' who first appears six years after this, in the New Year's Gift Roll of 1587/8. The latter was an older woman, the wife of Hugh Morgan the Apothecary royal, who on his appointment 15 July 1583 was sixty-six years of age.

Mistress Morgan would score. Even six or eight years later, when having plunged down the social scale she was well on her way from 'her Highness's Mistress Morgan' to 'that drab Black Luce', she was still often at her instrument:

> 128 *How oft, when thou, my music, music play'st*
> *Upon that blessèd wood whose motion sounds*
> *With thy sweet fingers when thou gently sway'st*
> *The wiry concord . . .*

Of her dancing Shakespeare says nothing, but one could hardly gain the Queen's favour without excelling in it. The date of her birth we do not know; but line 9 in the 1599 form of Sonnet 138, where Will and Luce outface each other with lies—*But wherefore says my love that she is young?*—indicates her as noticeably older than her lover, that 'untutor'd' youth. If we should conjecture her as nineteen in 1579, she would be four years older than Shakespeare, twenty-eight and -nine in the sonnet-years 1588–89.

Luce Morgan was undoubtedly a gentlewoman born, and in fancying her early training we may compare the account[1] Greene gives of an English courtesan, born of honest and wealthy parents about threescore miles from London:

My selfe am an instance, who after I grew to be sixe yeeres olde, was sette to Schoole, where I profited so much that I writ and read excellently well, playd upon the virginals, Lute and Cytron, and could sing prick-song at the first sight: in so much, as by that time I was twelve yeeres olde, I was holden for the most faire, and best qualitied young girle in all that Countrey, but with this, bewailed of my wel-wishers, in that my parents suffered me to be so wanton.

Queen Elizabeth well knew the instant temptations and dangers the women faced—despite her vigilance and punishments —in what Sir William Knollys calls 'the wolfish cruelty and fox-

---

[1] *A disputation betweene a hee conny-catcher and a shee conny-catcher* (1592), 44.

like subtlety of the tame beasts' of the Court, the scores of men tirelessly intent on debauching them.

> For there you shall be woo'd in other kinds
> Than yet your years have known;
> The chiefest men will seem to throw themselves
> As vassals at your service, kiss your hand . . .
> And they will praise your virtues; beware that!
> The only way to turn a woman whore
> Is to commend her chastity.[1]

Her women could not have lacked plenty of warning, both from her precepts and from examples immediately under their eyes. In 1579, during Luce Morgan's employment with the Queen, everybody at Court was reading John Lyly's best-seller *Euphues*, detailing the pitiful story of Lucilla, courtier turned courtesan, written by a man with an intimate knowledge of the Court's character:

Euphues to Philautus, Touching the deathe of Lucilla.

. . . thou seemest to take more thought for the losse of an harlot, then the life of an honest woman. . . . But where thou arte in the courte, there is more regard of beautie then honestie. . . . The court may as wel nourish vertuous Matrones as the lewde Minion. . . . I would have him ende as *Lucilla* began: without vyce, and not beginne as she ended, without honestie.

Some day we may learn when and how Mistress Morgan was banished from Queen Elizabeth's side. I am not writing another romancing biography of Shakespeare, and so far no trace of her has been found between Sir Thomas Heneage's note of 12 February 1581/2 and Shakespeare's record of 1588 or 1589. Her story is no uncommon one. In 1598 Greene is supplemented by John Dickinson's similar tale of the fall of 'The faire Valeria';[2]

---

[1] Beaumont, *The Woman-Hater* 1.3.
[2] *Greene in Conceipt.*

and John Aubrey tells of the actual Elizabeth Broughton, of an ancient Herefordshire family:

> She was a most exquisite beautie, as finely shaped as nature could frame; and had a delicate witt ... Richard, earle of Dorset, kept her. ... At last she grew common and infamous, and gott the pox, of which she died.

The milder venereal disease is more than hinted at by Shakespeare about 1589:

> 144   14   *Till my bad angel fire my good one out.*

And by 1595 Thomas Lodge (*A Figge for Momus*) reports the worse one: 'For I knew well, he had the poxe by *Luce*.'

We have seen Shakespeare's play on the woman's given name *Lucy*. Remembering the frequency of *Hat live*, can we believe that he neglected *Morgan*? For with English versifiers dealing in names embodying *Mor-*, the tendency to play upon them appears ingrained. When we read in Francis Davison's poem 'Pure and Endless'—on sending a ring to his love—the lines

> Shall make *more* precious, when you shall it wear ...
> Doth it the purer grow the *more* 'tis tried? ...
> That whereas gold, the *more* 'tis purified ...
> My love doth grow *more* pure by your *more* trying ...

it is safe to say that her name was not Cholmondeley. Similarly with the great Sir Thomas:

> When More two years had Chancellor been
> No *more* suits did remain;
> The same shall never *more* be seen
> Till More be there again.[1]

Also with the distinguished composer:

> Morley! would any try whither MORe LYeth[2]

---

[1] *Notes and Queries*, 1.10.393.
[2] Verses to Thomas Morley's *Madrigalls* ... 1594.

And in verses on John Morgan, who in January 1579/80 killed George Turberville's father in a brawl:

Ha misard [miserable wretch] Morgan *more then* madd . . .[1]

Now to look again at the sonnets on Luce Morgan:

40	2	*What hast thou then* more than *thou hadst before* . . .
	4	*All mine was thine before thou hadst this* more:
	5	Then *if for my love*
127	10	*Her eyes* . . . mourners *seem*
	13	*Yet so they* mourn
128	12	*Making dead wood* more *blest* than *living lips*
130	2	*Coral is far* more *red* than *her lips* . . .
	7	. . . *there is* more *delight*
	8	Than *in the breath* . . .
	10	. . . *a far* more *pleasing sound*
132	3	. . . *loving* mourners *be*
	5	. . . morning *sun*
	9	. . . *two* mourning *eyes*
	11	*To* mourn *for me, since* mourning *doth thee grace*
134	2	*And I myself am* mortgag'd[2] *to thy will*
135	3	More than *enough am I*
	12	. . . *to make thy large will* more.
139	7	. . . *thy might*
		Is more than *my o'erpress'd defense can bide*
147	10	*And frantic mad with ever*-more *unrest*
150	9	. . . *to make me love thee* more
	10	*The* more *I hear and see just cause of hate?* . . .
	14	More *worthy I to be belov'd of thee.*

---

[1] Pr. Norma H. Hodgson, *Modern Language Review* 33.520.

[2] In the Quarto, written 'morgag'd'. Note that this is the unique appearance of the word in all Shakespeare's works. He cannot do without it here, for it brings him within one letter of Black Luce's name.

This should be enough, but I am tempted to see *more than* this
—that is to say, some play upon the *meaning* of the Welsh name
Morgan. Referring again to Camden, we get '*Morgan*. Brit. . . .
The same with Pelagius, that is, Sea-man . . . and Mor signifies
the Sea among the Welsh.'[1] So Shakespeare compares Luce
Morgan with *the sea*, made *more*:

135   9   The sea, *all water, yet receives rain still,*
And in abundance addeth to his store;
So thou, being rich in will, add to thy will
One will of mine, to make thy large will more.

And he further calls her

137   6   . . . the bay *where all men ride* . . .

If anyone should go still farther, and find the Queen of the
land of Gore, Morgan le Fay, and her powerful 'negromantic' arts
in Luce Morgan's black eyes, and Morgan's stronghold *La Belle
Regard* in Luce Morgan's *pretty looks*, I shall not be the first to
quarrel with him:

133   9   *Prison my heart in thy steel bosom's ward*

139   4   *Use power with power and slay me not by art*
     10   *Her pretty looks have been my enemies*

150   1   *O, from what pow'r hast thou this pow'rful might* . . .

The rest of Black Luce's story mingles the sordid with the
pitiful. As reported in the *Gesta Grayorum*, the house she set up
was in Clerkenwell: more exactly, in St John Street. And not
without competition, for Luce had a notable rival in Elizabeth
Holland, trading near by in Islington. In the spring of 1595 we
hear in Star Chamber of a young gentleman from Somerset,
Sylvester Sedborough, who came up to London and fell into
roguish company. 'Then they carried him from daye to daye to
lewde and infamous houses, as namely Blacke Luce her house in

---

[1] Cf. James Howell, *Familiar Letters* (ed. Jacobs, p. 53): 'that Arch-
Heretick was called *Pelagius à Pelago*, his Name being *Morgan*.'

or neere London, M^ris Hollandes house at Islington' and else-where.[1]

A few months later, 'Elizabeth Holland of Islington, widow' was indicted in the Court of Queen's Bench of keeping 'a common howse of bawdrye'. She pleaded not guilty, and a day was set for trial, but I have not found any record that it took place.[2]

In the autumn of the year following, 1596, professional rivalry grew to a quarrel. Had Mistress Holland been luring away some of Black Luce's staff? At any rate, Bess Holland went before a justice of the Queen's Bench and 'swore the peace' against Henry Savadge, Hosaia his wife, Luce Morgan, Anne Scott, and John Kelly, for fear of her life, etc.[3] This doubtless annoyed them, but Elizabeth Holland's triumph was brief; for in this same Michael-mas term she was again indicted of the crime of brothel-keeping. On her trial at Middlesex Sessions 16 February 1596/7, she now pleaded guilty. Her sentence ran,

she shalbe put into a carte at Newgate and be carted with a paper on her hed shewing her offence, from thence to Smythfeilde, from thence to her howse, from thence to Cornehill, from thence to the Standerd in Cheepe, from thence to Bridewell, and all the waye basons to be runge before her, at Bridewell to be punished, and from thence to be broughte to Newgate, there to remaine untill she have payed a fyne of xl^li and put in sewerties for the same, and to be bounde to her good behaviour.[4]

Chapman's *An Humorous Day's Mirth* (probably acted 11 May 1597) has a tribute to Black Luce's eminent command in her profession:

Why, he was taken learning tricks at old Lucilla's house, the muster-mistress of all the smock-tearers in Paris ... [properly so called] for she hath them all trained up before her.

---

[1] Sta. Cha. 5/S61/21.
[2] K.B. 27/1335/Crown 15. Michaelmas 1595.
[3] K.B. 29/234, Mich. 1596.
[4] Middlesex Sessions Rolls (ed. J. C. Jeaffreson), 1.234.

And Heywood in his *1 Edward IV* (about 1599) gives his gallows-bird Spicing a gallant speech before being turned off the ladder:

Commend me to blacke *Luce*, bouncing *Besse*, & lusty *Kate*, and the other pretty morsels of mans flesh. Farewell Pink and Pinnesse, Flibote and Carvell, *Turnebull* and *Spittle*, I die like a man.

Bouncing Bess is either Mistress Holland or Bess Lister, and lusty Kate the well-known Kate Arden.

Black Luce must have enjoyed 'influence', for until 1600 (so far as I have found) she eluded punishment. Bridewell, however, had long been appointed as a house of correction 'for the Vagabond, ydle Strumpet, and unthrift'. The guardians of London's morals arrested her, and on 15 January 1599/1600 the Court of Aldermen passed sentence:

Item yt is ordered that Luce Morgan alias Parker for that she is a notorious and lewde woman of her bodye and otherwise of evill conversacion shalbe presentlie committed to Brydewell there to be sett to worke till she shall become bounde with good & sufficient sureties for her good behaviour during her naturall lief.[1]

Whether Luce also was received at Bridewell with the usual cruel initial punishment of the four-lashed and knotted whip is not revealed. But without a doubt she laboured for a time, dressed in the coarse blue gown and canvas coif, beating hemp with the delicate fingers which had so often played for Queen Elizabeth, and which Shakespeare had worshipped.

She seems at least to have escaped the terrible 'carting' through the streets, exposed to the missiles and blows of the merciless mob—'stinking Fish, Such as they beat Bawds with when they are Carted'. How long a term she served is not yet known, but Philip Gawdy's letter of December 1600 seems to see her still there:

There is heavy news out of Bridewell, for Mall Newberry and Mall Digby have been carted three days together, when one of them had

---

[1] Aldermen's Court Repertories No. 25, p. 24.

like to have been killed with a blow of a stone upon her forehead. . . .
Luce Morgan lives in reasonable discredit still, but yet she keeps herself from coaching or carting.[1]

For what it is worth, the evidence of the Lay Subsidy Roll dated 24 September 1600 shows 'Luce Morgan' in St John Street, assessed on 'Goods iij^{li}, with an *oneratur* marked against her name as 'not paid'.[2] Perhaps she simply defaulted, but more probably she was still in Bridewell. Bawds did not court trouble by defaulting in payment of taxes.

She was not yet to suffer the common fate—bawds 'live well and die well, for they live in Clerkenwell and die in Bridewell'— and soon enough she was back in Clerkenwell, 'traded in lust and gainful brothelry'. There is nothing new to be gleaned from the various references to Black Luce and the 'merry' squibs written on her in subsequent years,[3] including that of Barnabe Barnes's *Devil's Charter*, printed 1607:

I coniure thee by *Negra Luciaes* name.

Very possibly, like Lyly's '*Lucilla* . . . ended [died] without honestie', we are to take John Davies of Hereford's 'Luce . . . ended like a bawd' literally, and see her dead before 8 October 1610, perhaps even before the *Sonnets* were published in 1609. From the lewd epitaph printed 1656 no date can be gathered. Scurrility apart, it simply relates that she turned Roman Catholic, and died diseased.

---

[1] B.M. MS. Egerton 2804, f. 133^v. Spelling modernized.
[2] E 179/142/234.
[3] John Weever, *Epigrammes*, 1599 (ed. McKerrow, p. 73); Manningham's Diary (29 March 1602), B.M. MS. Harl. 5353, f. 1; Bodl. MS. Ashm. 38, f. 203; I. M., *Newe Metamorphosis* (MS. Addl. 14824), i, f. 23^v; John Davies of Hereford, *Scourge of Folly* (1611), 'Upon English Proverbes' No. 380; *Jonson* (ed. Simpson), viii. 608–609; xi. 257.

X

SPIRIT AND GHOST

THE major 'monster and thing indigest' which criticism has saddled us with is a stolid effigy of the Mercury-quick Shakespeare in ponderous plaster, labelled 'Mentally-retarded sonneteer, at least seven years slower than the average'. Grovelling under the weight of that enormity, and tethered to the middle 1590s, *after* Marlowe's death in 1593, students have been instructed to discover Shakespeare's successful Rival, that *better spirit* sped by *the proud full sail of his great verse*—the poet *by spirits taught to write above a mortal pitch*—in (God bless us) little Barnabe Barnes; or at most not to look any higher than the philosophical George Chapman with his *Shadow of Night* and *Ovid's Banquet*. Should any dare to doubt, they can be silenced with Psychology: 'Shakespeare's backwardness made him envy his inferiors, such as Barnes or Chapman.' Unanswerable.

Before that plaster effigy was imposed, however, it was plain to the most cursory eye that the poet here described could only be one man: the sole contemporary of Shakespeare's who surpassed him in reputation and popularity, Christopher Marlowe.[1]

In Sonnet 80 the Rival Poet is the *better spirit* who *spends all his might*. What Elizabethan poet of whom Shakespeare could feel envious wrote in the style described in Wilson's *Arte of Rhetorique* as 'the *great* or *mightie* kinde, when we use *great* wordes, or vehement figures'? Who but Marlowe of the '*mighty line*' and *elati furoris*, of proud poetical fury? Who wrote *Above a mortal pitch*? Who but the spirit bred of Merlin's race, maker of the sky-surmounting Tamburlaine and Faustus the necromant? Whose insolent verse, like a booming privateer, had its *proud full*

---

[1] The identification of the Rival Poet as Marlowe has stood in print for more than a century, ever since Robert Cartwright's edition of the Sonnets, 1859. The two paragraphs following I published in 1951.

sail bellied by the happy gale of popularity? Whose but Marlowe's,

> His stretchëd sails filled with the breath of men
> That through the world

admire his *Tamburlaine?* The year 1589 rapt English minds with the glorious thought of precious prizes won at sea. For in that one year their privateers brought in no fewer than ninety-one Spanish prizes: making it the moment *par excellence* for Shakespeare's metaphor

> *the proud full sail of his great verse,*
> *Bound for the prize of all-too-precious you . . .*

Nothing in the world but the imaginary tardiness of the Sonnets could have extracted a single vote for any poet but Marlowe. And when the true date is seen to be about 1589, we can only wonder that what has so long stood between the eye of criticism and the obvious is nothing more substantial than an artificial fog of fancy about a couple of Elizabethan earls.

The fact that Marlowe is obviously the Rival Poet—the other one of the *both* in

> 83 13 *There lives more life in one of your fair eyes*
> 14 *Than both your Poets can in praise devise . . .*

makes a close study of what Shakespeare has to say of him—and others—about 1589 a matter of importance: and we begin with Sonnet 78.

78

> *So oft have I invok'd thee for my Muse*
> *And found such fair assistance in my verse*
> *As every Alien pen hath got my use*
> *And under thee their poesy disperse.*
> *Thine eyes, that taught the dumb on high to sing*
> *And heavy ignorance aloft to fly,*
> *Have added feathers to the learned's wing,*
> *And given grace a double Majesty.*

Yet be most proud of that which I compile,
Whose influence is thine, and born of thee.
In others' works thou dost but mend the style,
And Arts with thy sweet graces gracèd be.
But thou art all my art, and dost advance
As high as learning my rude ignorance.

Before coming to the Rival Poet Marlowe, however, Shakespeare in his first quatrain mentions some other writer or writers. For in the third line the eye is arrested by the extremely rare epithet *Alien*, capitalized and italicized in the text, which recalls Portia's 'It is enacted in the laws of Venice, If it be proved against an alien . . .' The first sense carried to any Elizabethan reader here would not be 'pens belonging to others', but *the pen of every foreigner* or *every foreign-born versifier*. We can be sure that if Shakespeare did *not* mean to imply something of this (but only 'versifiers outside the circle of our friendship'), he would have avoided the statutory term *Alien*. The question therefore puts itself, Was there in 1588 or 1589 an English poet or sonneteer recognizable as an *Alien*?

The answer is supplied by the appearance in a list of 1581 of 'Strangers that goe not to Churche' of the name

Thomas Watson yom'   Busshoppes gate   St Hellens[1]

And again, in a list dated 26 May 1590 of 'Frenchmen dwelling in London', the name *Thomas Watson*.[2]

We gather from this that Watson (who speaks of England as *patria*, and whose father seems to have been a Worcestershireman) had been born in France, where as we know he spent many years. Also that at least up to 1590 he had not yet received the denization or been naturalized by the Private Act of Parliament[3] required

---

[1] 1581, 24 June. B.M. MS. Lansd. 33, ff. 140–144; qu. *Returns of Aliens*, Huguenot Soc. X pt. 2, p. 220. Cf. Mark Eccles, *Marlowe in London* (1939), 158, 'The Wise Man of St Helen's.'

[2] S.P. 12/232/29 (11).

[3] Cf. W. A. Shaw, *Letters of Denization and Acts of Naturalization 1509–1800*, 1923.

to make him an English citizen, and was therefore an alien. But this alien was also author of the *Passionate Centurie of Love*, a famous sonneteer, a playwright, a learned scholar, and a friend of Marlowe's. From Shakespeare's line I draw the inferences (*a*) that Watson imitated Shakespeare in the praise of Prince True-love, and (*b*) from the hostility of the term *Alien*, that Shakespeare was not pleased. In the reference to Watson we have still another testimony to the early date of the Sonnets. By the 'mid-1590s' the *Alien* pen had long ceased to write, for Watson died in 1592 or before.

Nor was Shakespeare pleased by the chief rivalry—of that *able spirit*, that *better spirit* Christopher Marlowe. Seekers after the identity of the Rival Poet do not seem to have realized that Sonnet 78 rules out of consideration *every poet who was not a Master of Arts*. The Rival therefore cannot be Daniel, Drayton, or Chapman, none of whom took a degree. But Kit Marlowe had been bred at Cambridge with Will Hatcliffe, and (with the aid of a letter from the Privy Council)[1] had proceeded M.A. in July 1587.

Shakespeare's topic in the final ten lines of this sonnet is *art* (*i.e.* scholarship)[2] in poetry: (*a*) formal, as learned in the University Schools, and (*b*) informal, as inspired or infused by the subject—the beautiful Friend. *Sans* university, Shakespeare the *dumb* or the *heavy* or *rude ignorance* has mastered the second so

---

[1] Hotson, *The Death of Christopher Marlowe*, 1925.
[2] Cf. schollers Learned in searching principles of art
Greene, *Friar Bacon and Friar Bungay* line 1094.

Boys of art, I have deceiv'd you both   *Merry Wives* 3.1.106.

It may be useful to recall that *artist* meant *scholar*, *Master of Arts*:

The wise and fool, the artist and unread   *Troilus and Cressida* 1.3.25.

Idiots that think themselves artists because they can English an obligation
Chettle, *Kind-Harts Dreame* (S.R. 8 Dec. 1592).

To the venerable artists and younger students in divinity in the famous University of Cambridge
Thomas James, *Strange and Dangerous Voyage*, 1633.

The man we call an artist they termed an *artisan*.

fully that his work rises as high as that of his university-bred Rival, the graduate *in Artibus Magister* or Master of Arts. The Rival's degree is stated in the lines

> [Thine eyes have] *given grace a double Majesty* . . .
> *And arts with thy sweet graces gracèd be.*

Grace is the University term for Congregation's permission to proceed to a degree. The recipient is said to be *graced*—'That shortly he was grac'd with doctor's name'[1]—and *Majesty* is the degree of *Magister*. As Jonson says,[2]

> But view her [Poesy] in her glorious ornaments,
> Attired in the majesty of art.

According to Shakespeare, then, the Friend's eyes have conferred a second full degree on the already-graced Rival—have doubled his Mastership of Arts.

Better spirit betrays an added bitterness, which makes Will Hatcliffe's preference peculiarly hard to bear: namely, this recent Cambridge M.A. of Marlowe's has now made the cobbler of Canterbury's son *a gentleman*, made him Shakespeare's *better*, raised him out of 'the meaner sort' to the class above the Stratford plebeian, who on the distaff side *was better born than Marlowe.*

---

[1] Marlowe, *Dr. Faustus* I Cho. 17.

He is a scholar . . .
Of good accompt in both our universities,
Either of which hath favour'd him with graces
                   Jonson, *Every Man in his Humour* 1.1.9–12.

Sir Edward Coke . . . afterwards proceeded by grace, Master of Arts
                   Hist. MSS. Comm., *Ninth Rep.*, App. 373*a*.

You Artlesse Bussard . . .
You that had never Doctorship in Schooles,
But got your grace from women or from Fooles
                   Rowlands, *Looke to it* . . . 1604.

Marry, here's grace and a cod-piece: that's a wise man and a fool
                   Lear 3.2.40.

A man of note . . . graced also with degrees of Schooles
                   Samuel Hieron, *The Preacher's plea*, 1604.

[2] *Every Man in his Humour* 5.3.324–325.

We recall that at Cambridge the fellow-commoners outranked the Bachelors of Arts, but were placed *below* the Masters. The first full degree had made the latter not only Regents of the University but also *gentlemen* by scholarship: 'scholars and gentlemen'.[1]

The certainty that we are hearing Shakespeare on this successful and recently gentilized Marlowe, when they were both twenty-five years old—about 1589—makes us read Sonnets 79, 80, and 85 with a new and vivid interest.

79

Whilst I alone did call upon thy aid,
My verse alone had all thy gentle grace;
But now my gracious numbers are decay'd,
And my sick Muse doth give another place.
I grant, sweet Love, thy lovely argument
Deserves the travail of a worthier pen;
Yet what of thee thy poet doth invent
He robs thee of, and pays it thee again.
He lends thee virtue, and he stole that word
From thy behaviour. Beauty doth he give,
And found it in thy cheek. He can afford
No praise to thee but what in thee doth live.
  Then thank him not for that which he doth say,
  Since what he owes thee thou thyself dost pay.

80

O, how I faint when I of you do write,
Knowing a better spirit doth use your name
And in the praise thereof spends all his might
To make me tongue-tied, speaking of your fame!
But since your worth, wide as the ocean is,
The humble as the proudest sail doth bear,
My saucy bark, inferior far to his,
On your broad main doth wilfully appear.

---

[1] 'Alsoe a man may obtaine beareing of Armes by Theology, Warrefare, Lawe, Physicke, Rhetoricke, Arithmeticke, Geometry, Astronomy, Musicke, Poetry.' *A Treaty of dignities* . . . B.M. MS. Addl. 25257, f. 184.

Your shallowest help will hold me up afloat
Whilst he upon your soundless deep doth ride;
Or, being wrack'd, I am a worthless boat,
He of tall building and of goodly pride.
    Then if he thrive, and I be cast away,
    The worst was this: my love was my decay.

We pause here on the terms *proudest* and *pride*, remembering that since *pride* both leads and includes the seven deadly sins, it is never a word of unalloyed approbation. The Elizabethan eye would see something less than pure admiration and confession of inferiority in *proudest sail, He of tall building and of goodly pride*, and *my saucy bark*. In 1589 the fate of the tall, goodly, proud Spanish men-of-war is fresh in mind. So also is the common legend that the magniloquent Dons at first contemptuously called the swift, yare, and lower-built English ships *pescadores*—'fishing-boats'.[1]

85

My tongue-tied Muse in manners holds her still
While comments of your praise, richly compil'd,
Reserve their character with golden quill
And precious phrase by all the Muses fil'd.
I think good thoughts whilst other write good words,
And, like unletter'd clerk, still cry 'Amen'
To every Hymn that able spirit affords
In polish'd form of well-refinëd pen.
Hearing you prais'd, I say ' 'Tis so, 'tis true!'
And to the most of praise add something more;
But that is in my thought, whose love to you,
Though words come hindmost, holds his rank before.
    Then others for the breath of words respect;
    Me for my dumb thoughts, speaking in effect.

---

[1] John Prime, *Consolation of David* (sermon, 17 November 1588) amusingly misread *pescadores* as '*peccatores . . . little poor sinners*. For so at first they could term our Navy & imagine of our ships'. But G. B., *A Fig for the Spaniard* (1591, D1ᵛ), has it correctly: 'at the first encounter with the mightie Spanish *Armada*, our simple Fleete of Fish-boates (as it pleased them to tearme it) tooke their Viceadmirall.' And Dekker (*Whore of Babylon* 4.4) has King Philip exclaim, 'We winne; our ships meete none but fisher-boates'.

Discouraged by Prince True-love's preferring Marlowe's scholarly verse to his own plain language, free of the *strainëd touches* [University] *rhetoric can lend*—though his thought rises higher than anyone's—Shakespeare yet gives unstinted praise to the *precious phrase by all the Muses fil'd* and

> *To every Hymn that able spirit affords*
> *In polish'd form of well-refinëd pen.*

But in the next sonnet the tone alters, and reverts to *proud*:

86

Was it the proud full sail of his great verse
Bound for the prize of all-too-precious you . . .

One is reminded of the ill-fated Pucelle's premature boast, 'Now am I like that proud insulting ship Which Caesar and his fortune bare at once.' *Proud full sail* also recalls the axiom 'pride must have a fall':—*drown Their full-sail'd pride, and headlong strike it down.*[1] And some readers may miss the force of *his great verse*. For this is not at all our vague modern encomium '*great* poetry', which is a sense never found in Shakespeare. *Great* is rather censure than praise, meaning 'big', 'proud', 'swelling', 'magniloquent'—as Wilson said, 'the *great* or *mightie* kinde, when we use *great* wordes'. '*Magnifica verba*, great, vaunting words' (Littleton); 'great wordes and bugge [terrible] lookes'.[2]

Another [preacher], as if his purpose were onely to amaze the vulgar, and to affright and astonish the multitude, mounteth aloft, and is all in his great words, and new-coyned phrases, more fit for some Mimicke or Tragedian, then a Minister of the Gospel.[3]

The 'swelling bombast of bragging blank verse' in Tamburlaine's high astounding terms rivals the Beast of the Apocalypse

---

[1] *The Faithful Friends*, 2.1.
[2] J[ames] L[ea], *A strange monster* . . . (1590), 9.
[3] Samuel Hieron, *The Preacher's plea*, 1604.

—'a mouth speaking great things and blasphemies'. As Greene says, 'daring God out of heaven with that Atheist *Tamburlan*'.

In sum, Shakespeare's view of Marlowe about 1589—*all his might . . . proud . . . great verse . . .* writing *above a mortal pitch*— resembles the considered and much later judgment of Ben Jonson: the age's best critic, who coined the phrase 'Marlowe's mighty line'. Jonson saw the large figure of Marlowe's Muse as *vegrandis* —'great but disproportion'd'. Perhaps the clue to *disproportion'd* lies in Marlowe's lack of humour, the quality often equated with 'a sense of proportion'.

86

> *Was it the proud full sail of his great verse,*
> *Bound for the prize of all-too-precious you,*
> *That did my ripe thoughts in my brain inhearse,*
> *Making their tomb the womb in which they grew?*
> *Was it his spirit, by spirits taught to write*
> *Above a mortal pitch, that struck me dead?*
> *No, neither he, nor his compeers by night*
> *Giving him aid, my verse astonishèd.*
> *He, nor that affable familiar ghost*
> *Which nightly gulls him with intelligence,*
> *As victors, of my silence cannot boast—*
> *I was not sick of any fear from thence;*
> > *But when your countenance fill'd up his line,*
> > *Then lack'd I matter; that enfeebled mine.*

Shakespeare implies that Will Hatcliffe's favouring reception improved Marlowe's verse—*fill'd up his line*. It was that supplement, not its essential worth, which gave it the victory.

Now what, we ask, was Marlowe's offering of *great verse, Bound for the prize of all-too-precious you*, which so effectively charmed Will Hatcliffe? Neither sonnets of personal praise nor *Hero and Leander* could be described as 'the proud full sail' of '*great* verse'. Has that offering gone among the wastes of time? Perhaps; but in view of Marlowe's high reputation, that offering is more likely to have been preserved than lost. And the one non-dramatic work of Marlowe's which can be described as *'great* verse' is *his blank-verse translation of the first book of Lucan.* Here is a sample of it:

> So thunder, which the wind tears from the clouds,
> With crack of riven air and hideous sound
> Filling the world, leaps out and throws forth fire,
> Affrights poor fearful men, and blasts their eyes
> With overthwarting flames, and raging shoots
> Alongst the air, and, nought resisting it,
> Falls, and returns, and shivers where it lights.

Marlowe's offering should certainly be something to flatter Prince True-love in his public character as the shadow-Pompey, *lov'd of more and less*—of both gentry and common people, as Shakespeare says. The favourite poet who makes a worshipped hero of Pompey is 'rich Lucan', 'learned Lucan',[1] in his heroic poem on the wars of Pompey and Caesar. No one has suggested a reason why Marlowe undertook to make a translation of Lucan into English verse. We may be sure that he did not enter upon the work by accident.

Would not a desire to please the Prince who bore Pompey's lion for his crest and (as I believe) chose the Pompey-hemistich *Dat poenas laudata fides* from this very Lucan for his *impresa*, give him that reason?

It was Thomas Thorpe who in 1600—seven years after the poet's violent death—secured this manuscript of 'that pure elemental wit, Chr. Marlowe' (as he calls him), to bring out as his first venture in publishing. The rights had passed to him via Wolfe, Blount, Linley, and Flasket. There may be significance here. For nine years later it was this same Thorpe who published Shakespeare's verse-offering to Prince True-love: the Sonnets. And he dedicated them in cipher *To the onlie begetter of these insuing sonnets Mr. W. H[atliv]*, doubtless in gratitude for having given him the manuscript. It is tempting to think that Thorpe's publication of Marlowe's offering would suggest him to Hatcliffe as the suitable publisher for Shakespeare's.

---

[1] His ninth book opens with an apotheosis of Pompey.

With Marlowe a certainty, his crony-and-deceiver the gulling *affable familiar ghost* is inescapable. There is only one English 'local ghost', *familiaris lar*, *Hausgeist*, or *duende de casa*. And that is *the shock-haired Robin Goodfellow*—otherwise called Puck-hairy or Hob[Rob]goblin, the shrewd and knavish sprite of the buttery where drink is kept, who plays hob with the wenches, and is a master of mischievous deception and hoax.

Similarly, in 1589 there is only one notable Londoner known as Robin Goodfellow, and that is the other Cambridge M.A. and dramatist the shock-haired Robin Greene,[1] who today is widely known for nothing but his envious attack on Shakespeare. After Greene's death in misery, Gabriel Harvey (in his *Foure Letters . . . especially touching Robert Greene*) calls him 'Robin-good-fellow,[2] and gentle Greene sleeves' and asks 'who in London hath not heard of his dissolute and licentious living; his fonde disguisinge of a Master of Arte with ruffianly haire,[3] unseemely apparell,

---

[1] *Greene*, who had in both Academies ta'ne
Degree of Master, yet could never gaine
To be call'd more than *Robin*: . . .
Marlo, renown'd for his rare art and wit,
Could ne're attaine beyond the name of *Kit*; . . .
Mellifluous *Shake-speare*, whose inchanting Quill
Commanded Mirth or Passion, was but *Will*.

Heywood, *Hierarchie of the Blessed Angells* (1635), 206.

[2] 'Good fellow' is something other than good:

T'is but an Ironized Tearme, good-Fellow so spells Theefe.

Warner, *Albions England* (1597), 241.

And take her cups, even with a courage downe,
Play the good fellow kindly . . .

Rowlands, *A . . . Crew of kinde Gossips* (1609), 4.

Averlan. A good fellow, a mad companion . . . sound drunkard.
Gale-bon-temps. A merry grig, a good fellow, good drunkard. . . .

Cotgrave, *French Dictionary* (1611).

No sonns of Belial, vitious and good-fellow ministers, as they call them, who are a kind of very vile and contemptible creatures.

Robert Bolton, *A Discourse of true happinesse* (1614), 204.

[3] 'A bushie beard therefore, & shocked haire, make not men seeme terrible, unlesse peradventure unto fearefull infants, in whose sight they appeere like Robin good fellowes, or Hobgoblins.'

A Paradoxe . . . of Baldnesse (1579), C7v.

and more unseemely Company?' And 'who like [drunken] *Elderton* for Ballating: *Greene* for pamphletting: both, for good-fellowship, and bad conditions?' Tom Nashe, in reply, calls himself 'a scholler and a good-fellow, a beggar', and defends Greene's memory with 'A good fellowe hee was'—ready to bet on himself in a drinking-contest. Even fourteen years afterwards, 'Robin Goodfellow' still connoted 'Greene': 'At which (as if *Robin Good-fellow* had been conjur'd up amongst them) the Wenches have falne into the hands of the Greene-sicknesse . . .'[1] The presence of Greene (as well as the *Alien* Watson) of course again shows that Shakespeare wrote this sonnet before Robin Goodfellow's death in 1592.

So much, then, for Shakespeare on that Robin (Greene) Good-fellow who later called him *Shake-scene*, that affable familiar ghost, compeer by night of that spirit Kit.

But what spirit Kit?

They have so fraid us with bull-beggars, spirits, . . . Kit with the canstick . . . Robin Goodfellow . . . the puckle . . .[2]

Urchins . . . Elves . . . Kitt-with-the-candlestick . . .[3]

Kit of the Candlestick. A vulgar name of the *ignis fatuus*, mentioned in Aubrey's Wilts.[4]

Here we have uncovered what looks like another bit of Shake-spearean criticism, A.D. 1589. For all his rare and shining art, that spirit Kit Marlowe is a Kit-with-the-candlestick, an *ignis fatuus*, a fool's fire which can lead benighted folk into trouble or danger—'Mislead night-wanderers, laughing at their harm'. Is this a side-glance at 'atheism'? I am inclined to think that it is.

On the difficult passage *that affable familiar ghost Which nightly*

---

[1] Dekker, *Seaven Deadly Sinnes* . . . 1606.
[2] Reginald Scot, *Discoverie of Witchcraft* (1584), VII. xv.
[3] Thomas Middleton, *The Witch* I.2.
[4] J. O. Halliwell, *Dict. of Archaic* . . . *Words*, 1847.

gulls him with intelligence J. Q. Adams cited Ford's *Broken Heart* 3.3:

> You have a spirit, sir, have you? a familiar
> That posts i' th' air for your intelligence?
> Some such hobgoblin . . .

Along with that we may consider the following:

The bruit . . . is transported to some good Taverne or Ordinarie, where . . . it is greedely snatcht up by some Dappert Mounsier Diego, who lives by telling of newes, & false dice.[1]

A Lying Knave.

. . . So full of newes, his braines and browes do swell:
He will your admiration entertaine
With secret things from *Rome*, from *France* and *Spaine*,
Barbary, Turkey, Indies East, and West:
He hath all Kingdomes businesse in his brest.[2]

A Corranto-coiner Is a state newes-monger. . . . It is strange to see . . . with what frontlesse insinuation he will scrue himselfe into the acquaintance of some knowing *Intelligencers*, who, trying the cask by his hollow sound, do familiarly gull him.[3]

I cannot pretend to be sure of Shakespeare's meaning here. But I suspect that at this date Marlowe was still employed (or wished to be again employed) in service for the government as an intelligencer or spy. Shakespeare is perhaps saying that Greene (who has a resourceful imagination as well as plenty of 'contacts', not only in the underworld of London) keeps feeding Kit important-sounding but baseless intelligence or 'top secret news', and that Marlowe swallows it whole.

In sum, there is rivalry from the learned Alien, and especially from the resoundingly popular Kit Marlowe—his degree and his gentility both still damp upon him—, aided by his crony, that raffish scribbler Robin Greene, M.A. These scholars show that they are gentlemen by scorning the plebeian poet. But Shakespeare knows his own worth. As for the Spirit and the Ghost, he has taken their measure.

---

[1] Nashe, *Terrors of the Night* (*Wks.* ed. McKerrow, 1.365).
[2] Rowlands, *The Knave of Harts*, 1610.   [3] Anon., *Whimzies* (1631), 15.

XI

SHAKESPEARE'S ORDER

ARE the Sonnets—or at least the main group numbered 1 to 126—properly numbered? That is to say, do they stand arranged in the order which Shakespeare (no matter in what order they were written) chose to give them? The world would give a good deal to know. For the question's importance needs no underlining: the poet's arrangement of the sequence is a matter just as essential to his art as his ordering of the thought within each poem.

This, however, is a question the great majority of readers do not trouble their heads about. For the arrangement as originally printed in Thorpe's quarto of 1609, and followed almost universally in later reprintings, satisfies them. It satisfies many an expert scholar and critic as well. To Sir Edmund Chambers it seems 'most likely that the arrangement of 1609 was his [Shakespeare's]. It does not, of course, follow that in putting them together he made no departure from the chronological order of composition'.[1] Similarly, for Northrop Frye 'It is a reasonable assumption that the Sonnets through 126 are in sequence. There is a logic and rightness in their order which is greatly superior to that of any proposed rearrangement'.[2]

But along with the preponderating *ayes*, we hear a muttering of *noes*. Some of these find the 1609 arrangement 'strongly suspect'. Why suspect? Because the *Sonnets* were brought out by a publisher, not by Shakespeare himself. We must allow suspicions when they are reasonable, but what grounds can be shown here?

We remember that Sidney's sonnets, five years after his death, were similarly brought out by an unauthorized publisher, Thomas Newman. Newman, however, did not treat Sidney a tenth as

---

[1] *William Shakespeare* (1930), 1.562.
[2] 'How True a Twain' in *The Riddle of Shakespeare's Sonnets* (1962), 39.

well as Thorpe later treated Shakespeare. For his edition appeared so vilely defaced with a swarm of errors that it had to be called in, and a far more correct one substituted. But here is the point to mark: that original wretched edition's *arrangement* of the Sonnets remained unaltered in the corrected one; and, moreover, that same arrangement was subsequently shown—by its reappearance in the *Arcadia* folio of 1598, prepared under the Countess of Pembroke's eye—to have been Sidney's own. If, however (like Thorpe for Shakespeare), we had no evidence but Newman for Sidney, what could deter a suspicious critic from finding Newman's arrangement 'strongly suspect'? And he would be wrong.

Among the minority who disapprove the order of Shakespeare's Sonnets as printed, some have the courage to document their discontent by setting out suggested rearrangements: all too often reaping more reviews than converts. Others stigmatize the 1609 order as 'unsatisfactory', but follow it—not venturing to offer their undisclosed improvements which would make it satisfactory.

Still, it is clear that neither camp contains ammunition much more forcible than a *reasonable assumption* or an *unsatisfactory*. No one, whether satisfied or disgruntled, has as yet produced for his belief the kind of 'grounds more relative than this' which all would accept.

In such a situation, it will be agreed that if anything at all turned up indicating that the order of the Sonnets as Thorpe printed them was Shakespeare's, or was not Shakespeare's, it should be submitted for consideration. Something has recently struck me as such a piece of evidence, and my purpose here is to present it.

As for this piece of evidence, I confess it took some time to penetrate to my consciousness. First, because I wasn't looking for it; and second, because it was embodied in a little-regarded feature, the *numbering* of individual sonnets.

Only wide reading of contemporary writings gave the preparation required—at the Armada crisis, for background to the understanding of Sonnet 107, and round the Babington Conspiracy and other plots of assassination for Sonnet 124, *the blow of thrallëd discontent.* For from these writings it was gradually borne in upon me that those same numbers, 107 and 124, kept turning up, in topical quotations from the book of Psalms.

Once the coincidence is seen, one realizes that it would have been noticed long ago, had we not overlooked an important area of mental background. Before coming to the evidence, therefore, let me first ask the reader to indulge me in a brief attempt to appreciate something of the astonishing intimacy of Shakespeare's Englishmen with the Psalms.[1]

We have heard it often enough, but have we made effective working knowledge of the fact that nothing in literature ever 'penetrated and permeated the hearts and speech of the English race' to compare with the Bible? And that its best-loved book— the lyrical Psalter—was the book of universal appeal, from Spenser's[2] *Magnificent Empresse Renowmed for Pietie . . . Elizabeth . . . Defendour of the Faith*—who set for her gentry and her poets the fashion of turning psalms into English metre,[3] and on occasion composed eclectic psalms or sacred songs herself— down to the humblest, 'so that now every Carter & Cobler can whistle and sing psalms'? One simplicity at least we can guard against. We shall not imagine the Elizabethans afflicted with the modern widespread ignorance of the Psalms of David.[4]

---

[1] As to their authorship, John Donne gives the contemporary view:
'those Psalms we call
(Though some have other Authors) *Davids* all'.

[2] Spenser's own works show thirty-nine borrowings from the Psalms— about twice as many as from any other book of the Old Testament.

[3] Surviving is her paraphrase of the 14th Psalm, *The fool hath said in his heart: There is no God.*

[4] Symptomatic is the recently published report of a brilliant Travelling Fellow from Britain on the following strange inscription he noted in Huntington, West Virginia, on a library's cornerstone:

THAT OUR SONS AND DAUGHTERS
MAY BE
AS CORNER STONES
POLISHED AFTER THE SIMILITUDE
OF A PALACE

The Book of Common Prayer, for the use of every parish in the land, begins 'The Psalter shall be read through once every Month, as it is appointed, both for Morning and Evening Prayer' —read through in the beautiful version of Myles Coverdale, who introduced into English the phrases *loving-kindness* and *tender mercy*. The Psalter's one hundred and fifty psalms were thus appointed to be distinctly and audibly read twelve times every year—an annual one thousand eight hundred psalms, or five psalms each day, in every church. And the reading was not all. For these same psalms, turned into rimed stanzas by Sternhold, Hopkins, and others, and set to music, were sung by all before and after services. At Paul's Cross in London, reports Bishop Jewel, you would hear them chanted by a throng of six thousand souls.

Psalm-singing parishioners included theatre-goers; and on the stage Shakespeare would treat them not only to a Falstaff (shocked at the world's badness) threatening to sing psalms himself, but also to a downhearted Parson Evans quavering the first line of Whittingham's 137th Psalm, *When as I sat in Pabylon*. For it would be surprising if Shakespeare should not share present memories with his audience. In his *Shakespeare's Biblical Knowledge* (1935), Richmond Noble lists some 150 Psalm-references from the plays. What dramatist of our day dares rely on even a slight acquaintance with the Psalter in a common theatre-crowd?

And what survivors of a wrecked ship today would (in more modern idiom) report that at the moment of crisis 'we committed ourselves unto the Lord, and began with doleful tune and heavy hearts to sing the Twelfth Psalm, *Help, Lord, for good and*

'I wondered why the inscription struck me; why you would only find such sentiments expressed thus in America. Not merely because the wording is infelicitous—plenty of monuments in Britain offend worse—but because of its belief in education, its aspiration, its desire for "polish"—*i.e.* for a successful worldliness on a par with New York.'

In kindness to this unworldly cousin-and-stranger, whose own education had stopped short of the Holy Bible, the library-inscribers should have supplied the source of these clumsily-worded and materialistic sentiments— *Ps.* 144:12. But to what purpose, if he had never heard of the Psalms?

godly men', as the crew of the *Tobie* did in 1593? Hitler's airborne Armada did not, like Spanish Philip's of 1588, carry for its slogan *Arise, O God, maintain thine own cause*—the 74th Psalm, nor was it met by the immortal Few with their forefathers' battle-cry from the 68th, *Let God arise, and let his enemies be scattered.*

Or what queen today—to try an ambassador's skill in compliment—would instinctively toss him a snatch from a psalm, and instantly receive a courtly volley in kind? Yet this is what Thomas Heywood reports[1] of Elizabeth Tudor:

The Queene sat then in state at the upper end of a long gallerie, which when the Ambassador should enter, the great Ladies of either side richly attired were placed; through the middest of whom as he passed along, he as amased at the state, or admiring at their beauties, cast his eye first on one side, then on the other (and that not without some pause, as if hee had beene to take a particular surveigh of all their features); but by degrees comming up towards the Queene, who sat like *Diana* amongst her nymphs, or *Ariadne* in her crowne of starres, instated above the lesser lights, to give him entertainement: and observing his eyes still to wander, she thus bespake him, *Averte oculos ne videas vanitatem: i.* Turne away your eyes lest you behold vanitie:[2] to whom he suddenly replyde, *Imo potius mirabilia opera Dei, i.* Nay rather the wonderfull workes of God.[3]

Merely an augmented charm, to recall that alongside this *marvellous are thy works* the Psalter's 139th adds *fearfully and wonderfully made.*

While the English might not perhaps match the Huguenots, with whom it was the sign of their religion to know all the Psalms by heart, yet their appetite for them was insatiable. Take the famous seven called Penitential, for example—*Ps.* 6, 32, 38, 51, 102, 130, and 143, the Ash Wednesday Psalms—the 51st repeated in the Commination, and the other six read as Proper Psalms for the day. Under their influence Petrarch composed seven Christian meditations he called *Salmi Penitentiali*, which George Chapman

---

[1] *Gunaikeion* (1624), 244–245.   [2] *Ps.* 119:37.   [3] *Ps.* 139:13.

turned into English and published. And while (among others) Sir Thomas Wyatt, Edmund Spenser, and John Davies of Hereford paraphrased the Psalter's Seven in metre, it was left to the versified version of William Hunnis to cruise down the age as a best-seller, under the irresistible title *Seven Sobs of a sorrowfull Soule for Sinne*.

The 51st stands out among the familiar Seven as the common psalm of confession. Lady Jane Grey recited the whole of it in English at her execution, while the Earl of Essex, at his, had patience only to repeat the first two verses. It begins

Have mercy upon me, O God, after thy great goodness:
according to the multitude of thy mercies do away mine offences.

This prayer for pardon is the famous 'neck verse', presented in black-letter Latin by the Bishop's Ordinary to the condemned felon claiming benefit of clergy—to judge whether he could read. When young Ben Jonson stood at the Newgate bar convicted of killing the actor Gabriel Spencer in a fight, it was only his unquestionable reading of *Miserere mei, Deus, secundum magnam misericordiam tuam* etc. which kept his vital thread from being 'cut With edge of penny cord and vile reproach'. The people's familiarity not only with the Seven Penitential but also with the Fifteen Gradual Psalms (*Psalms* 120–134) can be traced to the inclusion of both in the pre-Reformation Primer, the 'Lay Folks' Prayer Book'. This deep-rooted special familiarity has its bearing, as we shall find, on our present problem.

To round off this inadequate attempt at realizing the time's psalm-mindedness in its full reach and intensity, I cannot omit a fascinating proof of it which I have never seen pointed out. This was given by the Queen herself—often likened to David—of whom Shakespeare wrote, *Holy and heavenly thoughts still counsel her*: that Elizabeth who confesses, 'I walk many times in the pleasant fields of the Holy Scriptures, where I pluck up the goodlisome herbs of sentences. . . .'

In 1588 Queen Elizabeth wrote a song 'in manner of a thanksgiving to God for her and our deliverance from the Invincible

Navy of the Spaniard'. As a part of that great celebration on November 24th at Paul's Cross, 'Where prince and people did consent with joyful minds to meet, To glorify the God of heaven with psalms and voices sweet', choirs massed before their Queen lifted her song. And it began,

> *Look and bow down thine ear, O Lord,*
> *From thy bright sphere behold and see*
> *Thy handmaid and thy handiwork*
> *Among thy priests off'ring to thee.*

Few souls in that vast exalted throng could fail to recognize that in these words she drew on the 86th Psalm—which begins *Bow down thine ear, O Lord,* and later prays *help the son of thine handmaid*—or fail to see that she chose it *because the 86th is the first psalm* appointed in the Prayer Book *for Day 17*: the Queen's Accession Day, the 17th of November,[1] 'the day of the gladness of her heart', the day thirty years ago last Sunday when Mary's death both ended for us the burning of Christians for heresy and rid us of Spanish Philip; the day 'wherein our Nation received a new light after a fearful and bloody eclipse'. To the sound of *Bow down thine ear, O Lord* every bell in England this month rings out joy unceasing for Day 17, 'wherein God gave a rare Phoenix to rule this land'. In the royal choice of 'her own' psalm to render thanks for this second Great Deliverance, what felicity, what richness of evocation for her loving people!

With this introduction we come now to the two particular psalms deeply identified with the national crises of Dangers Averted: with the supreme moments when England like Israel was delivered by the mercy of God—from the blast of war by sea-borne invasion, and from the fox at her vitals, the king-killer. What praise could 'set forth their joys and thanksgiving for the same'? What but Psalms of the royal prophet David, 'so

---

[1] See 'November 17th', Sir John Neale's absorbing study in his *Essays in Elizabethan History*, 1958.

abundant in this behalf that neither old nor young can be ignorant thereof'?

It was the 107th and the 124th which all voices raised in times like these. Until 1859 the Prayer Book presented not only *Forms of Prayer to be used at Sea* but also *A Form of Prayer with Thanksgiving . . . for the happy Deliverance of King James I and the three Estates of England From the most traiterous and bloody intended Massacre by Gunpowder.*

In the first Form, the longer of the two psalms appointed for *Thanksgiving after a Storm* is the 107th, beginning

O give thanks unto the Lord, for he is gracious: and his mercy endureth for ever.
Let them give thanks whom the Lord hath redeemed; and delivered from the hand of the enemy.

And the *Psalm or Hymn of Praise and Thanksgiving, After Victory or Deliverance from an Enemy* begins with the first six verses of the 124th:

If the Lord had not been on our side, now may we say: if the Lord himself had not been on our side, when men rose up against us,
They had swallowed us up quick . . .

In the second, for use *upon the Fifth Day of November*, instead of the *Venite* is appointed a Hymn or eclectic psalm opening with the already quoted verses of the 107th; and to be read as one of three Proper Psalms is the 124th.

Before returning to the Elizabethans, we may note the unanimity of Jacobean divines in the 124th. Dr Daniel Dyke preached *Certain Comfortable Sermons Upon the 124. Psalme . . . Tending to stirre up to Thankefulnesse for our Deliverance from the late Gunpowder Treason.* Here he refers to God's former title or style as *The Lord that confounded the invincible Navie of the Spaniards.* Bishop William Bedell's *Protestant Memorial . . . of the Powder Plot* ends with a paraphrase of the 124th. Archdeacon Martin Fotherby at Paul's Cross on the Fifth of November 1607 exclaims, thrice blessed be the name of the Lord our God, *Who did not give us over as a prey into their teeth*, but miraculously delivered us. . . . So that we have great cause . . . to sing that joyful *melos* . . . *Our soule is escaped as a bird out of the snare: the snare is broken, and we are delivered.* [*Ps.* 124:6–8.]

Theodore Hering's *The Triumph of the Church over Water and Fire* (1625), as its title proclaims, includes both the great deliverances, Armada and Plot, in quoting the 124th Psalm: 'Let all *England* say, if the *Lord had not beene on our side*' etc.

Although no plot to kill Queen Elizabeth had matched the Gunpowder Treason for wholesale slaughter, she had survived many more than her successor. To her subjects, the sight of her fellow-kings William of Orange and Henri III of France both falling 'under the blow of thrallëd discontent', while she stood like some great cedar unmoved by assassins' repeated attempts, manifested God's protecting hand over Elizabeth:

The Queene of England . . . hath . . . escaped by Gods goodnes many great dangers, which for the defence of the Gospell have been complotted against her. They that doubt of this, let them but call to memory . . . Babingtons & Ballards conspiracy, Hardings imagery, Parries treasons, and unnatural cruelty . . . Lopez & Squires poisonable and venemous treachery. In the which doubtlesse we had al perished, & had bin swallowed up quicke, if the Lorde had not beene on our side. [*Ps.* 124.][1]

Looking back at *England's Elizabeth* in History's perspective from the reign of Charles I (1631), the frontispiece to Thomas Heywood's book sums up the nation's conviction. The speech shown issuing from the great Queen's mouth reads *If the Lord had not bene on my side*—the 124th Psalm.

Of all the efforts to strike her down, the Ballard–Babington Plot of 1586 encouraged by Mary Stuart most deeply shocked contemporary minds, because of the number of young Catholic gentlemen sworn to kill the Queen. When the traitors were caught, as Sir John Neale writes, 'it was as though England had

---

[1] Thomas Holland, *Panegyris Elizabethae Reginae* (1601), A4.

escaped a new St. Bartholomew'. Joy and relief burst out in a flood, irresistible.

They came together gladly all, and there did mery make,
And gave God thankes with cheereful hartes, for Queene Elizabeths sake.
In solempne Psalmes they sung full sweete the prayse of God on hie,
Who now and ever keepes our Queene from Traytors tyranny.

Inevitably, it was the 124th Psalm which sounded the keynote —whether incorporated in godly ditties 'to be sung for the Preservation of the Queene's most Excellent Majestie',

If on our side God had not beene
When traitours sought much blood to spill,
This day of joy we had not seene—

or quoted in Latin in a courtier's verses published 'In joy of the most happie disclosing of the most dangerous conspiracies . . . *Anima nostra sicut passer erepta est ex laqueo venantium Psal.* 124.'[1] 'Our soul is escaped even as a bird out of the snare of the fowler' —or recommended by authority for reading in *An Order of Prayer and Thanksgiving for the preservation of her Maiestie . . .* 'the 124. Psalme'.[2]

And just as inevitably less than two years later, when the deadly Spanish Moon of huge black men-of-war was driven northward into eclipse, it was the 107th, the 'Sailors' Psalm', which was universally raised in thanksgiving.[3] From the

---

[1] *Certaine English Verses* . . . 1586.
[2] 1586. (Ent. 25 Aug.) *STC* 16517.
[3] When on the shoals off Brill George Gascoigne had escaped shipwreck by a hair's breadth, he related

We fall on knees amyd the happy gale . . .
That pleasant song the hundreth and seventh psalme
There dyd we reade to comfort ouer annoye,
Which to my soule (me thought) was sweete as balme.

'Gascoignes voyage into Hollande An. *1572*.'
A Hundreth Sundrie Floures.

278

stationer John Wolfe, who upon the news of victory at once brought out an old work of Peter Baro's under the title *A special Treatise of Gods Providence . . . with an exposition of the 107. Psalm*, to the diarist Robert Comaundre, noting down the Armada story[1] with 'O that Men wold therefore prayse the Lorde for his goodnes, & declare the wonders that he doethe for the childerne of men!' it was still the 107th Psalm.

The Queen set aside Tuesday, November 19th—'kept holy-daie,' as Stow reports, 'throughout the realme, with sermons, singing of Psalmes, bone fires, &c. for joy, & a thanksgiving unto God for the overthrow of the Spanyardes our enemies on the sea.'[2] And the eclectic *Psalme and Collect of thanksgiving* published by authority as *not unmeet for this present time to be said or sung in Churches*[3] took for its framework the 107th Psalm.

Psalms, as we remember, were closely linked in the Elizabethan mind with lyrics called 'sonnets'.

> Twixt Poetry and best divinity
> There is such near and dear affinity . . .[4]

A triumphant Sonnet taken out of the Psalms of David.[5]

Sir Philip Sidney's works comprised his versions of the Psalms along with his sonnets; William Byrd in this very Armada year published *Psalms, Sonets, & songs*; Thomas Scot writes of a choir

> *Of solemne singers . . . all the ring*
> *Seemes Eccho-like, their sonnets to resing.*[6]

---

[1] B.M. MS. Egerton 2642, f. 123ᵛ.
[2] *Annals* (1615), 750a.
[3] 1588. *STC* 16520.
[4] John Taylor the Water Poet, *Works* (1630), 2d pagination, 247b.
[5] Walter Haddon, *Against Jerome Osorius* (tr. James Bell, 1581), 319.
[6] *Philomythie* (1616), 100.

In his *Sonnets to the fairest Coelia* (1594) William Percy asks

> *Have I not offered, Evening, and at Prime,*
> *My sighs, my Psalmes of invocations?*

Sonnets and psalms stood respectively as the typical expressions of human love and of sacred love—'For lovers Sonnettes, Davids Psalmes'[1]

> And Lover's Sonets, turn'd to holy Psalms.[2]

> Idolatrous Poetry let them invent,
> And into Sonnets change their Psalter.[3]

Recalling Chapter IV on the date of Shakespeare's Sonnets, the reader will have long perceived my present drift. I think he will agree that the numbering of Shakespeare's sonnet on the Armada as *107*, and of his sonnet *the blow of thrallèd discontent*—Love untouched by assassins' attempts—as *124* cannot be set down to accident. To call it chance would be asking too much of Fortune. We have seen that the 124th—one of the Fifteen Gradual Psalms—was among the most familiar.

For Shakespeare and for his readers, it is evident that the Psalms had identified the numbers 107 and 124 unalterably with the contemporary crises of Dangers Averted, the Great Deliverances. By employing those numbers from the Psalter, Shakespeare not only lent his meaning a power of association, but evoked in his reader the peculiar response he wished to summon.

If my conclusion is sound, we have here the contemporary evidence so long desired on the vexed question of the true, canonical order of Shakespeare's Sonnets. It will now be recognized that no one but their author would have given those two sonnets the numbers 107 and 124. And if in the sequence those two stand correctly numbered in their proper places, it follows

---

[1] Lyly, *Euphues* (*Works*, ed. Bond, 1.224).
[2] Peele, *His golden locks*, stanza 2, line 2.
[3] Joseph Beaumont, *Psyche* (1648), 2.80.

that the whole sequence 1 through 126 is correctly numbered: that the man who determined that order was therefore not Thomas Thorpe, nor anyone in the world but William Shakespeare.[1]

---

[1] For those who have forgotten the Elizabethans' intimate familiarity with the Penitential Psalms (*Ps.* 6, 32, 38, 51, 102), it is more than a little curious to compare them with their 'opposite numbers' in the Sonnets. To attribute all the following to accident or coincidence would strain credulity:

Psalm 6:7	My beauty is worn away because of mine enemies
Sonnet 6.1	*Then let not winter's ragged hand deface* [Beauty's *In thee thy summer ...* enemies, *treasure thou some place* winter and *With beauty's treasure ere it be self-kill'd.* death] *... thou art much too fair* *To be death's conquest ...*
Psalm 32:3	For while I held my tongue: my bones consumed away
Sonnet 32.2	*When that churl Death my bones with dust shall cover*
Psalm 38:13	I was ... as one that is dumb, who doth not open his mouth
Sonnet 38.7	*For who's so dumb that cannot write to thee*
Psalm 51:1	according to the multitude of thy mercies do away mine offences
Sonnet 51.1	*Thus can my love excuse the slow offence*
Sidney 51.1 *Ast. & Stella*	*Pardon mine ears, both I and they do pray*
Psalm 102:7	I ... am even as it were a sparrow: that sitteth alone upon the house-top
20	That he might hear the mournings
Sonnet 102.5	*When I was wont to greet it with my lays,* *As Philomel in summer's front doth sing,* *And stops his pipe in growth of riper days;* *Not that the summer is less pleasant now* *Than when her mournful hymns did hush the night ...*

XII
FORTY WINTERS

So all-absorbing is Shakespeare that one finds it hard to consider his Friend apart from him. But the fascination of learning more about this man who won the poet's heart is so great that no labour of delving for documents (the historian, too, holds up Adam's profession) has seemed too much. Archives have yielded something to my pickaxe and my spade.

Now, however, that Will Hatcliffe's identity is known to the world, so many will henceforth be watching for him, that the thousand sleepless eyes of the police will seem by comparison no more than a corporal's guard. In full confidence we shall be still nursing the unconquerable hope that more will be uncovered. And without requiring the industry of the weevil and the devil's own luck.

Joined to the watchers will be the former backers and handlers of the two noble contenders Southampton and Pembroke—two doughty would-be W. H.s whom Shakespeare, by his proud unvarying blazon of his friend Will as a *King*, has always shown to be some monster of the isle with four legs. Those fabulous beasts may leave off lion-and-unicorning, and munch consolatory plum cake. 'Let none presume To wear an undeservëd dignity.' After a century of bootless battling, however, their grievance is legitimate. Nobody told them that the Crown is not to be fought for—that from the beginning it has belonged to Shakespeare's sovereign, Will: *If there be any man that will say that my sovereign is not rightly Prince of Purpoole, I am ready here to maintain that he lieth.*

The long, dusty Earl-chase, as tiresome as it was tiring, proves to have been 'but a run after the drag of something that doth itch our senses: which when we have hunted home, we find a mere delusion'. For in retrospect one thing is unquestionable: if either one of these high-born children of an idle brain had been *right*, his identity must have thrown *some* light on some aspect of the Sonnets. And neither of them has ever shed so much as a glimmer.

> Yet am I terrified when well I weigh
> How some great Doctors did their wits undo,
> When they this mystery sought to bewray.

To correct the uncritical assumption that the dedications of *Venus and Adonis* and *Lucrece* reveal 'the intimacy of platonic affection' between peer and plebeian, it is enough to read similar patronage-seeking letters addressed to another magnate, Sir Robert Cecil. One finds an embarrassing number of 'lovers' entirely devoted to that cool little fish—'the one who governs this kingdom', as Don Virginio Orsino described him.[1]

It was *taking for granted* this Cinderella-story of one of 'the meaner sort' hob-nobbing *as an intimate* with a Right Honourable peer of the realm—that is, thoughtlessly accepting as a fact a folk-tale situation unexampled in real Elizabethan life—which misled even the sensible and the informed. One can, however, only envy the profound *expertise* which enabled the Southamptonite to recognize *Henry* (Wriothesley) in Shakespeare's *Will*. To the mind which can perform a feat like that, nothing is impossible.

'To err is proper unto men, but brutish to persist.'

Sherlock Holmes himself once fell into the error: 'But if I had not *taken things for granted*, if I had examined everything with the care which I should have shown had we approached the case *de novo* and had no cut-and-dried story to warp my mind, should I not then have found something definite to go upon?' To return, then, to our 'something definite'.

After *Love's Labour's Lost*, our next glimpse of Will Hatcliffe is in the Latin poetry of his friend Thomas Campion. To

---

[1] *The First Night of 'Twelfth Night'* (1954), 184, 226.

introduce it we can do no better than to quote the poet's biographer on Campion's friends at Gray's Inn:

... nearly all of those of whom he speaks in the language of affection were his actual contemporaries; as, for example, Edmund Bracy, Francis Manby, John Stanford, William Hattecliffe, George Gervis, Robert Castell, Thomas Michelborne, James Huishe, and others. He appears, indeed, to have been one of those persons in whom friendship rises almost to the level of a passion.[1]

Of these, Stanford had played *Clodius* to Campion's *Hidaspis* and *Melancholy* in the comedy presented to the lords by Prince Will Hatcliffe. To Hatcliffe's first cousin Francis Manby of Lincolnshire, Campion wrote poems: the last a sad one *in memoriam* when the young man, an Elizabethan Lycidas, had been lost in some expedition at sea before 1595.

In his 14th Elegy (printed 1595) written to his dear friends after an illness tortured with terrifying dreams, Campion relives the anguish of a vision: he saw his friends Hatcliffe, Stanford, Thurbarne, drowning from a ship smashed by a ferocious storm.

> *I watched thee now, Hatcliffe, in the swollen seas, hardly moving thy salt-wearied arms;*
> *And now at the wave-tops I glimpse thy limbs, Stanford, and thine, Thurbarne, rolling lifeless.*[2]

Waking, Campion found Hatcliffe not only safe and well, but his intimate friend in the sweet freedom of social equality. For Shakespeare, on the other hand, in his 'underfortune' of birth, the longed-for complete companionship with Will Hatcliffe possible to an equal such as Campion was only a dream:

> *Thus have I had thee, as a dream doth flatter,*
> *In sleep a king, but waking no such matter.*

---

[1] Vivian, p. xxvii.
[2] Te modo spectabam tumidas, Hattecliffe, per vndas
    Ægre versantem brachia fessa salo.
    Iamque tuos, Stanforde, tuos, Thurbarne, volutos
    Exanimes artus per vada summa lego.

As Purpoole's shadow-Pompey, Prince Will had triumphed thrice: first in his own palace, his guests the rulers of England; then in London, riding in state to dine with the Lord Mayor; and finally at Greenwich Palace, with *The Misfortunes of Arthur* and his mask, received by the Queen as her cousin, a visiting royalty. And for seven years—until the winter of 1594—he was Purpoole's king without competitor.

Meantime, however, poets who had rimed his praises at the brilliant opening of his reign had vanished from the London scene. The year 1592 saw the end of both the Alien Watson and the affable familiar Robin (Goodfellow) Greene. And in May 1593, at the height of the terrible pestilence, that other spirit Kit Marlowe had expired with the point of Ingram Frizer's dagger in his brain.[1]

---

[1] Hotson, *The Death of Christopher Marlowe,* 1925. In view of the 'exciting' interpretations too often put upon it, a footnote to this discovery of mine may perhaps be allowed me after forty years—particularly when I find a scholar (*Shakespeare Survey* 14, p. 9) presenting my book with a new and lurid title, *The Assassination of Christopher Marlowe.*

Sensational writers (more conversant with cloak-and-dagger literature than with Elizabethan life) have presumed to reject the sworn on-the-spot testimony of the coroner's sixteen jurors at Deptford Strand, in order to feed the credulous reader with a dark political Murder of Marlowe: his murder ordered by some high-placed rascal, because 'he knew too much'. Marlowe knew too much? We may doubt that Shakespeare—whose knowledge of the dead shepherd was a good deal more accurate than ours can be—would accept such a description of him. For he reports this Kit Marlowe, so far from knowing too much, as gulled (duped) nightly with 'intelligence' by Robin Greene.

The description more properly fits the sensation-mongers. They know too much that never was. As for the trifling item of murder, if Marlowe needed murdering (and the necessity has never been shown), it is safe to say that he would have met with an obscure accident on a dark night: not been killed in a public-house before witnesses in broad daylight.

One of the most entertaining of our murder-fanciers discovered melodrama in the fatal dagger-wound, described by the jury who viewed Marlowe's body as inflicted *super dexterum oculum suum. Super* obviously means *on* or *upon,* not 'above' or 'higher than'. Just like the two wounds Marlowe had inflicted on Frizer *super caput suum* (*on* his head) with the dagger which had hung *super tergum suum* (*at* or *on* Frizer's back).

But assuming this to mean *through the skull above the eye,* he inferred great force in the thrust, and therefore murderous intent. Enviable, the author whose readers will swallow stuff of this sort. Not even an idiot would attempt to kill a man with a dagger by driving its point through the frontal bone. The wound obviously was upon or over the right eye through the eye-socket into the brain. Had it been *through the bone of the skull*, so astonishing a wound would have been so described.

After supper, when this 'lamentable transaction' (as J. P. Collier calls it) took place, these fellow-dependants of Mr Thomas Walsingham's were evidently gambling to determine who should pay the bill. It was backgammon—called *Level-coil* or *Hitch-buttock*, since the loser had to get up and sit out. Three were left in the game. Frizer was seated at the board on a form between Poley and Skeres. Marlowe, apparently a bad loser, was behind him on a bed, bitterly disputing with Frizer the verdict of the dice— that *he* should pay the reckoning—and the words grew 'malicious'.

Rolling off the bed to the attack, Marlowe plucked out Frizer's long dagger where it hung at his back, and holding it by its dull blade—in the universal alehouse fashion of 'pummelling' an adversary—fell to beating Frizer over the head with the heavy pommel. To put a stop to this, Frizer rose up, twisted round (his legs hampered by the bench), and grabbed the hilt. Pulling it towards him turned the dangerous point in at Marlowe; and as long as both held on, the dagger still pointed at him. In the mad awkward back-and-forth struggle which followed, the worst happened: that point ran deep into Marlowe's eye-socket.

After long convivial hours in the tavern, both were probably more than half drunk. Thomas Kyd knew Marlowe too, and reports his reputation for 'rashness in attempting sudden privy injuries to men'. Marlowe was the assailant here, and his attack on Frizer was just that—what the Spanish call *antuvión: is when two men, falling at words, the one upon a sudden before the other can draw his weapon, hurteth, woundeth, or killeth him: or to come behind one and strike him . . . also any manner the like treachery* (Percivale).

This killing with both brawlers clutching the dagger was not murder, not suicide, but *chance-medley:* the casual killing of a man; homicide by misadventure. Very sad, but Marlowe had 'asked for it'. None of his friends saw anything suspicious in the manner of his death. And Frizer not only properly received a pardon, but continued in the favour of Mr Walsingham, something he never could have done had there been the slightest ground for suspecting him of foul play.

But reason and the facts carry no weight in this matter. Marlowe the youthful rebel, Marlowe of those brave translunary things, Marlowe slain untimely, Marlowe the darling of sentimental criticism? He *must* have been murdered, even if he wasn't. Murdered, that is to say, unless indeed he was only playing possum: got up while nobody was looking, sneaked off, and in hugger-mugger obligingly wrote all Shakespeare's plays for him—in the intervals (as Mr John Crow suggests) of composing the Works of Calvin and the Tales of Hoffmann.

setting fortune. As Sovereign, Will Hatcliffe's date was out. And in all these years he had not managed to gain a post at Court. He had found that good looks, good character, princely parts, and skill in dancing, without wealth or powerful friends, were not enough to secure advancement. Although he was the Hatcliffe heir, the expenses of his kingship at Gray's Inn had been a great drain. His father Thomas had four other sons and two daughters (out of at least eleven children, seven survived to grow up) to educate and provide for. Whether or not Will—like so many others in his position—in this extended period had been industriously angling for a wealthy match we do not know. But after looking about him for another year in a frustrate hope of rising in the world, in the winter of 1595–96, at the ripe age of twenty-seven—no longer now *the world's fresh ornament And only herald to the gaudy spring*—Will Hatcliffe turned definitely to marriage.

Shakespeare's story during these crucial years presents a notable contrast. The actor-poet had certainly not succumbed to cruel Fortune's oppression, which had seemed so bitter to him in 1588 and 1589. True, in 1595 he was still a plebeian player, excluded from full companionship with gentlemen. But nothing could conceal his real merit. His unique quality and accomplishment could not fail to 'rank him in the file of praise and honour', and were rapidly making his advancement. In the judgment of the gentle and the learned, his sonnets had set him in the first flight of poets. His plays, equalled by none, were now eagerly followed by the whole world, his published narrative poems had met instant and universal acclaim. Excellence in his profession had by this time made him sufficiently well-to-do to maintain a gentleman's port and state; and within a year he would have a coat of arms granted to his father, and be able to write himself *gentleman* —as poor deceased Kit Marlowe had done nine years before on proceeding *in Artibus Magister* at Cambridge.

Non sanz droict. Everyone knows this 'word' which appears at the head of the Shakespeare grant of arms. But what does it mean? If this was indeed the personal motto the poet chose for himself, it has so often been ignorantly mistaken for a vulgarian's vaunt—'*I have a right to a coat of arms*'—that it becomes necessary to recall the high thoughts proper to the mottoes of gentlemen.

The first precept heroical was 'worship God'; and we find it variously followed in motto. *Ung sans plus* (One God alone), King Henry VI; *I AM alone* (God alone, *Exod.* 3:14), King Henry IV; *Ung je serviray* (One God), Earl of Pembroke; *Ung pour tout, tout pour ung* (One God for all, all for one God), Earl of Southampton; *Esperance en dieu*, Earl of Northumberland; *Che sara sara* ('God's will shall be in heaven above and here', as George Whetstone translates it), Earl of Bedford.

As for *droit*, it is of course Right. *Draw thy sword in right . . . my right-drawn sword.* Harry of England will fight for his claim, but only if it is made *with right and conscience*.

'Shake spear' means 'Fight'. And Shakespeare's arms are *armes parlantes*. Playing or canting on his name, the noble falcon of his crest shakes the spear. As in an *impresa*, Shakespeare has here found 'a correspondency of the picture, which is as the body, and the motto, which as the soul giveth it life . . . short, and answerable thereunto, neither too obscure, nor too plain'. *Non sanz droict* is answerable to *Shake spear*, uttering the poet's heroical thought: 'I shake the spear, but *not without right*'—'put forth My rightful hand in a well-hallow'd cause.' In short, 'Fight—*not without right*.' A motto fit for a gentleman and a Shakespeare,

> Whose *Muse* full of high thoughts invention
> Doth like himselfe Heroically sound.

We return to Will Hatcliffe. Where did he find the wife to give him the children who would carry on his ancient name? We remember that the old Hatcliffe family tradition had been one of service in the royal household, chiefly as administrative and financial officers. His great-grandfather Thomas had been Clerk of the Green Cloth (or Counting House, part of the administrative board presided over by the Lord Steward) to Queen Elizabeth's father; his cousin and namesake William Hatcliffe of Greenwich under King James purveyed for the Stables as Avener royal, and no doubt had been carried over, like so many others, from the preceding reign.

Now another north-country family, the Kays of Woodsome Hall near Huddersfield,[1] Yorkshire, were associated with the Hatcliffes in the royal service. Matthew Kay of Greenwich— brother of Robert Kay of Woodsome, Esquire,[2]—left a legacy[3] to Will's cousin William Hatcliffe the Avener royal.

At the time of Prince Will's glory in 1587–88, another member of the family, John Kay of Hackney, Esquire (formerly Avener royal), had been one of the four Clerks of the Green Cloth. Mr Kay died in May 1589, the year after the Armada; and it was in his family six years later that Will Hatcliffe found his future wife. She was Dorothy Kay, the eighteen-year-old daughter of Queen Elizabeth's late Clerk.

In those days the village of Hackney—partly because of its attractive rural situation near the bird-haunted marshes of the River Lea which offered so much sport—was favoured for fashionable residence. Among those who chose it were numbered the Earl of Oxford, Edward Lord Zouch, Robert Lord Rich (Penelope's husband), Edward Lord Cromwell, and the Queen's Champion Sir Edward Dymoke, patron of the poet Samuel Daniel. And on progress with her Court, Queen Elizabeth repeatedly visited the wealthy Sir Rowland Hayward, twice Lord Mayor of London, at Hackney.

Dorothy Kay was Will's junior by nine years, christened 2 August 1577. In 1587–88 when the Privy Council of Purpoole and the poet Shakespeare had been urging their boy-sovereign to marry and get an heir, she had been a child of ten. We learn from her father John Kay's will[4] dated 7 May 1589 that he left her 'his

---

[1] At Farnley Tyas, until recent times the seat of the Earls of Dartmouth, whose ancestor married a Kay.

[2] Whose daughter Grace married Sir Richard Saltonstall, one of the founders of the Massachusetts Bay Colony. H. F. Waters, *Genealogical Gleanings*, 970.

[3] P.C.C. 77 Fenner. Dated 14 November 1610.

[4] P.C.C. 48 Leicester.

leases in messuages [dwellings and grounds] etc. in the manor of
Laleham, Middlesex' and £100 to be paid at her age twenty-one
or her marriage. This is certainly something, but Dorothy Kay
was clearly not a rich match.

On Hatcliffe's side we find that on 16 November 1595 'William
Hatteclyff of Hatteclyff, Lincs., gent.' acknowledged a debt of
1000 marks (£666 13s. 4d.) to his father, payable 30 November
following:[1] possibly a bond occasioned by the father's payment
of Will's debts. Also that on 8 January 1595/6 his father Thomas
'in consideration of a marriage to take place between William
Hatcliffe and Dorothy one of the daughters of Bridget Kay,
widow of John Kay, Esquire, granted to Sir Thomas Grantham
and George Hatcliffe the elder [Will's uncle], John Kay [Dorothy's
brother], and Thomas Marsh, Esquire, the manor and rectory of
West Ravendale [or "Randall", adjoining Hatcliffe], Lincolnshire,
in trust' for the use of his said son.[2] Thirty-six years later it was
at this manor of West Ravendale that Will Hatcliffe died and was
buried, followed after seven years by his widow Dorothy.

And Thomas Hatcliffe also settled on his son the inheritance of
his two adjoining manors of Hatcliffe and Gunnerby, with the
proviso that on coming into possession after his death the heir
was to pay out of their profits annuities of 20 marks (£13 6s. 4d.)
each to the four younger sons Francis, George, Edward, and
Christopher.[3]

In the light of Will Hatcliffe's subsequent history, it is significant that Thomas did not give his twenty-seven-year-old son the
manor of West Ravendale outright on his marriage, but made it
over to a quartet of trustees, probably to secure repayment of
sums advanced to Will, and certainly to preclude his prompt
disposal of the property—held to be worth £200 a year—for

---

[1] L. C. 4/193/43.
[2] C2 Chas. I./B75/34. Answer of Sir Thomas Grantham and William
Hatcliffe and Dorothy his wife to the bill of complaint of Sir Oliver Butler
et al. Cf. C21/B25/14 and C21/B82/22.
[3] C2 Chas. I./H35/8. *Francis Hatcliffe v. Thomas Hatcliffe and William
Butler*, 1641. Cf. depositions, C21/H26/15.

Will did not become the owner until his father's death. From information afforded by numerous Chancery proceedings in later years, it is clear that from the start young Hatcliffe proved incapable of husbanding his estate and keeping out of debt.

We need not infer from this that he was a reckless gambler, playing away his patrimony at cards. A habit of free spending and of living on an equality with gentlemen wealthier than himself would be enough to bring him down. The mere expense on dress, horses, coach, hawks, hounds, and hospitality—joined with neglect in overseeing and husbanding his estate—would readily dissipate a handsome inheritance. As John Aubrey confesses, in recounting the precipitate ruin he made of his own patrimony, 'I was never riotous or prodigal, but (as Sir E. Leech said) sloth and carelessness are equivalent to all other vices.'

If transferred to the painful economics of Will's later life, Shakespeare's lines

> *Unthrifty loveliness, why dost thou spend*
> *Upon thyself thy beauty's legacy . . .?*

touch the cardinal point. Will was an unthrift, one 'who if his father had left him nothing must have begg'd'. Easy enough to say that he should have shown more care and foresight. But if he was brought up in a class above his own, and thus learned to live on a scale too liberal for the size of his estate, he may not have been solely to blame. In a sense, therefore, the very gifts of nature, exceptional and enviable, which served to advance him in society proved his enemies. Without them he might possibly have made a life less tossed with trouble.

And if it was to his aunt the Earl of Lincoln's daughter that Will Hatcliffe had owed his early advancement, it was no doubt now to Henry the second Earl, or his heir Thomas, Lord Clinton, that his father was indebted for his election to the House of Commons.[1] The borough of Grimsby in 1597 elected Thomas

---

[1] Sir John Neale, *The Elizabethan House of Commons* (1949), 207.

Hatcliffe, Esquire, as one of its two burgesses, taking from him (as its custom was) a bond of forty pounds which insured 'John Hatcliffe, mayor, and the commonalty aforesaid' against any claim for 'fees, duties, sums of money, or expenses during all this next Parliament'[1]—signed, *Thomas Hatteclyff*. At Westminster he sat for Grimsby in the session 24 October 1597–9 February 1598.

Two daughters, Dorothy and Judith, were born to Will and Dorothy Hatcliffe before their son and surviving heir Thomas, who was baptized at St Mary's Hatcliffe 29 January 1605/6. Thus at a remove of eighteen years Will at last satisfied the demand of the Sonnets that he beget a son. In this same year, 16 September 1606, Will's sister Faith married Thomas Glapthorne of Whittlesey, Cambridgeshire, as his third wife. Her first surviving son, baptized 28 July 1610, was Henry Glapthorne, who afterwards became a minor Caroline dramatist.[2] Brother-in-law Thomas Glapthorne later took a hand in Will Hatcliffe's attempts to repair his ruinous estate, with results which satisfied neither. Meanwhile Will had lost both his mother-in-law the widowed Bridget Kay (buried at Hackney 2 May 1601) and his mother Judith Ayscough Hatcliffe (buried in Hatcliffe church 2 November 1604). Of the parents, only Thomas Hatcliffe was left.

Shakespeare's Sonnets had *not* been included in the spate of sonnet-printing in the middle 1590s. How did they come to belated publication in 1609? Will Hatcliffe's situation in that year suggests a reason. Thorpe's dedication to 'Mr. W. H[atliv]' is *prima facie* evidence of Will's interest in this publishing of his praise written twenty years ago. The passing of a generation had dimmed the memory of that glorious young Prince and his plebeian poet as they had seemed in 1588–89: had wrought such change that they were now hardly recognizable even to themselves.

---

[1] 27 September 1597. First Court Book, Town Hall, Grimsby. Spelling modernized.

[2] J. H. Walter, *The Times Literary Supplement*, 19 September 1956, p. 748, who also gives Faith's burial at Whittlesey, 27 September 1625.

In those early days Shakespeare could curse Fortune,

That did not better for my life provide
Than public means which public manners breeds ...

adding, *Thence ... my name receives a brand.* If an Elizabethan's name *receives a brand* from the *public means* of common stage-playing, that opprobrium did not prevent men of the calibre of Shakespeare and Alleyn from achieving both fortune and social dignity. Through his income as actor, playwright, and part-owner of the Globe, Shakespeare's *poor* and *outcast state* of 1588 had given place to prosperity. At Stratford for more than a decade he had been master of 'The Great House', and had since added lands, houses, and tithes to his ever-growing estate. In the literary realm he was now acknowledged King, not merely of Comedy as 'our English Terence', but of Tragedy as well— *M. William Shak-speare: His True Chronicle Historie of the life and death of King Lear ...* His name alone would sell a play-book.

As for Will Hatcliffe, who had been somebody when this same Shakespeare was nobody, in 1609 his inheritance was still in the future, and he still living beyond his means in Lincolnshire, one hundred and fifty road-miles from the metropolis. Where now was his London triumph of twenty years before—his youthful princely grace *lov'd of more and less*—when his poet-friend Shake-speare lived by a small part of all his glory? Vanished was the Court—gay, dignified, superb—to which he and his royal train had been welcomed by Gloriana. Whitehall and Greenwich were now given over to waste and drunken disorder under a dirty King whom none could either love or respect. With many an old courtier of the Queen's, Will might have been tempted to give his infant heir Thomas that bitter surname *Ichabod*, meaning 'The glory is departed'.

Thomas is three years old, and he himself, the *lovely boy* of 1588, is forty. From his desk he rummages out the bound manu-script, the sequence written out fair for him by his great renowner Shakespeare. To open it is to open a window on the lost realm

of his youth: *From fairest creatures we desire increase.* . . . And
turning the page, he reads

> *When forty winters shall besiege thy brow*
> *And dig deep trenches in thy beauty's field,*
> *Thy youth's proud livery, so gaz'd on now,*
> *Will be a tatter'd weed of small worth held.*
> *Then being ask'd where all thy beauty lies,*
> *Where all the treasure of thy lusty days,*
> *To say, within thine own deep-sunken eyes*
> *Were an all-eating shame and thriftless praise.*
> *How much more praise deserv'd thy beauty's use*
> *If thou couldst answer, 'This fair child of mine*
> *Shall sum my count and make my old excuse,'*
> *Proving his beauty by succession thine!*
>   *This were to be new made when thou art old*
>   *And see thy blood warm when thou feel'st it cold.*

Look in your glass, and there appears a face. . . . The look he now
takes is reluctantly realistic. Strange, to read 'these words now
prov'd a prophecy'. But is there not a second way *to be new made*
after twenty winters? To bring *the lovely gaze where every eye
doth dwell* back to the minds of those who once beheld the flower-
ing of that primrose, Prince True-love?

Setting forth on a day late in April 1609 for the Easter Term
in London, he slips the manuscript into a saddle-bag. On arrival
he goes to the same Thorpe who had published Marlowe's Lucan
nine years before, and now gives him Shakespeare's Sonnets
and also 'A Lover's Complaint'. The highly gratified Thorpe
offers to dedicate the book 'To Mr. William Hatcliffe Esquier'.
But as a former friend Will is sensitive about appearing as
a belated climber-on to the chariot of Shakespeare's fame. Beyond that, to spread his name on a dedication-page could not fail
to bring from the new generation of readers the awkward query,
'And *who* is Hatcliffe?' He desires something more discreet,
which will remind those who can remember, and no matter for
the rest. Thorpe begs him to be easy, and proceeds to produce

that very thing. The plan proves a success: for a year after the Sonnets have come out in print, John Davies makes it plain that Prince True-love's memory is again fresh in mind:

> To . . . Mr. Will. Shake-speare.
> Some say (good *Will*) . . .
> Had'st thou not plaid some Kingly parts in sport,
> Thou hadst bin a companion for a *King* . . .

Some such picture as this of the birth of the Quarto of 1609, I believe, satisfies the likelihoods; and unless contrary evidence turns up, it may serve.

Before John Davies's book came out, Thomas Hatcliffe died— 13 August 1610—aged about sixty-two. But it was only after a delay of nearly two years that administration of his estate was granted to his son and heir 'William Hatcliffe Esquire', 24 June 1612.[1] To his signature of the bond, Hatcliffe affixed his seal (see the illustration). Since his family crest was the Lion borrowed from Pompey the Great, Will not unnaturally chose a Roman head for his signet. The question whether he took this head to represent his great exemplar Pompey must be left to conjecture.

We shall not pause long over the details of Will's dissipation of the Hatcliffe estate. The three manors Hatcliffe, Gunnerby, and West Ravendale were each held to yield £200 a year, £600 in all, and the combined charge of his four brothers' annuities came to little more than £50: certainly a good estate. Almost at once, to raise a large sum, he sold Hatcliffe and Gunnerby to the Pierreponts of Nottinghamshire—Lady Frances and her son Robert (later Earl of Kingston)—with the condition that he should stay on as tenant at the low rent of £300 a year. Yet even this he failed to pay, and the Pierreponts re-entered the manors.[2]

---

[1] Lincolnshire Archives Office. Act Bk. XI. 48; Admon. 1612/B. 169.

[2] Four of Will's bonds I find recorded as follows: 1611, 29 June, to Frances Pierrepont and Christopher Molyneux of Gray's Inn, Esq., £1200; 1612, 31 Mar., to Francis Barne, of Woolwich, Kent, Esq., £800; 1612/3, 27 Feb., to Philip Gerard of Gray's Inn, Esq., £1000; and 1613, 27 May, to the same and Henry Travers of London, Gent., £4000. P.R.O. L.C.4/197, ff. 220, 293^v, 413^v, 443.

A couple of years more found him desperately deep. Will himself mentions debts due to George Alington and others totalling £1489.

In 1616 brother-in-law Thomas Glapthorne entered the picture, and (as Will says) in return for a seven-years' lease of West Ravendale undertook to pay the debts aforesaid within that period. But this was not enough. Later in 1616, to clear the debt to the Pierreponts, Glapthorne was to put up £1000, with which Hatcliffe was not only to satisfy them, but persuade them to grant Glapthorne a new lease of the two manors for 30 years at £400 a year rent. This scheme apparently went through, although Glapthorne protests that his dealings with Hatcliffe have ruined him, while Will complains that he has been cheated and robbed.[1] Thus two-thirds of Will's inheritance had gone for ever by the time that Shakespeare died.

If thou survive my well-contented day
When that churl Death my bones with dust shall cover . . .

We now move forward to the year 1629. By this date Will Hatcliffe had not only survived Shakespeare thirteen years, but James I as well. He was now an old man—sixty-one. Still famous for his 'fair parts'; but in extreme danger of losing by a suit in Chancery the last bit of property he could leave to his son. A supreme effort was necessary. I find strong evidence of his enduring charm in the fact that he was able to get from Lord Conway, President of the Council, a letter begging the Lord Keeper (Lord Coventry, the Chancery judge) to show him favour.

This was the way of it. His Lincolnshire contemporary Sir William Pelham had been at Gray's Inn when he was Prince of Purpoole. Pelham's heir, young Sir William, had married Frances, daughter of Lord Conway. To this young Lady Frances old Will now presented his misfortunes so movingly that she wrote

---

[1] C2 Jas. I. H10/23 *Hatcliffe v. Hatcliffe*, 1621. G7/72 *Glapthorne v. Grantham, Keyes, and Hatcliffe*, 1621.

her father a powerful appeal to intercede for him. And [this] intercession:

Lord Conway to Lord Coventry, 20 October 1629.

Right Honourable

I have been moved by a daughter of mine that is co[ntracted] matched in Lincolnshire to Sir Wm. Pelham, who is most ca[reful] to move in any unjust thing, and now moves this with [such] caution and so many arguments arising from the gentleman's f[ortune] and the good estate he hath had, out of which he hath n[ot] riotously or negligently . . . I am an humble suitor to your l[ordship] that you would be pleased to give the bearer Mr. Wm. Ha[tcliffe] favourable hearing; and if your lordship may not with your [honour] judge the cause for him, then my humble suit is that it may [please] your lordship to limit and bound your order as it may have resp[ect to] the livelihood of those that must be maintained out of it, and th[at] of the debts that must be paid from that revenue. And now I be[seech] your lordship to pardon me if the affection of a father hath transp[orted] me to trench upon my duty to your lordship by this particular [suit] which I will redeem by all the humble service to your lordship [ever]

While I have not learned whether or not this letter took eff[ect,] it is at least clear that in his final years Will was not ousted fr[om] his West Ravendale home.

To set beside Shakespeare's witness to his character, I ha[ve] saved for the last another most impressive testimony from int[i]mate knowledge. It is given by his neighbour Gervase Holles (1607–75) of Grimsby, the loyal Cavalier soldier and distinguished antiquary. No one can read Gervase's description and anecdote[s] of his father Frescheville Holles (1575–1630) without being drawn to admire and love that delightful spirit and independence, that open fearless honesty, merry wit, kindness, hospitality, and warm true heart. As for his person, even with comely Will Hatcliffe at hand, Gervase held his father Frescheville the nonpareil of

---

[1] S.P.16/150/79. Spelling modernized.
[2] *Memorials of the Holles Family* (ed. A. C. Wood, 1937), 63, 199–202.

manly beauty. And in support he quotes the verdict of Will's devoted wife:

I have heard my cozen [1] [Dorothy] Hatcliffe say (who could judge of a man very well, let it not be understood to her praejudice, for she was a gentlewoman of an unblemished honour), that when he first was suitor to my mother, shee believed him the most delicate piece of nature y^t ever she look'd upon.

His very presence lifted the company, and silenced base or evil talk. And although he had the Holles fault of a quick temper, and—doubtless like his crony Will Hatcliffe—'he loved game too much', I can think of few higher recommendations of a man than 'he has long been a dear friend of Frescheville Holles''. Gervase gives this title to three only, and Shakespeare's Will is one:

In his owne country he loved best and had the nearest freindship wth my cozen Wm Tyrwhit of Ketleby . . . Mr William Hattecliffe of Hattecliffe and Mr Christopher Smith of And[er]by.

Late in January 1629/30, some three months before he died, Frescheville Holles in his last illness made his will, copied out in the *Memorials* by Gervase, his sole executor. Here we read the item, 'I give to my cozen Mrs Dorothy Hattecliffe an olde Angell.' And 'Wm Hattecliffe Esq.' is one of five to whom he leaves 22s. in gold each 'for rings to weare in remembrance of my love', and whom he appoints supervisors of his will. All five were present and signed as witnesses.[2]

His dear friend Will Hatcliffe did not wear the ring long. For in the winter of 1631, aged sixty-three, in his turn he fell fatally ill, and made his brief testament.[3]

---

[1] Gervase's great-grandfather Peter Frescheville had married Margaret Kay of Woodsome as his second wife. *Memorials*, 163.
[2] The reproduction of the last page is from the original preserved at the Principal Probate Registry, Somerset House.
[3] Original spelling retained, except for modernizing *i, j,* and *u, v.*

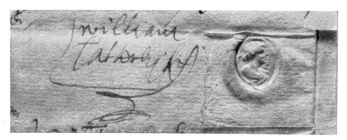

THE HAND AND SEAL OF WILLIAM HATCLIFFE

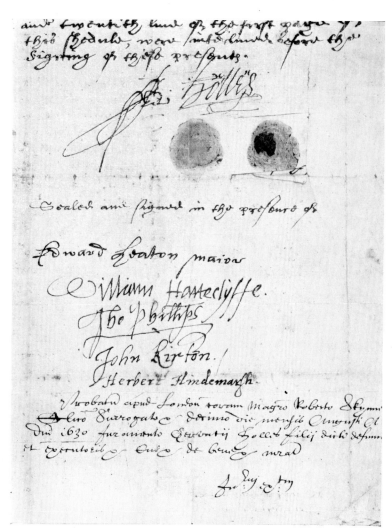

SIGNATURE OF WILLIAM HATCLIFFE

The last Will & Testament of Willyam Hatteclyff Esq made &
written the seaventeenth day of December in the yeare of our
Lord God 1631 as followeth

In the name of God Amen I Willyam Hatteclyffe of West Randall
in the countye of Lincoln being whole & sound in mind god be
thanked but sicke in body doe the day & yeare abovesayd make &
ordeyne this my last will & Testament in maner & forme following
First I doe give my soule to God my Creator who gave it mee,
praying his divine Majestie to receive it to his mercy and for Jesus
Christ his sake my Saviour and Redeemer in whom I onely assuredly
trust to be saved at the day of Judgment./
Next I Comitt my body to the earth to be buried in the Chappell of
West Randall; then Concerning my earthly goodes, my buriall &
Charges of that kind being discharged & my debtes payed, I doe
hereby make my deare & welbeloved wife Dorothy my Executor,
to whom for her paynes therein taken I doe give & bequeath all my
fine lynning of what kind soever, & all my other goodes whatsoever,
my debtes being discharged. And to whom likewise I Comend my
two daughters Dorothy & Judith, desiring her to give them theire
bringing up in the feare of God & to give them such maintenance as is
Convenient & to the better establishing of this my last will & Testament I have hereunto set to my hand & seale the day & yeare abovesayd./

Witnesses thereunto   *William Hatteclyffe*
 Francys Hatteclyffe   [Proved, and execution granted to
 Edward Skamon his mark   executrix, 13 February 1631/2.] [1]
 Thomas Lathorpe his mark

Is it too fanciful to trace character here? The making of the
will, forced upon him by sickness, not only shows no forethought,
but the mention of 'bringing up' two unmarried daughters who
were then about thirty years old suggests a mind already wander-
ing. His son and heir Thomas (who survived him twenty-one
years) appears nowhere in the will. He makes no mention of

---

[1] From the copy, L. A. O. Lincoln Consistory Court, Wills, 1631, f. 231.
For the inventory, together with his widow Dorothy's will and inventory
seven years later, see Appendix.

brothers or friends, though his brother Francis is present. Everything, including the payment of unspecified debts, is left to the care of his dear wife. The one particular in his mind is 'all my fine linen' (which the inventory lists as his most valuable asset next to the corn and hay in his barn). If Will Hatcliffe fleeted his time carelessly like a prince 'clothed in purple and fine linen', the disappearance of his heritage is no mystery.

More fortunate than his great Pompey, basely murdered by ingrates, Will departed attended with love. If his dying thought strayed back, some may fancy him saying with Darius

> *My best was but a momentary bliss . . .*
> *To think I was, and am not now a King.*

Others may give him the soft whisper of Isaac Barrow, 'I have seen the glories of the world'. But however it was, henceforth he will live a king for ever young and fair in the lines of a true friend famous beyond the utmost date of time.

Every reader will come to his own conclusion about this, perhaps the most interesting friendship in literature; and as one of his first questions will ask, I wonder how long it lasted?

The new fact to be reckoned with is that the Sonnets are concentrated within a period of little more than three years: 1587–89. As yet we have no evidence that the friendship lived or did not live beyond that span. In 1610 it was recalled that Shakespeare *might* (had he not been a player) have been a companion for his sovereign—meaning that social disparity set an insurmountable obstacle:

> *Let me confess that we two must be twain . . .*
> *Farewell: thou art too dear for my possessing.*

Since from Cicero down it was universally agreed that *equality* is indispensable for true friendship, the failure or impermanence of the tie was to be expected on this ground alone.[1]

---

[1] 'For perfect love can never be without equality'; 'In friendship there must be an equalitie of estates' (Pettie and Lyly, qu. among others by Tilley,

Another fresh consideration is the demonstrated youth (22–25) of the poet, to set beside the tenderer youth (18–22) of the Friend. In the poet we may now see youth's *extremes*, its intensity, its wholeheartedness—*thou hast all the all of me*—leading that unique soul into a land unreached by any. Alone among the critics, the late C. S. Lewis proved equal to describing it:

> The greatest of the sonnets are written from a region in which love abandons all claims and flowers into charity. . . . This patience . . . this transference of the whole self into another self without the demand for a return, have hardly a precedent in profane literature. In certain senses of the word 'love' Shakespeare is not so much our best but our only love poet.[1]

Shirley in one of his plays vainly gropes for some term to express it:

Clariana.	What thing's in him
	'Bove other friends?
Bellamente.	His love, his love, Clariana.
Clar.	That may be found in many.
Bel.	But not so rich . . . the name
	Of friend's too narrow for him, and I want
	A word that carries more divinity
	To express his love.[2]

The transparent truth and entirety of devotion expressed nowhere but in the Sonnets identified Shakespeare with Friendship, made him The Friend *par excellence*. Thus in Willobie's *Avisa* (1594) it is as much the phrase 'my faythfull frend' as the description 'the old player' which identifies W. S. as Shakespeare; and it is the

---

Dict. Prov., F761); '. . . disparitie of manners may for a time maske under the collour of amitie, but at last prooveth brittle' (Greene, *Wks.*, ed. Grosart, VII. 242); 'Parity or likenesse . . . in fortunes, *vid.* in the state and estimation & accompt they have in the world, as either in regard of their birth, of their riches, of their preferment, or finally of their credyt and renowne in it, in regard of their birth, for . . . to be borne of poore parents, this is vile and contemptible with them who are high borne' (H.H., *The Forme of Friendship and Love* (1608), 63.

[1] *Op. cit.*, 505.   [2] *Love's Cruelty*, 1.7.

Sonnets which suggest to Scoloker (1604) his epithet—'*Friendly Shakespeare's Tragedies*'.

But it takes more than one to make a friendship; and in considering the much more youthful Will, we must recall contemporary collective wisdom:

The mind of a young man is momentany, his fancy fading, his affections fickle, his love incertain, & his liking as light as the wind; his fancy fired with every new face, and his mind moved with a thousand sundry motions, loathing that which of late he did love, and liking that for which his longing mind doth lust, frying at the first, and freezing at the last.[1]

And the observations of Aristotle and Cicero as well:

It is generally acknowledged that youth is the golden period of friendship. Aristotle did not fail to notice, however, the impulsive tendency of youth to enter on and dissolve friendships in one day. . . . On this account Cicero observes that men must come to maturity before their friendships can be regarded as solid and permanent.

To the unhappy disparity in rank and circumstances, therefore, must be added the youth of both parties. A further obstacle to lasting and equal friendship might be seen in a possible disparity of emotional maturity: it took Will Hatcliffe nearly ten years longer than it took Will Shakespeare to find a mate and embark on marriage.

In sum, if the friendship came to an early end (and I believe it did), we need not seek to attach blame to Will Hatcliffe. To represent as cold or selfish a youth who could inspire not only universal affection but the particular devotion of Thomas Campion, and the lifelong friendship of Frescheville Holles, not to mention so unexampled a love as Shakespeare's, would be to deny Shakespeare's insight into the human heart and to make nonsense of the Sonnets.

If we are left in the dark about the friendship's dissolution, for

---

[1] Bodenham, *Politeuphuia* (1597), 190. Spelling modernized.
[2] W. M. Rankin in *Encycl. of Religion & Ethics* (1914), VI. 133.

its beginning, in like manner, we can do no more than grope. What magical combination in Will Hatcliffe was it which drew Will Shakespeare's heart so irresistibly? Love is subtle as sphinx. Most probably the poet himself could make no reply but Montaigne's, of Étienne de la Boétie: 'If a man urge me to tell wherefore I loved him, I feel it cannot be expressed but by answering, Because it was he, because it was I.'

As we know from his last instructions, Will Hatcliffe was not buried in the ancestral church, St Mary's Hatcliffe—where on a ledger-stone in the vestry one can see his grandsire's incised figure with his coat of arms, three quatrefoils or primroses. He was laid to rest in the ancient chapel standing on his own neighbouring manor of West Ravendale ('Randall'). In 1202 a priory for Premonstratensian canons (from Beauport, Brittany) was founded there. Four hundred years later all that remained of it was its chapel, in which under James and Charles a curate conducted services of worship for the Hatcliffes and their farm-people.

If you go out from Grimsby southwest some seven miles to West Ravendale, you will find the ruined chapel on high ground above the manor-house named Ravendale Priory. Somewhere within its overgrown fragments of wall—one of them containing the piscina south of the altar—lie the remains lost and forgotten of the Friend *fair, kind, and true,* to whom Shakespeare wrote

> *Thy bosom is endearèd with all hearts*
> *Which I by lacking have supposèd dead;*
> *And there reigns love, and all love's loving parts,*
> *And all those friends which I thought buried . . .*
> *But things remov'd tHAT hidden in thee lie.*
> *Thou art the grave where buried love doth LIVE,*
> *Hung with the trophies of my lovers gone,*
> *Who all their parts of me to thee did give;*
> *That due of many now is thine alone.*
> *Their images I lov'd I view in thee,*
> *And thou (all they) hast all the all of me.*

XIII

IN RETROSPECT

To look back over the road we have travelled is to be astonished. We have found those miscalled 'lost years' of Shakespeare's—1585–92, from twenty-one to twenty-eight, marked by amazing accomplishment. To add to his notably rapid advance in two exacting careers—of player and of dramatist—so far as to be reported 'excellent' in the first by Chettle in 1592, and as a dramatist envied by Greene in the same year, we have learned that he had also triumphed in a third. For by 1589 he had completed his Sonnets. And the depth and maturity of their 'high thought's invention', crowned by Spenser's unhesitating tribute, placed him at the age of twenty-five with the highest poets.

If assimilation of this fact—recognizing the leading creator as a leader—requires 'an almost Copernican revolution' in our self-contradicted concept of him, the time is ripe for it. The intelligent reader may well be weary of a worm's-eye view of Shakespeare which represents the quick Soul of the Age as its sluggish and backward follower.

For my part, the retrospect shows me how much I have had to learn about the proper search for Shakespeare. Some thirty-odd years ago that admirable critic Desmond MacCarthy wrote,

Unless the researcher's day-dream comes true, and a chest of Shakespeare's private papers is discovered, we must remain for ever dependent upon one source of further information—namely, legal and business records.[1]

Along with the rest of the world, I agreed with him. So fully, indeed, that I pictured the rest of my life devoted to ransacking the archives for more external biographical facts.

True, we were not quite so blindly complacent as Coleridge,

---

[1] *The Sunday Times* (London), 4 October 1931.

with his 'I believe Shakespeare was not a whit more intelligible in his own day than he is now to an educated man, except for a few local allusions of no consequence.' But we did assume that in their centuries of work scholars had detected and followed for us all the major clues presented by Shakespeare's words. Although the Sonnets, as Chambers observed, are 'full of personal hints', none of these had ever led to any solid information. With Cyril Connolly, we agreed that 'every impartial critic would be forced to admit that . . . the Sonnets are very nearly clueless'. Nothing, so we all believed, could throw any significant light but the discovery of some document.

Only in 1947 did I begin to suspect that there must still be words in Shakespeare's text carrying important meanings which time has concealed from the modern reader. In considering *The mortall Moone* of Sonnet 107, I felt certain that whatever it *did* mean, it could not mean Queen Elizabeth. An unprejudiced search for an Elizabethan *moon* promptly yielded 'fleet-formation' —notably *the crescent of the Spanish Armada*. At that time I was still ignorant of Samuel Butler's correct conclusion (1899) that Sonnet 107 reflects the terror and the relief of the Armada Year, 'the fatal year of fearful Eighty Eight'. It is therefore all the more striking to note that Butler arrived at this truth in spite of his unquestioning belief that 'Queen Elizabeth is intended by the words "The mortal moon".' His discovery of the Armada Year without the Armada recalls the performance of *Hamlet* with the Prince of Denmark left out. Time's *pyramids* of Sonnet 123 came next, for from the editors' notes it was evident that none of them had the slightest notion of what Shakespeare and his readers understood by the term.

Already in 1933 the first lesson had been set out by Leon Kellner: namely, that the mere language of Shakespeare is seldom understood by modern readers, and that the most important element in the Sonnets is *the meaning of Shakespeare's words*. This is difficult doctrine. Difficult, because when you think you know what a word means, few things can be harder than to act as though you don't: to stop and devote real effort to exploring it objectively. Does this process require humility, or instil it, or both? In scientific investigation it is of course indispensable. Speculation about the 'total meaning' of a poem will be better received when we know the meaning of its parts.

Certainly the effort to find correct answers to the insistent question *What does Shakespeare say?* is all-absorbing. It leaves one neither time nor inclination for final pronouncements such as Mackail's 'the boy is unidentifiable', or Beeching's on the Dark Woman, 'the Sonnets supply no possible clue by which the particular person can be identified'.

But to mistake, or fail to understand what Shakespeare says is more excusable than to assume that he does not mean what he says. For example, when he describes his native traditional theatre-in-the-round as *this wooden O*, to report that he means 'this wooden U with an Italianate scenic wall added'. Or when he says *sovereign*, to presume that he means 'earl'. To do this is to step out on to the slippery slope which ends in the rubbish-heaps of scholarship.

What in sum have we gained by attending closely to the meaning of Shakespeare's words?

We have learned that the poet, like John Keats, attained maturity as a young man. His Sonnets, so far from being scattered products of his middle age, were the concentrated utterance of his youth, completed when he was twenty-five. A true friend's noble love for the beautiful young Prince, and a base enslavement to the Dark Woman, both found their expression by his pupil pen.

We have learned that the Friend was William Hatcliffe of Lincolnshire, a youth so excellent in beauty, character, and princely parts as to be chosen as 'True-love', Gray's Inn's Christmas King; that Shakespeare's hyperbolic praise of his loveliness, and its expression in terms of a woman's beauty, are both normal and expected for an Elizabethan prince; that the puzzling sonnets urging marriage and an heir were addressed to him in his rôle as Prince of Purpoole, 'to secure the succession'; and that Shakespeare's *my sovereign* and *Love* are titles proper for this Prince.

Also that the symbol and badge of his reign was the True-love (quatrefoil or primrose—*only herald to the gaudy spring*), which embodies the theme of the Sonnets; that his coat of arms bore three True-loves or quatrefoil Primroses, the 'three fours' which his poet unvaryingly reproduced in the Sonnets' three quatrains —the *noted weed, ever the same.*

We have learned that the bewitching Woman was Luce Morgan, once a favourite of the Queen's, now grown common and infamous.

Together with confirmation of our knowledge that the Rival Poet was that spirit, the Master of Arts Kit Marlowe, we have learned that his crony *that affable familiar ghost* was Robin (Goodfellow) Greene, and the *Alien pen* was Thomas Watson.

We have learned from evidence contained in the numbering of the Sonnets that the order or sequence of Sonnets 1–126 as printed in 1609 was Shakespeare's own arrangement of them.

By establishing the date and the occasion of the Sonnets we have learned that *Love's Labour's Lost*—a Christmas play for Gray's Inn under its Prince *Love*—belongs in the sonnets-year 1588–89: which calls for serious revision of Shakespeare-chronology.

Perhaps even more important than the new facts, however, is the discovery and preliminary exploration of a region hitherto unsuspected: *Shakespeare's allusive and symbolic method* in his personal or lyrical poetry.

Yet the most startling and valuable gain is the subjective one. To contemplate this profusion of features always present before us in the Sonnets, but which we have not been able to see, is to realize that much more, both here and in the plays, is still waiting to be recognized:

> if 't be so good
> When heard alone, what is 't when understood!

We have only passed the threshold. There are many things within.

APPENDICES

Inventory [1] of William Hatcliffe's goods, 4 January 1631/2.

A true & perfect Inventory of all the goodes & Chattells aswell moveable as unmoveable of William Hatteclyffe late of West Randall in the County of Lincoln Esquire deceased taken valued and prised the Fourth day of January in the yeare of the Raigne of o[r] Soveraigne Lord Charles by the grace of God of England Scotland France & Ireland King defendo[r] of the Fayth &c the Seaventh by Thomas Mussendyne gent John Draper Richard Todd Thomas Hogg Richard Meares & Willm Scrimsey as followeth/

Imprimis his Purse & his apparell	vi[li]	xiii[s]	iiii[d]
Item all the Corne in the Barne	l	o	o
Item sparres & ouldwood under the Corne	o	x	o
Item Hay	xiii	vi	iiii
Item one payre of Bullockes	viii	o	o
Item 2 Kyne 1 Bull 6 Calves	viii	o	o
Item horses & one foale	vi	o	o
Item sheepe	iiii	o	o
Item Three acres of Wheat & Rye	iii	o	o
Item swyne	ii	o	o
Item wayne geares & plowe geares	iii	o	o
Item one ould Belfrey two tables two plankes one Creele wth other wood in the yard	iii	o	o
Item in the dyning Chamber 3 stooles & one Forme	o	x	o
Item in the lodgeing Chamber Two beddes & their Furniture wth other implem[tes]	vi	v	o
Item in one other Chamber Two bedsteades & one bedd	o	xiii	iiii
Item in the Kitching Chamber 2 bedds	o	x	o
Item brasse & pewter & one Lead in the Kitchin	ii	iii	iiii

---

[1] L. A. O. Consistory Court Lincoln Inventories, 138/257. Here and in Dorothy Hatcliffe's will and inventory I retain the original spelling, with the exception of modernization of *i, j,* and *u, v.*

Item	£	s	d
Item in the Hall & Parlor one Table & other thinges	o	x	o
Item bookes	i	x	o
Item one Gaflocke [? iron crowbar]	o	vi	viii
Item at Grimsby 4 brasse pottes	ii	o	o
Item Pewter	ii	o	o
Item 2 Pannes	o	vi	viii
Item one Trunke	i	o	o
Item Racke 1 dripping pann & some other ould things	i	xiii	iiii
Item in the lodging Chamber one flatt trunke wth the lining [linen] in it	xii	o	o
Item one round Trunke wth Two ould Carpettes & Cushinges in it	iii	o	o
Item the best bedd & furniture belonging	viii	o	o
Item one Trunke wth three ould bedds	iii	o	o
Item in the same Chamber Chaires & stooles & other odd things	i	o	o
Item one little Morter	o	v	o
Item in the great Chamber one bedd	i	vi	viii
Item 4 peeces of ould hangings	o	x	o
Item in the Parlor 1 Table & stooles & one paire of land Irons	ii	x	o
Item in the Kitchyn one payre of Rackes one spitt wth other ould Things	i	o	o
Item in the Kitchyn Chamber a Presse	o	x	o
Item in the Hall one ould Table	o	iii	iiii

Summa totalis   Clx^li   iii^s —./.

Will of Dorothy Hatcliffe, made 8 May 1638.[1]

In the name of god Amen May the eighth Anno domini 1638   I
Dorothee Hatcliffe of West Ravendale alias Randall in the countey of
Lincoln widow being weake in body but (thankes be to god) of perfect
minde and memory doe ordaine & make this my last will and testam^te
in manner & forme followinge   That is to say   First I commend my
soule into the handes of almighty god hopeing to be saved by his

---

[1] From the signed original, L.A.O. Consistory Court Lincoln, Wills,
1638, f. 384.

mercy in Christ my saviour and my body to the earth there to be decently buried   Itm I give to my sister Luce twenty poundes which I received with hir and one bed with all thinges pertaininge thereunto, the disposeinge of whome & of hir goodes I commit to ye care of my two daughters Dorothee and Judith.   Itm I give unto Thomas Hatcliffe my sonne all my wanes & ploughes with all other my implem^tes of husbandry & one featherbed of the best sorte, one square tablecloth of damaske sixe table napkins one cupboard cloth & one towell all of them also of damaske, all which damaske I will after the death of my saide sonne shall be left & remaine unto Thomas Hatcliffe my grandchilde   Itm I give unto Dorothee Chapman my daughter [1] one paire of fine holland sheetes two feather beds y^t is one of the best and one of the worst   a livery cupboard one drawing table one little table of firre wood   one turky worke cupboard cloth and one counterpoint coveringe.   Itm I give unto Dorothe Hatcliffe my grandchilde ten lambes which I will shall goe on and increase for hir use as god shall blesse them untill she shall accomplish the age of eighteene yeares or be maried: dureinge all which time I will that the saide sheepe with the increase of them shall remaine in the possession of my executour.   All the residue of my goodes & chattels moveable and unmoveable householde goodes and householde stuffe whatsoever my debtes and legacies being payde & my funerall expences discharged I give unto Judith Hatcliffe my daughter whome I make the full and sole executour of this my last will & testam^t   And I ordaine & make the noble kinsman Sir Edward Aiscough knight & Mr Alford minister at Briggesley supervisours desireinge them that as I have found them faithfull friendes unto me in the time of my widowhood so they will be pleased to continue their good affection and best advice to my executour   And I doe give unto each of them a twenty shillinges piece of golde intreatinge them to make thereof each of them a ringe & to weare them for my sake   In witness whereof I have hereunto put my hande and seale ye day & yeare first above written

in the presence of   [signed] *Dorothye Hattecliffe*
[signed] *Robert Alforde*
    „   *Constance Andrewe*   [fragment of seal]
    „   *Francis Hatteclyffe*
[Proved 19 March 1638/9.]

---

[1] In 1637 Dorothy had married Philemon Chapman, gentleman.

A true Inventarie of the goodes of Mrs Hattecliffe of Randall taken valued and prized the xi^th^ day of Februarie 1638.

	li	s	d
Imprimis her purse and apparrell	xiii^li^	vi^s^	viii^d^
Itm in the two Chambers ove*r* the kitchin two old bedsteades wth beddinge to them wth other implem^tes^	iii	xiii	iiii
Itm in the little chamber ove*r* the hall one old bedd wth bedding & a stoole	o	xx	o
Itm in the Chamber ove*r* the hall one table frame one chaire one forme one cupboard one peece of tapestrie	o	xx	o
Itm in the Chamber ove*r* the parler one bedstead wth the furniture	iii	o	o
Itm in the same Chamber 2 old chists two old trunckes 4 peeces of tapestrie wth other implem^tes^	iii	o	o
Itm in another Chamber one little bedd wth beddinge to it	o	xx	o
Itm in the hall one table frame one forme one stoole one cupboard	o	x	o
Itm in the butterie two hogsheades and other implem^tes^	o	v	o
Itm in the little parler one old fether bedd wth a rugg	o	x	o
Itm in the kitchin brasse & pewter	o	xxx	o
Itm rackes & spittes & other implem^tes^	o	x	o
Itm one Sowe & 4 piggs	o	xx	o
Itm six geese six turkies 3 hennes 2 cockes 4 duckes	o	xvi	o
Itm a coach wth the harnes	ii	xiii	iiii
Itm 7 acres of wheate & rie	viii	o	o
Itm 2 horses one cow & 3 quies [kine]	xii	o	o
Goods at Grimsbie			
Imprimis in the Chamber ove*r* the hall 1 bedstead 4 old fether bedds 2 bolsters wth other implem^tes^	iiii	o	o
Itm in the Closett one truncke wth bookes	o	x	o

---

[1] In 1637 Dorothy had married Philemon Chapman, gentleman. No. 147/46.

Itm in the Closett one truncke wth pewter xxxiii iiii

Itm 4 brasse pottes 2 morters, one little brasse pott
 wth other brasse xxxiii iiii

Itm one p*ai*re of Rackes wth a grate for a fire xiii iiii

Itm one little old table one cupboard & an old chist vii viii

Itm in the parler one drawinge table xvi o

Itm one forme one cupboard 3 little tables two chaires
 1 beddstead and an other table xx o

Itm at Mr Kirtons fine linnen in a truncke x o o

Itm in an other truncke carpettes cushions and other
 thinges v o o

Debts owing to her./

Imprimis Mr Chapman [her son-in-law] v x o

Itm Thomas Lathropp iiii o o

Itm Wm Claton ii v o

Itm John Overey xv o

Itm George Marflett xx o

Itm Robert Westroope xl o

Itm one old Waine wth other thinges forgotten xx o

Itm at Mrs Andrewes one beddstead & a tubb xx o

Summe is — 96^{li} 17^s o^d.

William Brighouse   Philemon Chapman
 [?Th] Hogg

[Inventory exhibited 19 Mar. 1638/9.]

INDEX

U   313

315

Dodoens' *Herbal*, 165 n.
Donne, John, 22, 67, 70, 71, 74, 93 n., 103, 131, 165, 166, 233 n., 241, 271 n.
Dorke, Walter, 210 n.
Douce, Francis, 233
Dowden, Edward, 239
Dowland, John, 176
Drake, Sir Francis, 101–2, 133
Draper, John, 308
Drayton, Michael, 36, 69, 259; *Amours*, 196 n.; *Legend of Matilda*, 27 n., 199; *Poly-olbion*, 112, 187
Drummond, William, of Hawthornden, 66
Dryden, John, 194 n., 245 n.
Dudley, Ambrose, *see* Warwick
Dudley, Robert, *see* Leicester
Durrell, Lawrence, 9
Dyke, Daniel, 276
Dymoke, Sir Edward, 116, 152, 289

Earle, John, 125, 131
Eccles, Mark, 258 n.
Edward III, The Reign of (Anon.), 244 n.
Edward III, King of England, 183, 184
Edward IV, King of England, 38, 115
Edward VI, King of England, 67
Ekwall, Eilert, 114 n.
Elderton, William, 267
Eleutherius, N., 88 n.
Eliot, T. S., 42, 98
Elizabeth I, Queen of England, as *sun, goddess, sea*, 27, 28, 54; not *mortal moon*, 74–6, 305; Pallas, 47; Astræa, 158; a great tree, 96–7; character, 83 n.; people's love, 216; as Queen, 143; praise of, 134; love of music, 247; as poet, 199; translates *Glasse*, 152, 165–6; quotes and paraphrases Psalms, 271, 273, 274–5; on Armada, 79; True-love jewels and badge, 166–9; urged to marry, 137; court

of, 46–7, 293; plots to kill her, 97–8, 277–8; and Prince of Purpoole, 52–6, 228–30; gifts to Luce Morgan, 246–7
Elvetham Entertainment, 28
Elyot, Sir Thomas, 134
Empedocles, 164
Emperor, at Inner Temple, 49
Erasmus, 138
Escorial, 82
Essex, Robert Devereux, Earl of, 16, 18, 19, 21, 274
Eye, Suffolk, 243 n.

Faithful Friends, 29 n., 219, 263
Falconet, E. M., 210
Farnley Tyas, Yorks., 289 n.
fellow-commoner, 119–21, 261
Ferne, Sir John, 130, 176, 201, 202
Ferro de' Rotarii, Giovanni, 129 n., 211 n.
Fitton, Mary, 239, 247
Flasket, John, 265
Fleay, F. G., 231
Fletcher, John, *Fair Maid of the Inn*, 195; *False One*, 97 n., 312 n.; *Honest Man's Fortune*, 177 n.
Fletcher and Massinger, *Elder Brother*, 60 n.
Fletcher, R. J., 108 n.
Florio, John, 66, 69, 104
Flower, Francis, 229
Fontana, Domenico, 87
Ford, John, *Broken Heart*, 268
Fortescue, Sir John, 46
Fotherby, Martin, 276
Francis I, King of France, 140
Frederick V, Count and Elector Palatine, 135–6
Frescheville, Peter, 298 n.
Friendship, symbolic figure of, 209–14; public theme in 1588, 210
Frizer, Ingram, 285–6 n.
Frye, Northrop, 197–8, 269
Fulbecke, William, 219–20, 228
Fulgentius, F. P., 210
Fuller, Thomas, 27 n., 58–9, 112–3

316

317

319

Oxford, Earl of, 289
Oxford University, 67 n., 119

Paris, Mrs Thomasina de, 247
Parker, husband of Luce Morgan, 245
Param, Alessandro Farnese, Duke of, 133
Parma, Ottavio Farnese, Duke of, 215
Parry, Mrs Blanche, 247
Parry, William, 277
Pasteur, Louis, 108
Paul's, children of, 218
Peacham, Henry, 122, 128, 184
Pearce, R. R., 108 n.
Peck, Francis, 39 n.
Peele, George, 25, 101, 216, 280
Pegasus, Honourable Order of, 47
Pelagius, 252
Pelham, Lady Frances, 296–7
Pelham, Sir William, sr., 296
Pelham, Sir William, jr., 296–7
Pembroke, Mary Sidney, Countess of, 270
Pembroke, William Herbert, 3rd Earl of, 11, 40, 68, 282, 288
Penruddock, John, 229
pensioner, 117, 119
Penson, William, 125
Pepys, Samuel, 245 n.
Percival, P. J., 207 n.
Percivale, Richard, 286 n.
Percy, William, 67, 280
Peretto, Francesco, 243 n.
Perient, Thomas, Prince of Purpoole, 50, 63, 106, 188 n.
Perne, Andrew, 121
Peterhouse, Cambridge, 115, 121
Petrarch, 71–2, 104, 157, 273
Pettie, George, 300 n.
Phidamore his fygure of fancye (Anon.), 177–8
Philip II, King of Spain, 76, 80, 82, 84, 93, 101, 273, 275
Phiston, William, 243 n.
Picinelli, Filippo, 203 n., 211 n.

Pierrepont, Lady Frances, 295
Pierrepont, Robert, later Earl of Kingston, 295
Pindar, 179
Pinto, Oreste, 37
Plato, 179
Pliny, 144, 195
Plutarch, 55, 171, 207, 216–18, 223
Poe, E. A., 25
Poley, Robert, 286 n.
Pompey the Great, and W. H., 212–20, 223–4, 227, 265, 300; his lion-insigne the Hatcliffe crest, 129–30, 215, 265; the 'people's love', 216–18, 227; in *Love's L. L.*, 233–4
Poole, Josiah, 81 n., 177 n., 222 n.
Pooler, C. K., 242 n.
Pope-Hennessy, John, 23, 163
Porter, Henry, 103
Pothinus, 213
Powle, Stephen, 39
pride, proud, meaning of, 262–3
Prime, John, 262 n.
Primer, The ('Lay Folks' Prayer Book), 274
primrose, heraldic, 127, 163, 169, 171, 173, 187, 307
'procreation' sonnets, reason for, 136–9, 307
Proteus and the Rock Adamantine (mask) 54
Psalms, Book of, 271–81; Gradual, 274, 280; Penitential, 273–4; *Ps. 6*, 281 n.; *12*, 272–3; *14*, 271 n.; *32*, 281 n.; *38*, 281 n.; *51*, 274, 281 n.; *68*, 273; *74*, 273; *86*, 275; *102*, 281 n.; *107*, 276, 278–80; *119*, 273 n.; *124*, 276–80; *137*, 272; *139*, 273 n.; *144*, 272 n.
Ptolemy, King of Egypt, 129, 213, 220, 223
Purpoole or Portpool, Prince of (*and see* Gray's Inn), 49, 54–5, 109, 132–4, 188–9; Barons of Four Ports, 141, 181–90; Champion, 192–3; Court of Exchequer, 182–

323

shadow under a shadow, explained, 63, 106, 199–200

Shakerley, Peter, 226, 228

Shakespeare, William: name, meaning of, 288; variants of, 146; arms and crest, 215, 288; motto explained, 287–8; appearance and character, 132; standing in 1595, 287; in 1609, 293; Sh. and Hatcliffe; their meeting, 131–2; relative ages, 73, 110, 132, 301; 'Companion of a King', 41, 63, 106; their friendship, 300–3; Sh. and Black Luce Morgan, 238–52

Sonnets: celebrate a King (not a peer), 26–41, 106, 282; therefore hyperbolic in praise, 134; royal youth as beautiful as a woman, 135–6; heir urged for 'succession', 136–9; three quatrains like Hatcliffe's three quatrefoils, 173, 175; plays on *Hat live*, 159–62; on *Lucy*, 240–4; on *Morgan*, 251–2; on Greene, Watson, and Marlowe, 256–68; sequence of, 270–1, 280–1; date of, 1587–89, 65–105; written in youth, 67, 70–3, 102–5, 238, 248; 'muse of azure dye', 198–9; early tributes 1589–94 to Sh. as sonneteer, 193, 200: publication of, 145, 292–5; date and occasion of *LLL*, 230–5; Sh.'s allusive and symbolic method discovered, 307

Sonnets quoted: *1:* 109, 138, 187, 201, 294, *2:* 29, 139, 294; *4:* 33, 159, 224, 291; *5:* 21; *6:* 29, 139, 159, 281 n. *7:* 224; *9:* 29, 30, 159; *10:* 139, 159, 185; *11:* 34, 159; *13:* 29, 159, 176, 185; *14:* 31, 185, 198; *16:* 22, 102, 140, 159; *17:* 159, 217; *18:* 186, 200, 201; *19:* 185; *20:* 21, 135, 136, 201–3; *21:* 198; *22:* 59, 160; *25:* 35, 100–2, 159, 200, 201; *26:* 33; *27:* 200; *28:* 34, 200, 201; *29:* 214; *30:* 182–3; *31:* 159, 303; *32:* 281 n., 296; *33:* 26, 200, 201; *34:* 26, 169,

221–2; *36:* 41 n., 158, 300; *37:* 28, 34, 63, 160, 214; *38:* 145, 146, 159, 177, 281 n. *39:* 160, 171–2; *40:* 176, 198, 251; *41:* 160, 240; *45:* 32; *46:* 37; *47:* 21; *51:* 59, 176, 281 n. *53:* 34, 201, 212; *54:* 160, 185, 198, 212; *55:* 158, 160, 162; *57:* 31, 35, 134; *58:* 32, 33; *60:* 185; *61:* 174, 198; *62:* 34, 72, 172; *63:* 21, 35, 72, 160, 201; *66:* 98–9, 160; *67:* 160, 187; *69:* 28; *70:* 21, 35, 93 n. *72:* 161, 174, 198; *73:* 161; *74:* 161, 172; *78:* 19, 24, 34, 35, 145–6, 177, 257–8, 259–60; *79:* 34, 160, 176, 261; *80:* 20, 27, 256, 261–2; *81:* 153, 158, 160, 162; *82:* 59, 158, 198; *83:* 257; *85:* 262–3; *86:* 257, 263, 264; *87:* 31, 32, 284, 300; *89:* 59, 162; *92:* 161; *93:* 59, 160, 176; *94:* 142–4, 160; *95:* 158, 162; *96:* 34; *97:* 160; *99:* 10, 20; *100:* 20; *101:* 185, 199, 201; *102:* 281 n. *104:* 64, 110; *105:* 23, 175, 176, 186, 198, 201; *107:* 73–84, 92, 176, 271, 280; *108:* 162; *109:* 161; *111:* 41 n., 161, 214, 293; *112:* 161; *113:* 161, 198, *114:* 28; *116:* 181, 198; *120:* 10, 222; *123:* 84–92, 198; *124:* 92–8, 271, 276–80; *125:* 10, 32, 35, 37–40, 141–2, 198; *126:* 236–7; *127:* 241, 251; *128:* 248, 251; *130:* 251; *132:* 241, 251; *133:* 241, 252; *134:* 251; *135:* 251–2; *136:* 242; *137:* 242, 252; *138:* 72, 248; *139:* 241, 252; *140:* 241; *141:* 241; *142:* 241; *143:* 123; *144:* 250; *145:* 161, 240; *146:* 161; *147:* 161, 240, 251; *148:* 242; *149:* 242; *150:* 240, 241, 252; *152:* 241; *153:* 242;

Plays quoted: *Ant. & Cleop.*, 86; *Errors*, 50; *Coriol.* 208; *Cymb.*, 26 n., 34 n.; *Haml.*, 33 n., 168, 208, 209, 305; *1 Hen. IV*, 34 n., 60 n., 272; *2 Hen. IV*, 27 n., 34 n., 61 n.; *Hen. V*, 26 n., 29 n., 30 n., 33 n., 34 n., 288; *1 Hen. VI*, 30 n.,